The Lost History of Cosmopolitanism

The Lost History of Cosmopolitanism

The Early Modern Origins of the Intellectual Ideal

Leigh T. I. Penman

BLOOMSBURY ACADEMIC
LONDON • NEW YORK • OXFORD • NEW DELHI • SYDNEY

BLOOMSBURY ACADEMIC
Bloomsbury Publishing Plc
50 Bedford Square, London, WC1B 3DP, UK
1385 Broadway, New York, NY 10018, USA
29 Earlsfort Terrace, Dublin 2, Ireland

BLOOMSBURY, BLOOMSBURY ACADEMIC and the Diana logo are trademarks of
Bloomsbury Publishing Plc

First published in Great Britain 2021
This paperback edition published in 2022

Copyright © Leigh T. I. Penman, 2021

Leigh T. I. Penman has asserted his right under the Copyright, Designs and Patents Act,
1988, to be identified as Author of this work.

Cover design: by Tjaša Krivec
Cover image: Construction of the Tower of Babel. Hendrick van Cleve (1525–1589)
Flemish artist.
(© World History Archive / Alamy Stock Photo)

All rights reserved. No part of this publication may be reproduced or transmitted
in any form or by any means, electronic or mechanical, including photocopying,
recording, or any information storage or retrieval system, without prior permission
in writing from the publishers.

Bloomsbury Publishing Plc does not have any control over, or responsibility for, any
third-party websites referred to or in this book. All internet addresses given in this
book were correct at the time of going to press. The author and publisher regret
any inconvenience caused if addresses have changed or sites have ceased to exist,
but can accept no responsibility for any such changes.

Every effort has been made to trace copyright holders and to obtain their permissions
for the use of copyright material. The publisher apologizes for any errors or omissions
and would be grateful if notified of any corrections that should be incorporated in
future reprints or editions of this book.

A catalogue record for this book is available from the British Library.

Library of Congress Cataloging-in-Publication Data
Names: Penman, Leigh, author.
Title: The lost history of cosmopolitanism: the early modern origins of
the intellectual ideal / Leigh T.I. Penman.
Description: London, UK; New York, NY: Bloomsbury Academic, 2020. |
Includes bibliographical references and index.
Identifiers: LCCN 2020029958 (print) | LCCN 2020029959 (ebook) | ISBN 9781350156968 (hardback) |
ISBN 9781350230934 (paperback) | ISBN 9781350156975 (ebook) | ISBN 9781350156982 (epub)
Subjects: LCSH: Cosmopolitanism–Philosophy. | Humanism–History. |
Europe–Intellectual life–16th century.
Classification: LCC JZ1308 .P47 2020 (print) | LCC JZ1308 (ebook) | DDC 306–dc23
LC record available at https://lccn.loc.gov/2020029958
LC ebook record available at https://lccn.loc.gov/2020029959

ISBN: HB: 978-1-3501-5696-8
PB: 978-1-3502-3093-4
ePDF: 978-1-3501-5697-5
eBook: 978-1-3501-5698-2

Typeset by RefineCatch Limited, Bungay, Suffolk

To find out more about our authors and books visit www.bloomsbury.com
and sign up for our newsletters.

For Ilona

Contents

List of illustrations		viii
Acknowledgements		ix
1	Strangers, citizens and sojourners: towards a vocabulary of the cosmopolitan	1
2	Hieroglyphics of empire	15
3	Theatres of the world	39
4	The cosmopolitan inversion	65
5	Sharing Diogenes's tub	85
6	Heavenly cities of the eighteenth-century philosophers	105
Epilogue		127
Notes		131
Bibliography		171
Index		201

Illustrations

2.1	John Dee, *Monas hieroglyphica* (1564), title page	27
3.1	Samuel Purchas, *Hakluytus Posthumus* (1624), vol. 1, title page	44
3.2	Anon., 'Nosce te ipsum' (*c.* 1590)	45
3.3	[Jean de Gourmont?], 'Congnois toy toy-mesme' (*c.* 1570)	48
3.4	Dirck Coornhert, 'Tempus ridendi tempus flendi' (1557)	50
3.5	Georg Braun, 'Weltkarte im Adlerform' (1574)	52
3.6	Jodocus Hondius, 'Typus totius orbis terrarum' (*c.* 1596)	54
3.7	Jeronimus Wierix, 'Spirituale Christiani Militis Certamen' (*c.* 1590)	55
3.8	Abraham Ortelius, 'Vtopiae typus, ex Narratione Raphaelis Hythlodæi' (1595)	58

Acknowledgements

Like the cosmopolitan itself, this project once existed only in the realm of the ideal. There it might still languish were it not for Ian Hesketh and Knox Peden, then fellow postdoctoral fellows at the Centre for the History of European Discourses at the University of Queensland, who in 2014 invited me to contribute a talk on the history of cosmopolitan ideas to their seminar series, 'Aesthetics of Scale'. This invitation jump-started this book by prompting its (initially) reluctant author to stop collating references, and start ordering his thoughts.

Many people have helped this project along the way. Ian Coller and Charles Zika encouraged my initial explorations of early-modern cosmopolitan expressions when I was still at the University of Melbourne. James Brown, Howard Hotson and Lyndal Roper, all at the University of Oxford, provided references and advice. At the University of Queensland, attendees of the regular WIP seminars at the Institute for Advanced Studies in the Humanities read parts of this work, and without exception provided valuable feedback. Ian Hunter, in particular, offered incisive comments on an early version of the first chapter, which helped refine the direction and arguments of the book as a whole. Otherwise I thank Marina Bollinger, Peter Cryle, Simon During, Peter Harrison, Nicholas Heron, Ian Hesketh, Gary Ianziti, Anna Johnston, Simon Kennedy, James Lancaster, Michael Ostling, Knox Peden, Lucia Pozzi, Trish Ross, Charlotte Rose Millar, Ryan Walter and Mike Zuber for their careful readership and commentary. Many others offered advice, references or expertise along the way, including Tom Aechtner, Cedric Beidatsch, Erik-Jan Bos, Geoff Boucher, Adam Bowles, Shannon Brincat, Anthony Grafton, Ortwin Grevel, Ariel Hessayon, Didier Kahn, Vera Keller, James Lancaster, Rafał Prinke, David Pritchard, Karin Sellberg, Rick Strelan, N.A.J. Taylor, James Ungureanu and Andrew Weeks. Production of this book was made easy by the editorial team at Bloomsbury, especially Laura Reeves and Rhodri Mogford. It's a pleasure to have the opportunity to thank them all here. But my greatest debt is saved for last: throughout the research and writing of this work, Ilona Fekete has been a wonderful companion, inspiration and muse, while Samu and Kata were always on hand to remind me of the relative importance of my research. This book is dedicated to Ilona.

1

Strangers, citizens and sojourners

Towards a vocabulary of the cosmopolitan

In September 1522 the celebrated Dutch humanist Erasmus of Rotterdam (1466–1536) declared that he was a 'citizen of the world'.[1] At first glance the statement appears to be a fitting self-designation for a figure widely considered to be an early modern archetype of the cosmopolitan. Erasmus was a polymath whose contributions to literature, philology, philosophy and ethics remain of interest and inspiration to scholars today.[2] Through his extensive travels and his epistolary activity Erasmus enmeshed himself in a transnational republic of letters, a virtual scholarly community extending across political, cultural and linguistic borders. Intimately familiar with the writings of antiquity, Erasmus frequently appealed to Stoic ideas to critique the status quo and created literary monuments to tolerance and thought free from religious dogmatism. In his *Querela pacis* (Complaint of Peace, 1521), he expounded at length on the subject of the brotherhood of all men, representing the conflicts of his age as a fracturing of natural law and divine order. A testament to the endurance of Erasmus's reputation as a model internationalist is the attachment of his name to the eponymous Erasmus Programme, established in 1987 as a European Union educational project dedicated to fostering student exchange at institutions of higher learning across the continent.

But this particular vision of Erasmus and his legacies is surprisingly modern. It first flourished in the decades after World War II, when the Dutch humanist was seized upon by scholars as a balsam for a modernity ailing from the excesses of totalitarian ideology and international conflict.[3] In recent decades, very different readings of Erasmus have emerged. Far from being a figure of unreserved internationality in outlook, some scholars now see in his work traces of nascent Dutch patriotism, and a figure whose dedication to Christian community outweighed his obligations to any transnational scholarly network.[4] Although Erasmus's declaration of world citizenship is often mentioned in this revisionist literature, it is rarely quoted or discussed in detail. This neglect is unfortunate, for Erasmus's statement provides further evidence towards the need for a reconceptualization of his motivations and, perhaps, his legacy. Indeed, Erasmus made his statement in a letter addressed to the Swiss reformer Huldrych Zwingli (1484–1531), in which he declined the offer of citizenship in the city of Zürich. Erasmus's words in his missive repay careful attention:

> I am most grateful to you and your city for your kindly thought. My own wish is to be a citizen of the world (*ego mundi civis esse cupio*), to be a fellow-citizen to all men, a pilgrim (*peregrinus*) better still. If only I might have the happiness of being enrolled in the city of heaven. For it is thither I make my way, under the constant attacks of all this illness.[5]

This statement is neither based on Erasmus's self-awareness of being part of a humanistic republic of letters, nor does it comprise a fundamentally 'secular … free declaration of acceptance of humanity and tolerance' that is 'connected to the antique tradition of Cosmopolitanism'.[6] Furthermore, it can hardly be read as suggesting his membership in 'a single political human brotherhood, fraternizing beyond the frontiers'.[7] The statement was exclusive, not inclusive, political not by intent but by implication, and sacred rather than secular. Indeed, Erasmus was a citizen of the world because he was a *peregrinus* – a pilgrim or stranger – making his way towards 'the city of heaven', where he 'might have the happiness of being enrolled'. While this resembles classical Stoic themes of the individual being enmeshed in obligations owed to the larger world, more centrally and perhaps more unexpectedly, it embodied the idea of the Christian *homo viator* sojourning through life towards the city of God, where he is enrolled in the books of Heaven (Hebrews 11:13). Similarly, Erasmus's desire to be a 'fellow-citizen to all men' derives from St. Paul's letter to the Ephesians 2:19.[8]

Seen in this light, Erasmus's statement does not appear to correspond at all with what one historian has recently identified as the core of cosmopolitanism in early modern Europe. 'Since at least the sixteenth century,' we are informed, '"cosmopolitanism" meant – as now – the ability to experience people of different nations, creeds and colors with pleasure, curiosity and interest, and not with suspicion, disdain, or simply a disinterest that could occasionally turn into loathing.' We are furthermore assured that this 'ability' was inspired by travel and intellectual exchange, leading 'some Europeans [to] approach those distinctly different from themselves hospitably, with a willingness to get to know them, even to like them. From at least the sixteenth century such an expansive person was called a *cosmopolite*, best defined as a citizen of the world'.[9] This statement has little in common with Erasmus's own conception of his world citizenship relating to a religious heavenly community. His words suggest rather that early modern Europeans could use the cosmopolitan terminology to designate a variety of concepts, none of which need be correlated with an ability or disposition to meet, greet and tolerate the people of the world, or to belong to a 'cosmopolitan movement'.[10] Although it was sometimes attached to the idea of an abstract world community, it could also be linked with concepts largely alien to modern conceptions of cosmopolitanism.

Situated at the intersection of conceptual history and intellectual history, the present volume provides a new history of the rise of cosmopolitan thought in early modern Europe. Rather than looking for antecedents of modern cosmopolitan conceptions in the past, it is dedicated instead to documenting the variety of meanings that early modern figures attached to the idea of the cosmopolitan. It considers and contextualizes statements made in letters, books and other documents between 1500 and 1800 from throughout Europe, which employ what I have chosen to call the 'cosmopolitan vocabulary'. This includes words like the Greek κοσμοπολίτης, the Latin *cosmopolitanus* and *mundanus*, the French *cosmopolite*, *cosmopolitain* and *citoyen du monde*, the Italian *cittadino del mondo*, the English cosmopolite, cosmopolitan and worldling, the German *Weltbürger*, the Dutch *Wereldburger* and other vernacular equivalents. Rather than providing an exhaustive catalogue of these usages – a largely antiquarian task that would fill several volumes – it focusses on a selection of key moments when meanings attached to the cosmopolitan vocabulary were contested, disputed or inverted by historical actors.[11] Alternatively, it pays attention to those moments when early modern conceptions of the cosmopolitan seem most alien to modern scholarly expectations.

What emerges is a new history of the intellectual origins of a cherished, though volatile, modern ideal. Far from being merely historical in interest, it tells a larger story about how we came to think about cosmopolitanism today, which challenges scholarly and popular conceptions of 'cosmopolitanism' and understandings of its origins. Additionally, this volume opens new avenues through which modern observers can approach the cosmopolitan, by demonstrating the crucial role played by early modernity in the formulation of a cherished ideal. Indeed, without the debates surrounding the cosmopolitan ideal in early modernity, modern cosmopolitanism would not exist.

Influenced by concerns religious, philological, scholarly, social, cultural and biographical, the cosmopolitan vocabulary was used by early modern actors to designate a diverse range of concepts. In the sixteenth century the vocabulary was used in an overwhelmingly religious register by Catholics and Protestants alike, often to designate concepts related to a spiritual *ecclesia*. But in the course of the seventeenth century, influential clerical authors, especially in Protestant countries, began to associate the vocabulary instead with worldliness, thus inverting its associations. By the beginning of the eighteenth century, the cosmopolitan vocabulary was the almost exclusive preserve of deists and secular philosophers.

Two crucial arguments emerge from this history. The first is that, historically, the cosmopolitan vocabulary was used to impose difference, instead of to efface it. Furthermore, there has never existed a single, stable cosmopolitan concept; but rather a range of concepts designated with the cosmopolitan vocabulary. The second argument is that the Enlightenment ideals of cosmopolitanism would be unthinkable without the early modern discourse on the cosmopolitan. In France, the *philosophes* reflected on historical usages of the cosmopolitan vocabulary, and attempted to appropriate the terminology to designate their own endeavours, thereby creating a meta-discourse of 'cosmopolitanism'. As such, this study provides not only a history of how early modern Europeans used the cosmopolitan vocabulary in shifting registers to designate sometimes surprising concepts. It also demonstrates that the diversity of expressions of early modernity were a crucial precursor for European thinkers to conceive of an abstract modern 'cosmopolitanism' in the first place.

The cosmopolitan vocabulary

The cosmopolitan vocabulary first appeared in antiquity. Although the Greek word κοσμοπολίτης (hereafter *kosmopolitēs*) is said to have been coined by the Cynic philosopher Diogenes of Sinope (fl. fourth century BCE), the earliest extant usages of this word only date to the first few centuries of the Common Era.[12] Even during this period, the vocabulary was already applied to designate a variety of partially conflicting concepts. Transmitted in an influential prosopographical work of the fourth century CE, Diogenes's aphoristic declaration that he was *kosmopolitēs* was intended to demonstrate his sovereignty over self and indifference to the rest of the world.[13] As H.C. Baldry has pointed out in his classic study of Greek thought, this statement was a manifestation of Diogenes' desire to eschew connections with fellow men, not to establish them.[14] Several centuries before Diogenes's expression was being popularized, Roman Stoics – influenced by Plato's foundational metaphor of the world as a 'city whose home is in the ideal' – used the cosmopolitan vocabulary to express the concept of an individual's citizenship in the *oikumene*, or civilized world.[15] The Stoics Cicero (104–43 BCE) and Epictetus (50–135 CE) attributed Diogenes' aphorism to their spiritual forefather Socrates (d. 399 BCE) who, when asked from whence he originated, supposedly declared that he was a πολίτης του κόσμου (*politēs tou kosmou*, citizen of the world). In other accounts, Socrates was said to have used the words κοσμίος or *mundanus* (worldling) in his response. According to these classical sources, Socrates's conviction derived from his exercise of reason, and the enmeshment of his philosophical obligations in a metaphorical 'great city of the world'.[16] This is something very different from what was meant by Diogenes.

But the cosmopolitan vocabulary was not only employed in a secular register. The Hebrew philosopher and theologian Philo of Alexandria (*c.* 25 BCE–*c.* 75 CE) described the Biblical Adam as the 'only cosmopolitan (τῷ κοσμοπολίτην) . . . for the world was his household and city'. However, following his exile from Eden on account of fracturing the divine law, Adam was forced to relinquish his claim to such a title. This special status was only regained by Moses for the Hebrews after he accepted the covenant atop Mt. Sinai (Exodus 20:1–17, Deuteronomy 5:6–21).[17] In his *De confusione linguarum*, Philo included a lengthy gloss on the story of the patriarch Abraham, the archetypal pilgrim of the Old Testament. Abraham's declaration that he was 'a foreigner and stranger among you' (Genesis 23:4, similarly Exodus 6:3–4) were portrayed by Philo as part of a valorizing discourse of heavenly citizenship, in which the experience of worldly exile was justified by the promise of eternal repose in a heavenly New Jerusalem (Ezekiel 40–48; Isaiah 54:11–14). For Philo, figures like Abraham, 'after they have stayed a while in their bodies, and beheld through them all that sense and mortality has to show, they make their way back to the place from which they set out at first. To them the heavenly region, where their citizenship lies, is their native land, the earthly region in which they became sojourners is a foreign country'.[18]

Concepts of strangerhood and the cosmopolitan New Jerusalem also proved appealing to some Christians, who in addition to seeing their fledgling religion as a fulfilment of Hebrew prophecy, were also influenced by Platonic and Stoic metaphors of the spiritual city.[19] For example, the Gnostic apocalypse *Allogenes the Stranger* (c. 300 CE) played on Abrahamic themes of strangerhood crucial to the status of the chosen.[20] The Greek-language *Apostolic Constitutions* (c. 380 CE), a document originating in Syria and belonging to the genre of Church Orders, echoed Philo in its call for Christians to remember that they were 'constituted to be citizens of the world' (κοσμοπολίτης).[21] Nevertheless, the Christian belief that Christ's grace alone was capable of absolving sin meant that they tended to relate the cosmopolitan idea to an active, missionary identity, as opposed to a passive covenantal one, conferred by adherence to the Law. One of the final extant usages of the cosmopolitan vocabulary in late antiquity appeared in the works of Ambrose (337–397 CE), the Bishop of Milan. Reasoning in a firmly supercessionist mode, Ambrose considered Platonic, Stoic and Hebrew statements concerning the cosmopolitan to comprise a uniform concept entirely consonant with doctrines of his faith:

> Even today, wherever the wise man goes, he is a citizen and knows his own, nowhere considering himself a mere pilgrim or foreigner, how much more was that first man [*sc.* Adam] an inhabitant of all the world, and as the Greeks say, a cosmopolite (*cosmopolites*), for he was the final work of God, continually talking with God, a fellow citizen of the saints, a ground-bed of virtues? Placed over all the creatures of the earth, sea, and sky, he considered the whole world his dominion.[22]

Ambrose's statement was novel because it equated a plethora of Stoic, Hebrew and Christian conceptions of the cosmopolitan, linking them with imagery drawn from the Deutero-Pauline epistle to the Ephesians (first century CE). This epistle declared that by accepting Jesus of Nazareth as the prophesied messiah, the Ephesians were 'no longer foreigners and strangers', but had become 'fellow citizens of the Saints' (2:19–20). By so doing, Ambrose retrospectively linked the cosmopolitan vocabulary to the New Testament concept of 'heavenly citizenship' (Philippians 3:20; Hebrews 11:13–16, etc.). This citizenship was in the spiritual *ecclesia* of the 'Jerusalem above' (Galatians 4:26), which in the prophecy of John in Revelation 21:2, merged with the earth at the end of time. At the same time that Ambrose made his interpretative innovation, the clause *ut Græci dicunt* ('as the Greeks say') earmarked the word 'cosmopolitan' as just one of many possible designations for the concept of membership in the Christian *ecclesia spiritualis*. While Ambrose's sentiments would endure in Christianity – reappearing most notably in a work by his protégé, Augustine's *City of God* (fifth century) – the cosmopolitan vocabulary itself fell into abeyance with the rise of Latinate Christianity.[23]

It would not be rediscovered until the late fifteenth or early sixteenth century, when Europeans devoted renewed attention to the literary and philosophical works of antiquity.[24] In the fourteenth century ardent bibliophiles like Poggio Bracciolini (1380–1459) scoured the monastic libraries of Europe in search of long-neglected works of antiquity, returning them to scholarly attention.[25] In addition to contributing to the nascent humanist movement – which emphasized man as the central figure in affairs physical and metaphysical – the efforts of translators, linguists and philologists to edit, publish and popularize works of classical antiquity led to the reintroduction of many obscure Greek and Latin words into scholarly discourse.[26] This included the cosmopolitan vocabulary. In 1516 Francisco Maria Grapaldi's (c. 1464–1515) *De partibus aedium*, a philological tract first issued in 1494 which doubled as a dictionary of ancient architectural terminology, included reference to Socrates as 'Cosmopolites ciuis mundi'.[27] It was not the only work to do so. The late fifteenth and early sixteenth centuries saw the publication of a variety of editions, translations and commentaries on works of antiquity that employed the cosmopolitan vocabulary, including texts by Diogenes Laërtius, Philo, Cicero, Epictetus, Ambrose and others.[28]

Following the reappearance of the cosmopolitan vocabulary in editions of ancient texts and scholarly literature in the early sixteenth century, vernacular assimilations like the French *cosmopolite, cosmopolitain* or *citoyen du monde*, the Italian *cittadino del mondo*, the English 'worldling', 'citizen of the world' or 'citizen of the universe', the Dutch *Wereldboerger*, the German *Weltmann* or *Weltbürger*, soon followed.[29] All of these terms, in addition to the Greek and Latin words above, comprise the cosmopolitan vocabulary considered in the present study.

What did early modern figures mean when they employed this cosmopolitan vocabulary? The example of Erasmus invites us to look beyond the typical conceptual fields associated with modern 'cosmopolitanism' or any real or imagined 'cosmopolitan movement' for answers. Early modern editors and translators not only rediscovered the cosmopolitan vocabulary of antiquity. In the spirit of Ambrose, they also expanded its conceptual boundaries. Incrementally, these early-modern commentators began to expand the associations of the vocabulary. For example, they designated Democritus of Abdera's (fifth century BCE) decidedly Stoic sentiment that 'to a wise man the whole earth is open; for the native land of a good soul is the whole earth' with the cosmopolitan vocabulary.[30] Others lingered over the words of the Roman Stoic Gaius Musonius Rufus (first century CE) – who applauded Socrates's exile from Athens by identifying the world as a common fatherland where all might consider themselves 'a citizen of the city of God which is made up of men and gods' – to express the same concept as that described by Cicero or Epictetus when they spoke of Socrates.[31] In his influential *Physiologia Stoicorum* (1604) the Flemish scholar Justus Lipsius (1547–1606) dedicated a whole chapter to documenting what he considered to be manifestations of the idea of the 'City of the World' in ancient Stoic literature. His work not only became a *locus classicus*, informing a host of seventeenth-century discussions of the cosmopolitan vocabulary; it also influenced Denis Diderot's thought on the subject.[32] The upshot of the efforts of Lipsius and others is this: many of the statements, ideas and associations of classical antiquity that are today routinely designated as 'cosmopolitan' are product of the intellectual and philological groundwork laid by sixteenth- and seventeenth-century commentators. In other words, the 'cosmopolitanism' of pagan antiquity, as it is presently understood, is to a large degree a creation of early modern scholarship.

This is a crucial realization with potentially far-reaching implications, because the approach of many early modern scholars to the Stoic, Cynic and even Platonic statements of antiquity was conditioned by concepts of strangerhood, peregrination and heavenly citizenship derived from their native Christian traditions.[33] Indeed, their uses of the cosmopolitan vocabulary subtly imposed a supercessionist continuity through classical, Hebrew and Christian conceptions of the cosmopolitan. This was a legacy which eighteenth-century writers would have to negotiate, and which modern scholars and commentators have often overlooked. Arguably, the ameliorative impulse at the core of modern cosmopolitan visions is itself an unwitting inheritance from early modernity.

In light of the diverse conceptual background that inspired or underwrote usage of the cosmopolitan vocabulary in early modern Europe, it is important to recognize that the cosmopolitan vocabulary was not, or not typically, used as a noun describing a distinct ideology or philosophy. It was more often employed to describe the attributes of an individual or group, and was thus related intrinsically to identity. As the present work demonstrates, early modernity was a time when a cosmopolitan might be an exalted citizen of heaven, a learned traveller, a despised stranger, a globetrotting sojourner, a paragon of reason, an instrument of divine law, a promoter of natural harmony, an ideal political subject, a political insurrectionist, a patriot, a divinely inspired prophet or a lowly sinner. He – and very occasionally she – could be a citizen everywhere in the world, or indeed a citizen nowhere in the world. All of these meanings were conditioned by political, social, religious, legal, cultural, biographical and linguistic circumstances.

The cosmopolitan vocabulary could be employed in this fashion because, as Karen O'Brien has argued, it possessed – and possesses – no fixed referent.[34] Although it was interpreted against a backdrop of associations, the words that constituted the vocabulary lacked what Reinhart Koselleck has described as a semantic 'carrying capacity', which made possible their reliable association with any particular concept. For there were no actual citizens of the world; there existed no cosmopolis. Except, of course, in the imagination.[35] As in antiquity, the cosmopolitan was an idea and an ideal, variously ethical, moral, religious or political, formulated afresh in the mind of every thinker. No two observers who employed the cosmopolitan vocabulary meant precisely the same thing by it, even if they drew on the same sources. If there is a thread that binds together early modern statements on the cosmopolitan, it is not related to their conception of an inclusive world community, but rather in the establishment of difference: in exclusion, rather than inclusion.

Early modernity has not typically been the subject of modern scholarship on cosmopolitanism. In pursuit of inclusionary lived experiences, the origins of tolerance, or of the roots of secular global thought – products all of late twentieth-century intellectual preoccupations – the exclusionary and contradictory expressions of early modernity appear confronting, contradictory and confusing, and are not easily reconciled with such narratives. Even in the relatively few studies of the history of cosmopolitanism that do consider early modernity, scholars have variously portrayed the period as an 'intermezzo' to a grander unified tradition of secular cosmopolitanism, as a teleological 'prehistory' of Kantian cosmopolitanism, as a 'medieval footnote' to ideas of world citizenship, or have indeed represented statements from this period as 'spurious and superficial manifestations of the cosmopolitan spirit'.[36]

One of the major reasons for this neglect of the often divisive early modern cosmopolitan expressions is historical. The current trend of scholarly interest in cosmopolitanism first emerged in the 1990s, in the wake of communism's collapse. While some western commentators, like Francis Fukuyama, celebrated the apparently terminal victory of liberal democracy, others reflected on questions of nationalism, patriotism and ethics, and on conceptions of community in the new economy of global politics and interrelations.[37] Some postulated that the world had entered a 'post national' moment, where artificial ideological boundaries had been cleared away for new conceptions of global community to flourish in their stead.[38] The British historian Eric Hobsbawm (1917–2012) predicted that, in the future, 'nations and nationalism will be present ... but in subordinate, and often rather minor roles', while Samuel Huntington argued that the recession of ideology in world politics would prompt conflicts along civilizational lines.[39] In a 1994 issue of the *Boston Review*, the American philosopher Martha C. Nussbaum proposed an alternative. In her influential essay 'Patriotism and Cosmopolitanism', she argued that national, political and ethnic boundaries were 'morally irrelevant' in the new political order, and suggested that the individual owed an allegiance not to any *patria*, but 'to the worldwide community of human beings'.⁴⁰ Based on an impression of cosmopolitanism drawn from the Stoics and Immanuel Kant, Nussbaum argued that this form of world citizenship could be inculcated via a system of liberal education. As a perceived attack on American 'politics of difference', Nussbaum's essay prompted considerable debate, and popularized the idea of cosmopolitanism as a radical alternative to nationalistic sentiment; a new humanistic ideology for the post-communist era.⁴¹

In the years following, a string of works that used the word 'cosmopolitan' followed, which dissolved Nussbaum's antagonism of cosmopolitanism and nationalism. Today, the word appears in the titles of works in fields as diverse as international finance, Puritanism, philosophy, gender, ethics, opera, German literature, international relations and global governance, to name only a few.⁴² Some observers have been troubled by the multiplication of associations that the cosmopolitan had taken on. Already by 1998 the American philosopher Bruce Robbins remarked that 'something has happened to cosmopolitanism', which by that time could be understood as a positive 'fundamental devotion to the interests of humanity as a whole', or alternatively linked to a variety of lived experiences. 'Cosmopolitanisms,' he remarked, 'are now plural and particular.'⁴³ Yet Robbins' diagnosis of the concept's ills is based on a wrongful assumption that there ever did exist a homogenous cosmopolitanism, either in the 1990s, or indeed in history more generally.

A survey of cosmopolitan expressions of early modernity demonstrates that this was never the case, and that recent scholarly engagement with the historical particularities of the cosmopolitan has been limited. Indeed, many seem to have been satisfied with Nussbaum's hasty genealogy connecting the Stoics to Kant as an adequate summary of the extent of its historical dimension, with the long centuries between omitted.⁴⁴ But as Galin Tihanov has argued powerfully, while this attempt to 'cast a bridge' across the millennia might be useful from a philosophical perspective, for an intellectual historian 'the sense of break and discontinuity is overwhelming'.⁴⁵ Another factor conditioning scholarly neglect of early modernity seems to be the application of essentialist definitions of cosmopolitanism applied by scholars. Tihanov has suggested, I think rightly, that many scholars are 'anxious to endow cosmopolitanism with a "positive" genealogy' that is both 'optimistic and ameliorative'.⁴⁶ This anxiety has arguably been manifested in the tendency of scholars to project modern ideals and understandings of cosmopolitanism back into the past, in anachronistic quest of 'anticipations' of modern cosmopolitan ideas. While this has resulted in valuable accounts of the emergence of 'cosmopolitan mores' in early modernity, it has also obscured some of the historical complexities that made the identification of such mores possible in the first place.[47] In particular, the secular register of modern cosmopolitan scholarship has meant that the sacred aspects of this complex history have remained underemphasized or indeed unnoticed.

The present work adopts the position taken by Pauline Kleingeld in her ground-breaking study of cosmopolitan ideas in Immanuel Kant's work. There, Kleingeld argued that 'rather than attempting to craft a substantive definition of cosmopolitanism ... it is better to draw the appropriate distinctions and to acknowledge that there is a plurality of approaches that are justifiably called cosmopolitan'.[48] In the present study, the 'plurality of approaches' is presented through the words of the historical actors.[49] As such, it is not intended as a prescriptive history of cosmopolitanism, for it does not seek to trace the history of a particular conception of the cosmopolitan thought back to early modern roots. Nor does it seek to judge the relative merits of these. Instead, taking Quentin Skinner's common-sense proposition that 'the terms we use to express our concepts have a history', it considers the diversity of concepts that the cosmopolitan vocabulary was employed to designate in early modernity, concentrating on those moments when the meaning or significance of this vocabulary was disputed, changed, or called into question by historical actors.[50] It is, then, primarily a history of early modern expressions of the cosmopolitan, but also about how we came to think about, and with, the cosmopolitan vocabulary today.

Arranged thematically and largely chronologically, the study begins with a consideration of the influential imperialist and religious cosmopolitan ideas of sixteenth-century thinkers like John Dee and Guillaume Postel, who have both long been thought to have reintroduced the cosmopolitan vocabulary back into European thought. Chapter 3 builds on this analysis by examining the influence of the cosmopolitan idea on early modern geography and cartography, demonstrating how Christian ideas of heavenly citizenship folded into knowledge terrestrial and heavenly. The fourth chapter charts the decline of the appeal of the cosmopolitan vocabulary across Protestant Europe in the course of the seventeenth century, while the fifth documents its continued appeal among neo-Stoics like Justus Lipsius, jurists, natural philosophers and the French Pyrrhonists. Despite often working in nominally secular contexts, these figures continued to use the cosmopolitan vocabulary to describe sacred ideals of world community. Chapter 6 concludes the work by tracing the emergence of a cosmopolitan meta-discourse in the eighteenth century, showing how the influential conceptions of Diderot and Kant, among others, were influenced by the sacred and secular visions of the sixteenth and seventeenth centuries.

2

Hieroglyphics of empire

I have appointed you a prophet to all nations.

Jeremiah 1:5

This gospel of the kingdom shall be preached in all the world for a witness unto all nations; and then shall the end come.

Matthew 24:14

For historians of cosmopolitanism the year 1560 marks a watershed moment. For it was in this year that the word 'Cosmopolite' – a repurposing of the Greek *kosmopolitēs* – reappeared in a European language for the first time in more than a millennium.[1] The context of its use suggests that it could be connected in some way to modern conceptions of world community. The word featured on the title page of a slim volume concerning the Ottoman Empire that was printed in Poitiers in France. Titled *De la République des Turcs*, the book was authored by the French polymath and Hebraist Guillaume Postel (1510–1581), and detailed the history, customs and laws of Ottoman civilization.[2] The author signed his name as 'Guillaume Postel, Cosmopolite'.

Prompted by this unusual epithet, scholars have characterized both Postel and his cosmopolitanism in a variety of ways. One saw him as the archetypal expansive world traveller, who wished to establish 'a universal peace, especially in religion and with the Turks'.[3] One has argued that Postel's work represents a landmark in cross-religious reconciliation and interfaith dialogue unrivalled in Europe before the twentieth century.[4] Another scholar suggests that the word indicated Postel's secular conception of being a person who felt himself 'bound to no nation' perhaps on account of having 'lived in a variety of countries'.[5] Yet another scholar has claimed that the word represented his 'sense of dedication to the service of the whole human race'.[6] In these views, Postel is a determinedly modern cosmopolite, an expansive 'stranger nowhere in the world'. The content of some of Postel's other works, such as his volumes praising the virtues of women, reinforce the impressions of the inherent modernity of his thought.[7]

But the scholarly consensus is built on two misconceptions. First, Postel was far from the first European to employ the term 'cosmopolite', which had appeared in humanistic works since the beginning of the sixteenth century. Second, a re-examination of Postel's life and work makes evident that he used the cosmopolitan vocabulary to designate very different concepts from those anticipated by modern scholars of cosmopolitanism. Indeed, Postel's *De la République* makes clear that his self-designation was neither product of a benevolent desire to learn about other civilizations, nor to foster interreligious understanding. Instead, prompted by considerations messianic and apocalyptic, the book intended to arm Christian missionaries with knowledge of Ottoman society sufficient to effect their conversion to Christianity, and thereby provoke an apocalyptic universal peace. In other words, Postel's goal was to eradicate a Muslim 'enemy' – to borrow his own term – by establishing Christian dominion throughout the world, beginning with its most powerful enemy. This victory, in turn, was couched by Postel within an elaborate imperial vision, in which the final victory of Christianity would be instituted by a European political power.

The present chapter re-examines Postel's cosmopolitan vision alongside that of his English counterpart, the Elizabethan cosmographer and 'magus' John Dee (1527–1608). Inspired by the topos of the Christian as a stranger, and influenced by both Stoic antiquity and humanist scholarship, both men presented imperial interpretations of the cosmopolitan idea, fashioned within distinctly prophetic matrices. Although the particulars of their visions differed, their work united several themes – including strangerhood, pilgrimage and heavenly citizenship – which have comprised the history of the cosmopolitan idea since antiquity. Recently, Anthony Pagden has suggested that cosmopolitanism is an idea 'whose fortunes have been linked, for far longer than has generally been supposed, with the history of European universalism'.[8] An analysis of the visions of Dee and Postel supports Pagden's contention, showing the long-standing relationship between empire, Christianity and the cosmopolitan conceived of as both identity and world community.

The most accursed and unhappy man who ever lived

Guillaume Postel's conception of the cosmopolitan is intimately tied to the details of his life. At the time of the publication of his *De la République* in 1560, the Frenchman was in disgrace. In the 1530s, he had been widely recognized and hailed as one of the most brilliant young scholars in Europe, and was a celebrated orientalist, cartographer and mathematician. But a series of reversals of fortune paired with mental illness led him into a labyrinth, and by the time he deposited the manuscript of *De la République* at the printery of Enguilbert de Marnef in provincial Poitiers in 1559, far from the intellectual capital in Paris both literally and figuratively, he had already been imprisoned on several occasions and accused of heresy. Thus while Postel called himself a 'Cosmopolitan Gaulois' on account of the fact that he had 'cures and cares for all the world', it was not for nothing that a contemporary described him as 'the most accursed and unhappy man who ever lived'.[9]

A consideration of the course of Postel's life provides valuable insight into some features of his thought. Postel was born in 1510 at Dolerie, a small village in the parish of Barenton in rural Normandy. Something of a child prodigy, in the 1520s he relocated to Paris where he enrolled at the Collège de Sainte-Barbe. Established in 1460, the institution trained Catholic missionaries for the New World, and its *alma mater* included Ignatius Loyola (1491–1556) and Francis Xavier (1506–1552). At Sainte-Barbe, Postel excelled in classical scholarship, philology, mathematics and languages, including Hebrew. In 1536 Postel's missionary zeal was acknowledged by a commission to accompany a French diplomatic retinue to Constantinople. In the Levant, Postel hired a tutor in Arabic, who claimed to be a member of a secret community of Ottoman Christians numbering some 300,000 adherents. This startling revelation meshed with Postel's latent apocalyptic commitments and missionary education, and gradually coalesced into an outlandish project to unite this island of believers with their brethren elsewhere by ensuring the universal victory of Christianity. The beginnings of this project were, perhaps surprisingly, scholarly in character.[10] First, Postel worked on a Syriac translation of the New Testament for missionary purposes. Thereafter he authored a *Description de la Syrie* (1542), a guide for missionaries, pilgrims and travellers in the Holy Land.

Postel outlined his plans in his early masterwork, *De orbis terrae concordia libri quatuor* (1543). Written at breakneck speed in the winter of 1542–1543, this volume sought to move contemporaries to action against the enemies of Catholicism wherever they might be found. The volume itself outlined a two-pronged approach to the conversion of the enemies of Christianity. First, Postel argued that scholars should invoke rational discourse to demonstrate the truths of Christian doctrine to their enemies in a moderate and straightforward fashion. Second, these same scholars should study the laws and mores of the Turks and Arabs, in particular the Koran, the better to refute them.[11] The results of this course of action would be the creation of a single world community both divine and human in character. The work was ultimately printed in Basel after being rejected by censors at the Sorbonne. Discouraged by the lack of interest in his schemes, Postel decided to depart France for Italy, in a vain attempt to interest the Jesuits in his visions of world harmony.

Upon reaching Rome, Postel publicly proclaimed that the French monarchy was the divine power chosen to lead the world to concord. This choice, in light of the contemporary unification of Habsburg Spain and the Holy Roman Empire from 1519 under Emperor Charles V (1500–1558), was largely a by-product of Postel's abstruse scriptural and humanistic studies. In his *Raisons de la monarchie* (1552), Postel argued that the French royal family was descended from Gomer, the grandson of Noah, who had been granted dominion over all the earth (Genesis 10). According to Postel, after the flood Gomer settled in what was then France, and his authority had devolved by means of Salic law to the French. All other Europeans, including the Habsburgs and their subjects, thus owed allegiance to the descendants of Gomer.[12] As such, Postel's initial choice of the French to lead the charge to a cosmopolitan universal peace was itself a manifestation of the same Christian universalist ideology which prompted his vision of world community.[13]

Although Postel indeed joined the Jesuits in Rome, he quickly courted controversy. In early 1545 Ignatius Loyola, who had grown suspicious of Postel's views on *concordia* and the French monarchy, ordered that Postel submit to an inquisitorial procedure. In December 1545 Postel was expelled from the order.[14] Dejected, he wandered the streets of Rome, until he began to perceive a calling previously 'hidden in the Orient'.[15] This realization came after

Postel obtained a manuscript of the *Zohar*, the foundational Jewish kabbalistic work. He studied the work intensely, and began translating it into Latin. The driving force to Postel's industry was his belief that the kabbalah furnished a new basis for the rational defence of Christian doctrine, which could help in demonstrating its truth to Muslims, Hebrews and others. At the beginning of 1547 Postel arrived in Venice, where he became chaplain in the hospital of Sts. John and Paul. It was here that his prophetic convictions blossomed into messianic fantasy. He authored a volume under the pseudonym 'Elias Pandocheus', identifying himself with the prophet Elias as a harbinger of universal harmony.[16] Postel's strivings were granted further impetus by his encounter with 'the virgin of Venice', the penniless and illiterate Mother Zuana, who impressed Postel so much on account of her piety that he came to believe that she was the embodiment of the divine *Shekinah* of kabbalistic doctrine. Soon Postel also became convinced that she was the 'bride of Christ', the embodiment of the Heavenly City of Jerusalem, prophesied to descend to earth at the end of time (Revelation 21:2).[17] The culminating events of history were nigh, and Postel descended into messianic fervour.

In the summer of 1549 he travelled to the near east where he spent some eighteen months acquiring books and manuscripts to further his missionary and scholarly endeavours. When he returned to France in 1550 or 1551, he learned that Mother Zuana had died during his sojourn. Distraught, Postel eventually became convinced that he was now possessed by the spirit of the Venetian virgin. Thereafter the Frenchman issued numerous works in which he petitioned not only the French, but also the Holy Roman Emperor to sponsor his sacred visions of concord. In 1555 Postel learned that several of his books had been placed on the Papal index, landing a crushing blow to his missionary and messianic pretensions. When Postel rushed to Venice to defend himself, he became the subject of an inquisitorial trial, during which it was decided that he was not a heretic, but insane. Freed from imprisonment in 1559, Postel hastened back to France. By this time calling himself 'Cosmopolite' to designate his peculiar messianic status, he deposited several manuscripts with a printer in Poitiers, including his *De la République des Turcs*. In the same year, he advertised his services in a letter to the Holy Roman Emperor Ferdinand I (1503–1564, ruled from 1558). In this missive, which was influenced by Stoic as well as Christian cosmopolitan discourse, Postel described his life's mission:

> Led by the *mater mundi*, who is right reason, I have proposed a method by which the Christian Republic may be preserved uninjured and undisturbed. This is to be accomplished by a universal empire, which will enable the teachings of the Christian religion, confirmed by right reason, to be disseminated. In this way, Christ will be seen to restore as much as Satan has destroyed, and it will be as though Adam had never sinned.[18]

In his *De orbis concordia,* Postel outlined that a first step to establishing this Christian Republic would be to promote 'right reason', by which he meant facilitating an informed discussion of scripture between Christian missionaries and the unenlightened. To this end he advocated the printing of sacred texts – for example the Koran and New Testament – in the language of each faction, so that all could adjudicate the truth of their opponent's claims. In 1553, he printed a volume showing the concord between doctrines in the Koran and the gospels, intended to better demonstrate the truth of the Christian faith.[19] Postel insisted that members of different faiths engage with one another peacefully, and even declared that 'the truth will out', declaring that he would happily convert to the religion of his opponent, for instance Islam, if he were reasonably convinced of its inherent truth.[20]

But Postel never truly countenanced any such circumstance, for he believed that the rectitude of his mission could be proved as irrefutably as a Euclidean formula.[21] This is demonstrated by the second aspect of Postel's project for restitution. For if missionary activity failed to achieve its desired outcomes, then military action would be used to compel world concord. This had been signalled by Postel as early as the 1550s. For example, in his *L'histoire memorable* (1552), Postel called himself a new Peter the Hermit (*c.* 1050–1115), a reference to the French ascetic preacher who inspired the First Crusade (1095–1099) to retake Jerusalem from the ruling Umayyad Caliphate.[22] Shortly thereafter, he created a map of the Holy Land dedicated to Catherine of Medici (1519–1589), which attempted to inspire Catholic powers 'to recover and re-establish Christ's dominion.'[23] Not content with this, in 1560 Postel outlined a rough military strategy by which the Ottoman Empire might be defeated, which drew on his first-hand geographical knowledge of the region.[24] According to Postel, to defeat the enemies of Christianity in the Levant,

> these things are needed: sobriety, patience, obedience, wealth, numbers, speed, and to have every part of the enemy's country filled with men; and to

pursue the victory without leaving off, once it is begun; and to attack at such a point, if possible, that the forces in Asia and Europe are cut off from each other, by occupying the strait of the sea [*sc.* the Bosporus] and their castles, and preventing any vessel from passing on pain of death. And the chief thing is to be secret in the affair, for in ten or twenty days they [*sc.* the Turks] can assemble a hundred thousand men around Constantinople if they have some little warning.[25]

As this passage makes abundantly clear, Postel's cosmopolitan vision of world concord anticipated the violent extirpation of Christ's enemies, be they Protestant, Jewish, or Muslim. We are here very far from the moral and ethical cosmopolitanism that is sometimes attributed to him by modern scholars.

By the 1560s, however, Postel was descending into insanity, his behaviour becoming noticeably erratic. At this time he again advertised his cosmopolitan plans to the Holy Roman Emperor Ferdinand I, but received no response.[26] Finally, after a series of incidents, Postel was imprisoned in Paris by royal decree on 29 January 1563, allegedly for his own protection. But this did not put a stop to his activities. Postel soon found a collaborator, another man who designated himself a cosmopolite, the priest and minor Hebraist Jehan Boulaese.[27] Together, the pair laboured with other scholars on a Syriac translation of the New Testament for missionary purposes. But shortly thereafter, both men became propagandists of the so-called 'miracle of Laon'.[28] In 1566, in Laon, a young nun named Nicole d'Obry was possessed by a host of demons, including Beelzebub himself. Ultimately, after a harrowing series of public exorcisms had failed to free the young girl, the devil was finally expelled by the sight of the host brandished by Laon's bishop. Boulaese collaborated with Postel on several tracts concerning the miracle, all of which insisted that Beelzebub's defeat in Laon signified the presaged world concord and 'restitution of all things' in 1566.[29] Their accounts were printed in parallel Latin, French, Italian, Spanish and German texts, ensuring that its message reached all the descendants of Gomer.[30] Ottoman Turkish and Hebrew editions were also planned, but were never printed.

Despite the grand hopes of Boulaese and Postel, the appointed year came and went without the desired cosmopolitan concord. Boulaese descended into obscurity, while Postel remained a prisoner in the Parisian monastery of St. Martin until his death in 1581. It was a sad and lonely end for this scholar of prodigious intellect and learning, who saw himself as a prophetic figure, chosen to usher the world into a glorious new age.

Postel as cosmopolite

Postel's self-identification as a cosmopolite might appear strange in light of the trajectory of his life. But the very fact that Postel was blown from pillar to post on account of his lifelong dedication to achieving world peace and concord appears to have been the crucial component of his cosmopolitan identity. As we have seen, in antiquity the self-designation of an individual as *kosmopolitēs*, could evoke different associations. For Diogenes the Cynic, it represented self-sovereignty. Within early Christianity, narratives of strangerhood valorized persecuted Christians, whose sufferings would be redressed by citizenship in the heavenly Jerusalem. In his 1553 work *Des merveilles du monde* – written after his recognition of Mother Zuana as the virgin of Venice – Postel complained that 'when people see anyone with some fervour or zeal to begin some sort of reformation, or live more according to God than is customary, he is immediately scorned or mocked … is reputed mad and senseless, and finally killed or imprisoned'.[31] In 1580, an elderly Postel declared himself the 'ass of God' because of his sufferings, a circumstance that informed his cosmopolitan identity (*sic asinus iste cosmopolites Postellus filius asinarum omnium*).[32]

As a formidable humanistic scholar, Postel was familiar with Stoic and Cynic philosophical traditions. Nevertheless, his cosmopolitan identity was heavily informed by Christian thought. Postel did not use the epithet solely to designate his outsider status; indeed, the evidence suggests that he also linked the idea of the cosmopolite to his projects for world concord. Let us consider a key statement from his *De la République des Turcs* (1560), the work in which Postel first publicly used the epithet 'Cosmopolite'. In a preface addressed to the French Dauphin, he wrote:

> Insofar as one cannot, when it is a matter of concord in the world (for universal peace, by reason of which I call myself a *Cosmopolite*, desiring to see it become established, under the Crown of France), in any way speak for the purposes of reason with the enemy without knowing his whole condition

as he himself does, and given that among either religion [*sc.* Christianity and Islam] the Ishmaelite empire is the greatest empire and armed power, and that among the Ishmaelites [the greatest empire] is the Turkesque one, I shall here grant you knowledge about it.[33]

It is because Postel seeks world peace through the conversion of Muslims that he calls himself a cosmopolitan. While it is possible to read Postel's intentions to 'grant knowledge' about other religions as a manifestation of Stoic ideals – namely to know and engage with everything according to reason – such readings overlook the matrix of prophetic and apocalyptic ideas from which Postel's statement emerged, as well as the civilizational and religious objections that informed them.[34]

This position can be seen more clearly in Postel's works documenting his conviction of the Hebrew origins of civilization. Like Philo of Alexandria before him, Postel's *De originibus* (1553) represented the Hebrew patriarch Abraham as a *civis mundi* and 'father of truth' who gave up his worldly possessions to prove himself to God.[35] Traditionally recognized as the fathers of Judaism, Christianity and Islam, Postel claimed that Abraham's sons in fact fathered all the world's religions, and that their progeny carried with them the secret and true godly teachings. This meant that the world's religions could be rationally reconciled with Christianity with little effort by missionaries.[36] As such, for Postel the cosmopolitan designation was flexible, but was centred on the idea of an apocalyptic world unity under Christianity, led by a new messianic figure.

Over the years, Postel had seen various others playing this messianic role, including the French King, the Holy Roman Emperor and Mother Zuana of Venice. Eventually, however, he realized that he himself was the key figure in the restitution of the world. This gradual realization is documented by the epithets Postel used in his print and manuscript works. In his earliest publications he identified himself simply as *Barentonius*, a reference to his parish of birth. Following his prophetic awakening of the 1540s, however, Postel began to designate himself in other ways. In his *Panthenôsia* (1547) he designated himself 'Elias Pandocheus', a reference to his self-identification with the prophet Elias, the shepherd of all nations and the 'restorer of all things' announced in Matthew 17:11. This designation reappeared in his *Signorum coelestium* (1553), where he added the epithet 'Restitutionis omnium curator et admolitore' to his name. The intensification of Postel's messianic pretensions from 1559 coincides with the first appearance of the designation 'Cosmopolite', such as in his *De le République des Turcs*. Later, in a c.1580 manuscript, he signed his name as 'Goileelmo Postello Rorispergio Cosmopolita'.[37] 'Rorispergus' was a bold Latin reformulation of his own surname as the apocalyptic 'dew scatterer' (Hosea 14:5) who would restore divine order.[38] Here, Postel wrote that he called himself 'Cosmopolite' because he strove to unite mankind 'into a single city' and to establish a 'peace throughout the world' under Christ.[39] Postel's apocalyptic cosmopolitan identity thus maintained the eclecticism of cosmopolitan associations in antiquity, even as it was employed in pursuit of a decidedly Christian messianic fantasy.

But Postel did not only use this cosmopolitan vocabulary in an epithetical sense. If we revisit his 1556 claim to have become possessed by the spirit of Mother Zuana of Venice, there emerges another, more disturbing, dimension. Postel believed that Zuana was the *mater mundi*, and that she was the bride of Christ, the fleshly embodiment of the heavenly Jerusalem (Revelation 21:2). After 1556, then, Postel was not only a cosmopolite on account of prosecuting his mission of world concord, or suffering for his beliefs. Possessed by the spirit of Zuana, Postel was not merely a citizen of the heavenly Jerusalem, he was the *cosmopolis* itself.

The arch conjuror of England

In May 1571 the English magus and cosmographer John Dee sojourned for several days in Paris. While there, Dee purchased two books by Guillaume Postel, one of them his *De originibus* (1553).[40] Both works concerned the mystical significance of Hebrew and the legitimacy of kabbalistic speculations as being capable of unlocking the secrets of the universe and demonstrating the ultimate truth of Christianity. This was not Dee's first encounter with Postel or his work. Dee had even met Postel in Paris in 1550, while lecturing on Euclid's *Elements of Geometry*, and his famous library in Mortlake already contained several of Postel's books and broadsheets.[41] But what is of most interest to us at present is an *adversarium* that Dee added to page fifty-seven of *De originibus*, where Postel discussed the status of the patriarch Abraham as '*ciuis mundi*'. In the margin of this page, Dee added the endorsement '*Cosmopolites*'.⁴²

Like Postel, Dee was a prodigiously learned scholar in the humanist mould, who studied intently the Stoic works of antiquity. As an ordained Catholic priest, he was also intimately familiar with the Judaeo-Christian cosmopolitan tradition. Scholars have disagreed on how to assess his cosmopolitan ideas, and indeed what Dee actually meant when he used the cosmopolitan vocabulary. Part of the disagreement is prompted by the fact that Dee's most extensive statement on the subject appears in his *General and Rare Memorials Pertayning to the Perfect Arte of Navigation* (1577), a tract practical in title if not object, which was ostensibly dedicated to encouraging the establishment of British naval power. The reputation of this volume has encouraged several scholars to see in Dee an important ideologue of British imperial expansionism at the Elizabethan court.⁴³ While Graham Yewbrey linked Dee's 'cosmopolitical' thought to his magical philosophy, William Sherman has argued that readers of Dee should be wary of seeing 'too much of the "cosmic"' in Dee's cosmopolitics, which he claims was English in its focus, Stoic in its inspiration and 'intensely patriotic'.⁴⁴ More recently, Glyn Parry has challenged the position of both scholars, arguing that there is a wealth of evidence to demonstrate that Dee's vision of empire was ineluctably 'cosmic' in character.⁴⁵ Parry has demonstrated conclusively that Dee's writings 'foreshadowed an empire that would be ecumenical, apocalyptic, territorial and absolute'.⁴⁶ Furthermore, in the course of his career, Dee had offered his services not only to rulers in England, but – like Postel before him – to a variety of European regents and emperors. Yet another position is articulated by Brian Lockey in his study of competing notions of the 'Christian Commonwealth' in England, who has shown that Dee was one of several contemporary figures using the cosmopolitan vocabulary to designate their thought.⁴⁷

A reassessment of Dee's writings on the cosmopolitan idea and its origins allows us to nuance the approaches of Yewbrey, Parry and Sherman. Dee's cosmopolitan visions were propped up by twin poles of Christian and Stoic ideals. These ideals were not only inspired by and consonant with his humanistic and magical worldviews, but were also inspired by a perhaps unlikely source: the practical language of sixteenth-century statesmanship.

The hieroglyphic monad

Although most discussion of the cosmopolitan aspects of Dee's thought has focussed on his post 1575 writings concerning the British Empire, I argue that the most crucial document for understanding Dee's cosmopolitan ideas was issued more than a decade earlier, in his *Monas hieroglyphica* or 'hieroglyphic monad' (1564). Authored over a period of thirteen days in Antwerp in January 1564, Dee's book was neither a cosmographical treatise nor a practical statement of imperialist strategy: it was instead an explication of the 'most secret symbol' of divine authority (Fig 2.1). As advertised on the title page, this work was dedicated to the King of Hungary, and soon to be Holy Roman Emperor, Maximilian II (1527–1576).

The *Monas* unites Dee's magical philosophy with his commitments to Christian empire and the contemporary language of state. It was written only a couple of years after Postel had designated himself a cosmopolite on the title page of his *De la République des Turcs* (1560). One scholar has suggested that Dee's book was influenced by Postel's thoughts on world concord.[48] Fittingly, then, Dee's *Monas* is a riddling, dense and difficult work. In its preface, which might be read as an elaborate job application, Dee announces to Maximilian II that he is one of the few members of the republic of letters who has 'aspired to an exploration and understanding of the supercelestial virtues and metaphysical influences' which can guide and influence the destiny of rulers and of nations.[49] Somewhat eccentrically, Dee chose to unfold the significance of these virtues and influences by means of explanation of the mysterious hieroglyphic monad.

For Dee, the hieroglyphic monad symbolized the harmony of secret heavenly laws with those of the 'terrestrial body'. The symbol, Dee informed Maximilian II, allowed its master to wield earthly power in concord with divine will. Indeed, the tract itself was supposedly written 'in the name of Jesus Christ … the pen merely of Whose Spirit, quickly writing these things through me, I wish and I hope to be'.[50] Dee declared that 'I give not only the principles but the demonstration' of the monad symbol, so that Maximilian II may heed 'the Voice of the Creator of the Universe' so that those 'godly-minded and born of God' can act in concord with the 'theological and mystical language'. While expressed in a Christian register, this was a sentiment consonant with Stoicism. Maximilian II, as a European ruler and inheritor of this knowledge, would not

Figure 2.1 John Dee, *Monas hieroglyphica* (1564). Title page. Courtesy of Library of Congress, Rare Book and Special Collections Division.

need to 'travel to the inhabitants of India or America' to grasp its implications, but could understand all from his own throne.[51]

Dee announced that this wisdom had been revealed for the purpose of making great Maximilian II's name, or that of 'some [other] member of the house of Austria', and he would in turn grow 'very great' by the 'interpretation of these mysteries'.[52] But Dee did not reveal this wisdom merely for the benefit of the Habsburgs. By aligning his prophetic talent with the political ambitions of a European leader, he hoped to avert 'great harm to the Christian polity'.[53] Later in the work, Dee made reference to 'still greater mysteries', which he claims to 'have described in our cosmopoliticall theories'. While C.H. Josten argued that this passage refers to now lost tracts by Dee on 'cosmopolitics', it could just as well refer to texts then unwritten.[54] In any event, we encounter here Dee's first invocation of the cosmopolitan vocabulary, embedded in a political and magical discourse. Read against the background of Dee's prophetic self-understanding, his use of 'cosmopoliticall' is decidedly reminiscent of Postel.

Dee's *Monas* offered an occult means by which to expand Maximilian's earthly power, in concert with divine will. As such, it combined aspects of Stoic as well as Christian thought on the idea. Although the text contained no explicit references to the practical means by which Maximilian's power could be expanded, it nevertheless allows us to contextualize Dee's later use of the cosmopolitan vocabulary, upon which he would discourse in some detail.

General and rare memorials

Six months after the publication of *Monas hieroglyphica*, Maximilian II was duly elected Holy Roman Emperor. His reaction to Dee's tract is unrecorded, but the book enjoyed a substantial reception among European alchemists and adventurers of all kinds.[55] Although the work was dedicated to a foreign ruler, its theories of right rulership and divine authority could be offered to any monarch. Thus it is unsurprising to learn that upon his return to England in the year of *Monas*'s publication, Dee claims to have discussed its content with Elizabeth I. He may even have promised to reveal to her some of the 'cosmopolitical' secrets only hinted at in the *Monas*.[56]

Although Dee was often present at the English royal court from the 1570s, his reputation and influence ebbed and flowed. His changing fortunes were partially attributable to rumours concerning his alleged conjuring and spell-making circulated by fellow courtiers, but in truth his status was not assisted by the fact that he was an ordained Catholic priest. To counter this, Dee set about crafting a series of works concerning the expansion of the British Empire. In distinction to his earlier *Monas*, these works were practical in nature. The most important of these was his *General and Rare Memorials Pertayning to the Perfect Arte of Navigation*. First dictated by Dee in early August 1576, it would only be printed, with substantial changes, in 1577.[57] The *Memorials* was the first in which Dee invoked the idea of the cosmopolitan in connection with Elizabethan imperial ideology. As several historians have observed, the book is unashamedly a promotion of British Empire, and even included the promotion of explicitly military strategies, such as the establishment of a standing English navy.[58] But it also wove together its cosmographical concerns with the occult lessons of *Monas hieroglyphica*.

Dee's *Memorials* contains his most unambiguous and complete statement on the subject of the cosmopolitan. This passage occurs in a rare moment of reflection that interrupts his propositions concerning the growth, defence and prosperity of England and her imperial possessions:

> I have oftentymes ... and many wayes, looked into the State of Earthly Kingdoms, Generally, the whole World over (as far, as it may, yet, be known to Christen Men, Commonly) being a Study, of no great Difficulty: But, rather, a purpose, somewhat answerable, to a perfect Cosmographer: to fynde hymself, *Cosmopolites*: A Citizen and member, of the whole and only one MYSTICALL CITY UNIVERSALL: And so, consequently, to meditate of the Cosmopoliticall Government thereof, under the King Almighty.[59]

The historian William Sherman has parsed this statement as a paraphrase of Cicero's *On the Laws*, arguing that it was intended to promote 'a matter of engaging the individual in the world and of stressing one's membership (and responsibilities towards) a global community'.[60] However, as Dee's *Monas hieroglyphica* demonstrates, the idea of the cosmopolitical was not simply mundane in its nature, and not merely indebted to Stoic notions. In the passage above, Dee makes clear that cosmopolitical ideas are a microcosmic reflection of the heavenly politics of 'the King Almighty', namely God. Therefore, any earthly politics, to be just and true, must reflect divine order. This order is embodied in the 'whole and only one MYSTICALL CITY UNIVERSALL' in which Dee holds his citizenship. While this idea is thoroughly Stoic in character, it is not exclusively so. Indeed, the imagery likely appealed to Dee above all because of its consonance with the Hebrew and Christian traditions of the Heavenly Jerusalem.

Dee's self-designation 'cosmopolites' also invites further comment. At one level there is again an undeniable Stoic influence. But like Postel before him, he also uses the designation to emphasize his prophetic status as an interpreter of divine wisdom. In this context, it is interesting to note that *Memorials* begins with a statement by Dee rejecting accusations of impropriety and frivolous conjuring that had been circulating at court, and invokes the metaphorical pilgrim to highlight his status as a maligned philosopher.[61] Dee announced that he had suffered through an 'extraordinary, and most painfull, and very costly Course of Philosophicall Enquiries' to fulfil his commitments of heavenly citizenship. In other words, he had suffered ridicule and slander for his toils in service of God. But if Dee's 'Cosmopolites' is maligned, this is all for the better, for it was a circumstance that allowed him privileged insights and understanding into reality. In a now-lost section of his undated manuscript work 'Famous and Rich Discoverie', Dee wrote that in order to produce cosmopolitical insights, it was necessary for the true philosopher to 'look on earth … with a spiritual and heavenly eye' and become a 'perfect Cosmographer'.[62] Again, the prophetic aspect of Dee's pronunciations is emphasized here, establishing the frame of his discourse as specifically Christian.

The articulation of Dee's and Postel's eclectic cosmopolitan discourses of empire building and world government invites questions about how prominent these discourses were at this time. While in the seventeenth century figures like Tomasso Campanella, Christoph Besold and Quirinus Kuhlmann would use the cosmopolitan vocabulary when describing a political universal monarchy, further light is shed on this question by the discovery of Dee's source for his statement in *Memorials*. For this declaration appears to have been inspired by *De optimo senatore* (1568), an influential manual for statesmen authored by the Polish humanist, jurist, diplomat and Catholic bishop, Wawrzyniec Gryzmała Goślicki, better known as Laurentius Grimaldus (1530–1607). This was a book that was in Dee's personal library.[63] Citing Cicero, Grimaldus justified the lot of man in the following fashion:

Among all creatures contayned within the circle of the earth, that which we call man, is the chiefest and of most reputation. For he alone, of all other living thinges of what nature so ever, is made not onely an inhabitant and Citizen of the world, but also a Lorde and Prince therein. Which authoritie, honour and greatnesse, from God the supreame governour of heaven and earth is given, who hath also vouchsafed to receive him, as it were a companion in the government of this universall Citie common to God and men, adorning him with divine understanding, to the end that through his godly reason and councell, this worldly Empyre, might be wisely, holily and justly governed.[64]

The resemblance to Dee's declaration should be readily apparent. In his work, Grimaldus emphasized the peculiarly Stoic notion that the connection between divine and human authority was one which 'proceedeth through reason, which beeing perfect, doth make men like unto God, and seem as it were mortall Gods'.[65] This vaguely antinomian sentiment indicates that Grimaldus's inspiration was more Stoic than Judaeo-Christian. Nevertheless, we can see that Dee's addition of a distinctly religious and prophetic aspect to Grimaldus's generic 'man' is necessary before an individual can begin to describe himself as a 'perfect Cosmographer' or cosmopolite.

'Filling the whole cosmographicall frame'

Dee's cosmopolitan self-identity as a prophetic mediator of divine wisdom demonstrates that his proposed service to the British crown was in fact foremost service to God and therefore to the Christian polity as a whole. To conquer the world, any political regime – be it led by Elizabeth I or Maximilian II – would have to act in harmony with divine will. This much is made apparent in the second half of his *Memorials*, where Dee engaged with the topic of British territorial expansion in the old world. Echoing Postel's arguments about the true birth-right of the French regents, Dee's abstruse discussions of genealogy and the vicissitudes of Salic law suggest that Elizabeth I could 'Royally, Justly, and Triumphantly' claim vast territories on the European continent once held by her ancestors. While at the one level Dee thereby emphasized Britain's putative rights to territorial expansion based on legal precedent – even if somewhat broadly and dubiously interpreted – it also emphasized at a deeper level the common Christian inheritance of European people. Twice Dee invoked Psalm 147 to equate the rights of Britain's body politic with the citizens of the Heavenly Jerusalem: 'O Hierusalem, prayse the Lord: Prayse thy God, O Syon. For, he hath Strengthened the Barres of thy Gates, And hath blessed thy Children within thee: He hath made all thy Borders *PEACE*.'[66] For Dee, the 'Fruit and end of Naturall philosophy' was for wisdom to be 'used, as Christen men ought to use it', and thus the security and expansion of Britain's influence was simultaneously for the benefit of 'all the whole, and universall world over, dispersed ... Filling the whole Cosmographicall frame, and Orbe'. Dee claimed that his studies 'in sundry affayres Philosophicall, and Cosmopoliticall', no matter to which monarch they had been offered, had been undertaken for the furtherance of 'Veritie, Justice, and Peace'.[67] As explored in *Memorials*, his 'Brytish Microcosmus' was a precursor to Christian victory throughout the globe.[68] In true apocalyptic fashion, this victory was mandated by none other than God himself, for as Dee remarks; 'our King' has bestowed upon the world a 'Mercifull Providence' that 'at no tyme, is wanting in matters Cosmopoliticall, of great importance' and which in Dee's eyes 'surpasseth all Humayn Policie'.[69] While it should be clear that Dee advertised his work as the furthering of Christianity as a whole, we should not lose sight of the rhetorical utility of such a move in a work that was, essentially, intended as a defence of his reputation at court and a demonstration of his usefulness to the British crown. As such, a representation of Elizabeth I as an arbiter of divine right was not merely prudent.

Between 1577 and 1578, Dee composed an unpublished sequel to *Memorials*, a manuscript treatise titled 'Brytanici Imperii Limites' (The Limits of the British Empire).[70] In it, he deepened his commitments to British imperialism, and deepened the nexus between royal authority and religious obligation. Building on his genealogical arguments concerning royal descent, Dee invoked the historical navigations and explorations of Edgar the Peaceful (943–975) and the mythical King Arthur as a legal wedge to justify British imperial expansion in Europe and the Atlantic worlds. Old lands once belonging to the British on the continent could be reclaimed, while claims to new lands could be justified on a variety of legal bases, which included not only civil and national jurisdictions, but also divine law (*iure divino*). As this last aspect indicates, what remained central to Dee's 'Brytishe discovery, and recovery Enterprise' was the commitment to furthering God's will, above and beyond any merely patriotic concerns:

> And generallie by the same order that other Christian princes do nowe a dayes make entrances and conquestes upon the heathen people, your highnes hath also to procead herein, both to recover the premisses and likewise by conquest to enlarge the bowndes of your Majesties forsaid title royall ... And cheiflie this recovery & discovery enterprise is speedely and carefully to be taken in hand and followed with the intent of settinge forth the glorie of Christ and spreadinge abro[a]de the heavenly tydinges of the gospell among the heathen, which pointe of all Christian princes ougth more to be esteemed then all their most glorious worldlye tryumphes.[71]

Although such bluster was absent from his earlier *Monas hieroglyphica*, the message articulated here is consonant with that work, whose dedicatee, Maximilian II, as Dee well knew, would have possessed historical claims to the territories of the Roman Empire under the same principles described to Elizabeth I.

Whether Dee truly believed that Britain would lead military expeditions to retake ancestral lands in Europe or elsewhere in the world is unknown, but the presentation of such a scenario to Elizabeth I was at least politically pointed. Just as Postel's fantasy of Gomer was designed to lure the French monarchy to support his prophetic speculations, the historical dimension of Dee's arguments provided a justification for the universality of his projection of British imperial power, bolstering contemporary associations of Elizabeth I with traditions of a last world emperor.

But there is an aspect of capriciousness, and self-interest, at work here. Dee considered Elizabeth I – and Maximilian II before her – to be inheritors of divine power only if their rulership existed in consonance with revealed divine laws. Should they stray from the path of true Christianity, a position ultimately and modestly mediated by himself, they risked losing divine favour. It was for this reason that Dee called himself 'cosmopolites'. Like Postel's 'cosmopolite', Dee claimed to be a prophet, a potentially messianic figure, and yet an outcast on account of his talents and claims.[72] A true biblical stranger in the tradition of Abraham.

Dee would remain so until his death. In the 1580s he travelled with his family and household to central Europe: first to Cracow, and then to Třeboň in

Bohemia. From there he made important contacts at the Prague court of Maximilian II's successor, Emperor Rudolf II (1552–1612). Dee sought patronage once more, this time by magical means. Having summoned angelic intelligences to appear in his 'shewstone', the conjured angels left behind glib glossolalogical pronouncements. These pronouncements, in turn, were interpreted and elaborated by Dee's 'scryer', a sometime miscreant, likely thief and brilliant manipulator named Edward Kelley (1555–1597). While although their alchemical expertise opened doors in Prague, and although Dee had studied manuals of state like Grimaldus's *De optimo senatore* to find a diplomatic idiom to bolster his profile as a prophetic builder of empire, he ultimately bungled his chances at the imperial capital. The same cannot be said for Kelley, who on account of his performance of multiple 'successful' alchemical transmutations was able to panhandle a position as a privy counsellor to the Emperor.[73] Although it is unlikely that Kelley ever actually offered counsel to the emperor on any matter at all, this circumstance is a reminder of the tight nexus between early modern politics and the occult sciences; precisely the nexus that Dee sought to exploit. Yet where Kelley transmuted 'gold' to establish his credentials, Dee's own bona fides were documented only in promises and potentialities.

In 1589 Dee returned to England. Again he sought to attract the attention of the royal court, but again his efforts were all but ignored by Elizabeth I, who appeared far more interested in tempting Kelley to return from Bohemia, presumably to bolster royal coffers. Dee, on the other hand, continued to attract little more than the scorn of his peers, especially in the political realm, who continued to accuse him of witchcraft, devil-conjuring and imposture. Doggedly, Dee defended himself from such calumnies, by invoking once more his citizenship in the heavenly city. The last of these efforts was his *Discourse Apologeticall* (1599). In this pamphlet, Dee provided a curriculum vitae of his many achievements, including a bibliography of his publications.[74] In a sworn statement that concludes his discourse, Dee declares that he had always prosecuted his studies

> as a true, faithfull, and most sincerely dutifull servant, to our most gratious and incomparable Queene Elizabeth, and as a very comfortable fellow-member of the body politique, governed under the scepter Royal of our earthly Supreame head (Queene Elizabeth) and as a lively sympathicall, and

true symetricall fellow-member, of that holy and mysticall body, Catholicklie extended and placed (wheresoever) on the earth.⁷⁵

While several scholars have seen a contradiction between national and universal obligations in Dee's cosmopolitics, this passage shows that Dee himself perceived no contradiction between his citizenships political and heavenly. Dee is a true subject to Elizabeth I, but remains a 'symetricall fellow-member' – a turn of phrase evoking Paul's *sumpolitai* (Ephesians 2:19) – of the heavenly city. Dee correlated earthly dominion with divine right; the power and authority of Elizabeth I – or Maximilian II for that matter – was subject to God. Dee's prophetic Cosmopolite was, as such, the mediator between the realms of the human and the divine.

Conclusions

Dee and Postel provide two sixteenth-century examples of a largely unfamiliar cosmopolitan identity. While scholars of both figures have sometimes interpreted their cosmopolitan pronouncements in light of discourses of religious tolerance (Postel) or the building of a British empire (Dee), the reality was significantly more complex. Their invocation of the cosmopolitan vocabulary was conditioned by knowledge of the works of antiquity, but was shaped decisively by Christian ideas. Both Dee and Postel conceived of the cosmopolitan in at least two separate ways. First, both men used the cosmopolitan vocabulary to designate their self-understanding as prophets, linking it to ideas of heavenly citizenship and the maligned *peregrinus*, to highlight their own special status. Second, their works saw a political valence in the cosmopolitan vocabulary, and indeed both pursued political influence through the postulation of visions of universal Christian empire coloured by its sentiments.

Postel and Dee were by no means the only figures who understood the cosmopolitan identity in a prophetic sense in early modernity, or who associated it with the establishment of imperial power.⁷⁶ As indicated above, around 1600 the Dominican friar Tomasso Campanella (1568–1639) authored his 'De monarchia Hispanica discursus'.⁷⁷ Like Postel before him, Campanella offered a Catholic take on the notion of universal monarchy, describing an apocalyptic world empire ruled by a *señor del mundo todo* from the Spanish Habsburgs. As John Headley has argued, this vision was informed by Giovanni Botero's (c. 1544–1617) theories on the reason of state, albeit fired by a peculiar prophetic urgency.[78] Campanella's tract inspired a host of reactions, among them one by the Lutheran jurist Christoph Besold (1577–1638). In a 1623 commentary on Campanella's work, he briefly surveyed arguments for and against the existence of a universal monarchy and Spain's pretension to such a title. For Besold, worldly power was ripe for abuse by worldly authorities, who were intent on pursuing self-serving policies of reason of state rather than a principle of divine or natural law. Indeed, the jurist concluded that only Antichrist would pretend to a universal monarchy before the Last Judgment.[79] Besold therefore advised readers to shun the prophecies of pretended political and religious messiahs who promised a world empire; their appropriation of divine prophecy led irrevocably to damnation.[80]

A remarkable demonstration of Besold's conviction appeared late in the seventeenth century in the person of Quirinus Kuhlmann (1651–1689), a hermeticist, poet and prophet of Breslau (Wrocław) in Silesia.[81] After flirting with militant prophetic scenarios, in the 1670s Kuhlmann read *Lux e tenebris* (1665), a profusely illustrated collection of prophecies edited by the Moravian pedagogue Jan Amos Comenius (1592–1670).[82] Coming to understand himself as a messianic figure called upon to fulfil its prophecies of universal Christian dominion, Kuhlmann began a restless prophetic activism. Eventually, he came to believe himself the prophet of a *Kühlreich* or 'cool empire' that would ultimately span the world. While this designation punned on Kuhlmann's own name, it simultaneously referred to the 'times of refreshing' (*tempora refrigerii*) of Acts 3:20–22, which the Silesian believed presaged his own coming.

One of the prophecies in *Lux e tenebris*, by the Moravian Mikuláš Drabík (1588–1671), envisioned the apocalyptic conversion of all peoples of the world to Christianity (cf. Psalm 86:9).[83] For Kuhlmann, Drabík's prophecy presaged a '*Cooling-Revelation* for the *Jews*, *Turks* and *Heathens*'.[84] On his travels, he adopted the pseudonym 'Salomon à Kaiserstein, Cosmopolita', linking his cosmopolitan mission to the Hebrew King Solomon and the 'stone-kingdom' of Daniel 2, which would establish God's eternal empire.[85] Kuhlmann's most audacious attempt to fulfil these prophecies occurred in 1678 when he sailed to the Ottoman Empire with a copy of *Lux e tenebris*, intending to use it to convert Sultan Mehmed IV (1642–1693) to Protestantism, after which the Ottoman troops could be used to establish a universal Christian empire. Rebuffed without an audience, Kuhlmann returned to Europe. But the political nature of his visions soon brought him into conflict with authorities elsewhere. In 1689 he travelled to Russia, where he apparently intended to convert the Tatars to Christianity. His efforts were checked by authorities in Moscow, who, finding seditious material in Kuhlmann's possession, condemned him to death at the stake for treason.[86] His immolation on Moscow's Red Square was the ultimate contradiction of the prophesied *tempora refrigerii*.

Kuhlmann differed from Postel and Dee in that he deliberately sought to work outside the political systems of his time to realize his visions. Nevertheless, his efforts demonstrate again the close, and apparently enduring, nexus between apocalyptic religious belief, cosmopolitan identity and political action, which circumscribed the ambitions of his predecessors.

3

Theatres of the world

The world is a comedy to those that think, and a tragedy to those that feel.
Horace Walpole

The apocalyptic visions of Guillaume Postel and John Dee combined the cosmopolitan vocabulary with strains of Christian messianism, classical Stoicism and humanist learning. In the background to their endeavours were actual geographical discoveries, products of a series of voyages of discovery, which set their imperial fantasies on the cutting edge of the European imagination. These voyages brought new cartographical knowledge, in addition to knowledge of the peoples of the earth previously unknown, which fundamentally changed or challenged the way that Europeans came to conceive of and engage with the world.[1] It is thus unsurprising to note that Dee's and Postel's literary works encompassed the production of cartographic works, and of course Dee himself authored a variety of books on the practicalities of navigation and the office of the 'perfect Cosmographer'. The messianic and apocalyptic interpretation of history that dominated the Protestant and Reformist worldviews of the period meant that geographical exploration and expansion could be read and understood as a manifestation of end-time prophecies, particularly those which anticipated that the 'Gospel would be preached throughout the world' (cf. Mark 13:10, Mark 16:15, Matthew 24:14). There is perhaps no better demonstration of the nexus between geographical discovery and apocalyptic speculation than Postel. Two years before his 1581 death, the elderly scholar attempted to pass on his messianic title to the Antwerp cartographer Abraham Ortelius (1527–1598). Postel claimed that in his masterwork, the proto-atlas *Theatrum orbis terrae* (Theatre of the world), Ortelius had created the most significant book since the Bible, an achievement that proved his messianic lineage.[2]

While Ortelius was presumably bemused by this bizarre declaration – no response is extant – the episode indicates that, as far was Postel was concerned, there was a conceptual connection between geographical knowledge, discovery and the cosmopolitan imagination. The present chapter examines the presence of the cosmopolitan vocabulary, and the various concepts that it was used to designate in geographical, cosmographical and cartographical works of the sixteenth and seventeenth centuries. In addition to considering the reception of the works of Dee and Postel, it surveys cartographical works which employed the cosmopolitan vocabulary or trod similar metaphorical and conceptual ground as the pilgrims and sojourners on their way to the heavenly Jerusalem. Finally, it also examines examples of devotional and utopian literature that used the cosmopolitan vocabulary to express anxieties concerning the place of mankind in the world. By so doing, this chapter illustrates the further breadth of associations the cosmopolitan vocabulary could possess, as well demonstrating the enduring influence of Christian concepts of heavenly citizenship as a conditioning factor in these associations.

Navigators, diplomats and merchants

Although to modern observers the works of Postel and Dee appear to be somewhat bizarre, the origins of Dee's cosmopolitan pronunciations in Grimaldus's *De optimo senatore* (1568) indicate that both men were drawing on idioms not entirely foreign to the vocabulary of the contemporary European statesman, and thus to the practice of statecraft. This impression is reinforced when we consider the reception of their works. Thus in 1567 the decorated French soldier, diplomat and 'geographer in ordinary to the king', Nicolas de Nicolay (1517–1583) began his landmark volume of accounts of travellers in the Levant by invoking Philo of Alexandria's foundational discourse concerning Adam as the first cosmopolite.[3] In the preface to this work, which makes explicit reference to Christian tropes of *peregrinatio*, Nicolay articulates the manifold duties of the Christian cosmopolitan to the world at large. For Nicolay, the true Christian was obliged to imitate the great strangers and voyagers of the past – like Noah, Jason, Hercules, Pythagoras and Marco Polo (1254–1324) – and experience the world before returning to the dominion of true belief. One of the prophets of such a course of action, according to Nicolay, was none other than Guillaume Postel. Indeed, Nicolay considered Postel's efforts to translate the Koran as a crucial prophetic undertaking that would bolster the reputation of France and secure the destiny of Christianity as a whole.[4]

There is some evidence to show the influence of Postel's thought on the influential political philosopher and jurist Jean Bodin (1530–1596). Famed for his works on political economy, Bodin also authored tracts dedicated to demonology and world government. One volume, unpublished during his lifetime, was the 'Colloquium heptaplomeres de rerum sublimium arcanis abditis' (*The Colloquium of the Seven about Secrets of the Sublime*, ca. 1588). This text recounted a fictional meeting of the heads of seven religions who attempted to determine the fundaments of true faith.[5] Some readers noticed that Bodin's arguments concerning the origin of religious society in Hebrew scripture resembled those of Postel. Some decades later, the Parisian humanist Gabriel Naudé (1600–1653) declared that Bodin had inherited Postel's manuscripts, which 'became the material for the book titled *About the Hidden Secrets of Sublime Things*'.[6] While Postel's works don't seem to have influenced Bodin's economic writings, Naudé's claim draws our attention again to the complex interrelations between theories of world community, prophecy and the cosmopolitan in French humanist thought.

Dee's cosmopolitan ideas were also readily discussed in England, an enthusiasm fuelled by nascent imperial pretensions, as well as the excitement fostered by contemporary voyages of discovery. Suggestively, the majority of this literature was penned not by diplomats or statesmen, but by clergymen. An early indication of the ready interchange between cosmographical and cosmopolitan ideas is demonstrated in the work of Richard Hakluyt (1553–1616), an English explorer and promoter of imperial pretensions in North America. In his influential *Principal Navigations, Voyages, and Traffiques, and Discoveries of the English Nation* (1598), a work written to promote England's explorations 'in these latter dayes', Hakluyt pillaged Dee's *General and Rare Memorials* to provide readers with an account of the navigations of King Edgar the Peaceful (943–975 CE).[7] This excerpt included Dee's reference to being 'Cosmopolites' and citizen in the 'mysticall citie universall'.[8] Hakluyt's appropriation of Dee's passage indicates that the conjuror was not the only contemporary who connected cosmopolitan discourse to providential early modern voyages of discovery, or even England's political future.

This lingering impression is confirmed by the case of the Lichfield minister William Barlow (d. 1625), who was inspired by the same passage in Dee's *Memorialls* in his *The Navigators Supply* (1597). This tract was intended for practical cosmographical application, namely to demonstrate the utility of the compass and lodestone for seafarers.[9] However, the presence of Psalm 107 on the title page: 'They that goe downe to the Sea in Ships, and employ their labour in the great waters, They see the workes of the Lord, and his wonders in the deepe' also suggests the pervasive presence of Barlow's religious concerns. In the dedicatory epistle – offered to the powerful courtier Robert Devereux, 2nd Earl of Essex (1565–1601) – Barlow praised 'the sayling Compasse' as a providential device which had become 'the notable meanes and Instrument' of English exploration and discovery. The invention was inspired by God not only to increase England's wealth and standing, but also 'to joyne dispersed Nations, not onely into the Civill or rather Cosmopoliticall union of human societie; but also (as Christian hope bindeth us to thinke) through the knowledge and faith of the Gospel, into the spirituall and mysticall fellowship of that Heavenly Jerusalem'.[10] Here Barlow appears to distinguish more firmly than did Dee between the cosmopolitical and the divine realms of contemporary politics. For Barlow, the 'Civill or rather Cosmopoliticall' represents worldly traffic between peoples of different races 'in many exceeding remote Ilands in the Ocean Sea'. This is a precursor to the creation of a 'mysticall fellowship' in the New Jerusalem, which could only be achieved through the glorious spread of the gospel. It is perhaps for this reason that Barlow saw fit to write his book in the first place: 'I did therefore judge it a matter not unfit for a Preacher of the Gospel, to set to his helping hand for advauncing a Faculty that so much tendeth to Gods glorie in the spreading of the Gospell.'[11] In other words, navigation and exploration, whether or not they carried with them imperial pretensions, countenanced a coincidence of sacred and secular history and endeavour. Another prominent feature of Barlow's *The Navigators Supply* is its firm apocalyptic background, where the discovery of new geographical locales takes place 'now towardes the ende of the world'.[12]

The most prominent thinker who followed in the footsteps of Dee, Hakluyt and Barlow was Samuel Purchas (*c.* 1577–1626), Anglican curate of Essex. In

1613, he issued his *Purchas his Pilgrimage*. Structured in several broadly chronological volumes, the work comprised 'a theologicall and geographicall historie of Asia, Africa, and America, with the Ilands Adjacent' and therefore a 'history of religions'.[13] For Purchas, the work provided the canvas for illustrating the rise of 'the Truth of Christianitie as it is now professed and established in our Church, under the Great *Defender of the Faith*', by which he meant King James I (1566–1625). As such, against the background of contemporary voyages of exploration and the unfolding of geographical wisdom, Britain's monarch could be cast in the grand role of the defender of the Christian faith across the globe.[14]

These microcosmic and macrocosmic concerns were amplified in his *Hakluytus Posthumus* (1624–1626), a five volume continuation of the documentary work of Richard Hakluyt. The first volume featured an engraved title page which united Purchas's sacred and secular concerns (Fig. 3.1).

Several vignettes indicate Purchas's understanding of the British as the chosen people, a new tribe of Israelites. On the left-hand side of the page, King James I is depicted alongside text adapted from Psalm 147: 'He sheweth his word unto *Jacob*, his statutes and his judgments unto Israel. He hath not dealt so with any nation.' Jacob, of course, was the Latinized form of James. To this Purchas added references apocalyptic and cosmopolitan. At the centre of the top panel is a depiction of the Heavenly Jerusalem of Revelation 21, accompanied by Hebrews 11:13–16: 'They were strangers and pilgrims on the Earth. God hath prepared for them a Citty.' Beneath the Heavenly Jerusalem appears an illustration of the Israelites departing the Holy Land (Numbers 9:17), a complex of ideas again intended to identify the British as God's chosen people. In the bottom third of the title page is a portrait of Purchas, together with a world map surrounded by inscriptions intended to demonstrate the vanity of the world. The message is clear. For Purchas, sacred and secular histories were intertwined. Geographical and cartographical advances by means of voyages of discovery simultaneously told the story of the apocalyptic advance of Christianity across the globe, led by the British. This was Dee's 'cosmopolitical' stage write large.

The works of Nicolay, Bodin, Hakluyt, Barlow and Purchas reflect the appeal of the cosmopolitan messages of Postel and Dee, as well as something of broader contemporary complex of interests and concerns of their audiences.

44 *The Lost History of Cosmopolitanism*

Figure 3.1 Samuel Purchas, *Hakluytus Posthumus* (1624), vol. 1, title page. Courtesy of Beinecke Library, Yale University.

Here, the cosmopolitan vocabulary was nigh inextricable from descriptions of voyages of discovery, as well as apocalyptic discourses concerning the progression of Christianity and the health of worldly polities that forwarded this progression.

Know thyself

As the title page of Purchas's *Hakluytus Posthumus* suggests, geo-political discourse on the cosmopolitan idea was also mapped in early modern cartography. By studying several of these maps in greater detail, we gain a better appreciation of the contemporary power and associations of the cosmopolitan vocabulary. One of the most prominent examples of this marriage of cartographical and cosmopolitan knowledges is simultaneously one of the most striking images in all of early modern visual culture; the so-called 'Fool's Cap' world map (Fig 3.2).

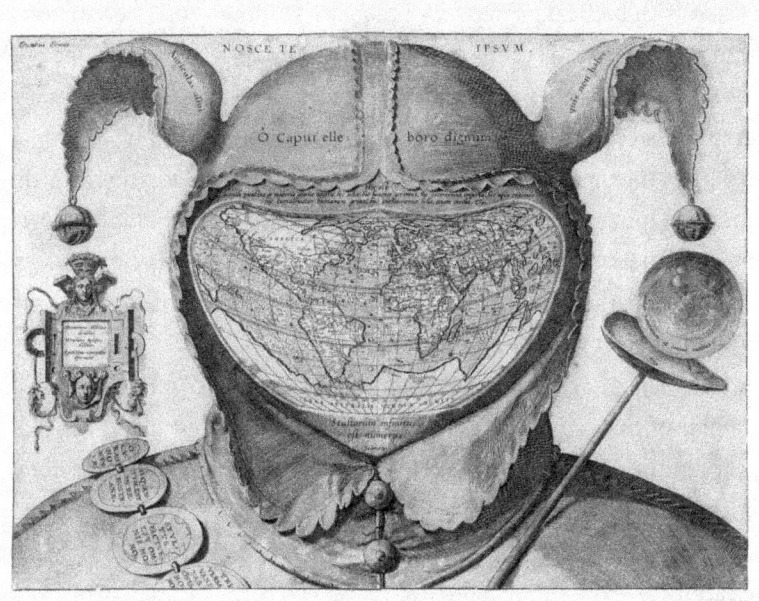

Figure 3.2 Anon., 'Nosce te ipsum' (*c.* 1590). Engraving, 350 × 480 mm. Courtesy of Alamy.

This elaborate engraving portrays a jester, clad in a 'fool's cap', whose visage is provided by a cordiform world map.[15] The image is festooned with imprecations intended to demonstrate the vanity of the world. At the head of the representation appears the ostensible title *Nosce te ipsum* ('know thyself'). Emphasizing the meditative aspect to the work, it derives from Juvenal's satires (first to second century CE), and was reputed to have been the saying which adorned the lintel of the temple of the oracle at Delphi.[16] On the cap appears a line from Pliny: 'For in the whole universe the Earth is nothing else and this is the substance of our glory, this is its habitation, here it is that we fill positions of power and covet wealth, and throw mankind into an uproar, and launch wars, even civil ones.'[17] Pliny's indictment of worldly pursuits is reinforced by Ecclesiastes 1:15: 'The number of fools is infinite.' On the cap's ears is a rhetorical question posed by the Stoic philosopher Lucius Annaeus Cornutus (20–65 CE); 'Who does not possess dunce's ears?' (*Auriculas asini quis non habet?*). The jester holds in his left hand a marotte topped by a reflective bauble inscribed with Ecclesiastes 1:2, 'vanity of vanities; all is vanity'. With the same hand the jester points to a bandolier slung over his right shoulder. This is again decorated with biblical passages: 'All men are without sense' (Jeremiah 10:14); 'All things are vanity, by every man living' (Psalm 39:6), as well as the opening line of Stoic philosopher Aulus Persius Flaccus's *Satires*; 'Oh the toils of men, the emptiness of life!' (*O curas hominum, O quantum est in rebus inane*). The imprecation on the fool's cap itself reads 'This head is worthy of a dose of hellebore,' a potent poison. Adding a distinctly apocalyptic valence, this statement indicates that the world will, indeed needs, to pass away, to be killed. The world of human endeavour is thus by definition a mortal world, and ephemeral, subject to the Last Judgment.

This unusual image has invited interpretations from commentators who see all manner of things reflected in its mute cartographical visage.[18] In 1621, the English dramatist Robert Burton (1577–1640) commented in his *Anatomy of Melancholy* that the image proved that 'all the world is mad'.[19] More recently one scholar has seen a 'moralized geography ... designed to emphasize the imbrication of exploration and vanity' reflected in its lines, while another recognized that 'all universal truths, all trustworthy knowledge is at the same time partial and untrustworthy because it conceals an imposed social ordering'.[20] Peter Whitfield has concentrated on the figure of the fool, through whom the viewer is forced 'to confront the possibility that the whole created order is irrational, alien and threatening'.[21] While there is something to all of these interpretations, I believe that the key to unlocking the meaning and intentions behind the map is provided in the cartouche to the left of the image. Here we read: 'Democritus of Abdera laughed at [the world], Heraclitus of Ephesus wept over it, [and] Epichtonius Cosmopolites engraved it.' The reference to the pre-Socratic philosophers Democritus (fifth century CE) and Heraclitus (535–475) indicates the influence of the Stoic tradition on the print's designer.

But who was this designer? The name 'Epichtonius Cosmopolites' is an obvious pseudonym, uniting the Greek *epikhthonios*, meaning roughly 'he who dwells on earth', with *kosmopolitēs*, a cosmopolite or 'citizen of the world'. In other words, the creator or 'engraver' of the image, the person who was in a position to best recognize the folly of the world, was a 'cosmopolite who dwells on earth'.[22] In addition to the Stoic inheritance, then, we are dealing with another manifestation of Christian identity, one who viewed their true home as being not on earth, but in heaven, the only true Cosmopolis.

The actual identity of Epichtonius Cosmopolites has remained elusive. However, researchers have determined that the cartographical projection which provides the visage of the fool is based on the 'Typus orbis terrarum', the third world map produced in 1587 by the influential Antwerp cartographer Abraham Ortelius, a circumstance which might suggest his involvement.[23] At first glance, this conclusion appears plausible. The reader will recall that in 1579 Guillaume Postel attempted to anoint Ortelius as a new messiah, an indication that the pair shared similar interests, and perhaps a shared conception of cosmopolitan identity. Furthermore, there are thematic connections between Ortelius's cartographical work and the 'Fool's Cap' map. First, Ortelius's maps were often adorned with a passage from Cicero condemning the vanity of the world.[24] Second, many of his cartographical masterpieces bore the title *Theatrum orbis terrarum*, depicting the world as a theatre. This metaphor has been refracted into common parlance thanks to Shakespeare's memorable axiom, 'All the world's a stage, and all the men and women merely players,' in his *As You Like It* (1599). Be that as it may, Ortelius's vision aligns in several respects with the central thematic and visual tropes of the 'Fool's Cap' map.

However, what is not typically recognized is that the 'Fool's Cap' was based on an earlier image issued around 1570 by the Parisian cartographer Jean de Gourmont Jr. (*c.* 1537–1598), titled *Congnois toy toy-mesme* (Fig. 3.3). In many respects identical to the later engraved version, de Gourmont's woodcut contains additional text, including the maudlin reminder in the hem of the jester's bib announcing 'there is no happiness after death' (*Nul eureux qu'apres la mort*). As Yona Pinson has argued, this Parisian woodcut is best understood within the context of the fool's journey, a motif prominent throughout European culture from the late fifteenth century. This tradition resulted in the publication of such influential works as Sebastian Brant's *Das Narrenschiff* (1494) and Erasmus's *In Praise of Folly* (1509).[25] Richard Helgerson has drawn attention to the fact that when modern observers examine de Gourmont's *Congnois toy toy-mesme* they see foremost the map itself; a practical object

Figure 3.3 [Jean de Gourmont?], 'Congnois toy toy-mesme' (*c.* 1570). Engraving, 90 × 150 mm. Courtesy of Beinecke Library, Yale University.

dressed in the incongruous motley of the fool. However as Lucia Nutti has argued, for early modern observers, to whom a world map would have been of limited practical value, they saw the cartographical image as symbolic: an invitation to contemplate God's creation and their place in it.[26]

The publisher of this striking image, Jean de Gourmont, was perhaps also its creator, and may well therefore be identified with Epichthonius Cosmopolites himself.[27] He certainly possessed an openness to a variety of religious traditions, which might typify the cosmopolitan type. From 1569 he created woodcuts for Christophe Plantin's *Quarante Tableaux* (1569–1570), a publishing project based in Protestant Geneva that documented the French wars of religion.[28] De Gourmont also specialized in cartography. In 1578 he cut the plates for *Polo aptata nova charta universi*, a world map based on a polar projection created by none other than Guillaume Postel.[29] As Ayesha Ramachandran has speculated, it is therefore possible that *Congnois toy toy-mesme*, and its cosmopolitan associations, emerged from within Postel's Parisian networks.[30]

To laugh or to cry?

Both de Gourmont's broadsheet and the later Dutch version of the 'Fool's Cap' map unite concepts of the cosmopolitan with moralizing allegorical discourses, among them the theatre of the world, the folly of humankind, and – by means of references to Democritus and Heraclitus – to the Stoic philosophical tradition. If we follow this last tradition, we gain further insight into the manifold backgrounds which informed contemporary cosmopolitan discourse, particularly in its cartographical dimensions.

The legend of the philosophers Heraclitus and Democritus coming together to lament the state of the world dates from antiquity, but the tale held a particular attraction for early modern humanists, who explored its significance in poesy, prose and art.[31] That the tale was known to the creator of the 'Fool's Cap' map is suggested by the fact that its striking visual conceit appeared in a 1557 Antwerp print concerning Heraclitus and Democritus, created by Dirck Volckertszoon Coornhert (1522–1590) after Maarten van Heemskerck (Fig 3.4).

Figure 3.4 Dirck Coornhert, 'Tempus ridendi tempus flendi' (1557). Engraving, 191 × 258 mm. Courtesy of Houghton Library, Harvard University.

Titled *Tempus ridendi tempus flendi* (a time to laugh and a time to cry, cf. Ecclesiastes 3:4), the image depicts Heraclitus weeping, and Democritus derisively amused by the state of the world. The world itself is depicted as a *globus cruciger*, a traditional symbol of Christian authority carried by European monarchs. Of greater pertinence is the fact that a jester's costume has been draped over the globe. This juxtaposition suggests the foolishness of mundane pretence towards divine authority, and reminds us of the folly of worldly endeavour compared with the eternity governed by God.

As the cartouche in *Congnois toy toy-mesme* shows, Jean de Gourmont was familiar with the tradition of Democritus and Heraclitus, and, given his professional connections to Antwerp, likely knew Coornhert's engraving. But whether or not this is the case, de Gourmont's print emerges from within a moralizing tradition that united cosmopolitan discourse with representations of worldly folly, the better to remind observers that their true home, where they shall dwell for eternity, was in heaven.

Cartographies of power

When observing de Gourmont's *Congnois toy toy-mesme*, one may ask why, if the object of the image was merely to demonstrate the folly of the world, a map featured in it at all. One answer is that the cartographic aspect represented the vanities of mankind in a very specific way, by contextualizing the profits and knowledge won through voyages of discovery with the riches of eternal life. Denis Cosgrove has suggested that the image suggests 'the moral implications of mapping humanity onto global space', which is certainly true.[32] But a further answer may be that the 'Fool's Cap' map was intended as a riposte to, or part of, a contemporary trend of figural cartography.

One of the most striking examples of this trend is the 'Weltkarte im Adlerform', issued in Cologne in 1574 and created by Georg Braun (1541–1622). This map features a cartographical projection of the world on the breast of a double-headed eagle, the heraldic symbol of the Holy Roman Empire (Fig 3.5). As Rodney Shirley has pointed out, Braun's map may well have been inspired by an image which the cartographer Henri Pontanus in Mechelen had desired to produce several years earlier, depicting 'a *mappemonde* in the form of an eagle of the empire'.[33] Braun's map might, therefore, be considered evidence of a pre-existing cartographical tradition.

The feathers in the eagle's wings contain the heraldic emblems of the constituent polities of the Empire. Surrounding the eagle are allegorical representations of the planets, the pagan gods and zodiacal signs. What is conspicuously absent in Braun's image is presence of any overtly Christian motif, a circumstance which might have prompted de Gourmont's creation of a cartographical riposte intended to demonstrate the world's vanity.

Nevertheless, if we adopt a framework of Dee or Postel, then Braun's map could well have been intended as a representation of Christian imperial dominion. In 1516, Charles I of Spain (1500–1558) ascended to the Spanish throne, and in 1519 was elected as Charles V, Holy Roman Emperor. As such, he not only possessed territories across Europe, but was also the inheritor of the Spanish colonial possessions in the Americas, Africa and Asia. By the time of Braun's map, these possessions, spread across the globe, remained the rightful inheritance of the Holy Roman Emperor.

Figure 3.5 Georg Braun, 'Weltkarte im Adlerform' (1574). Engraving, 860 × 1,000 mm. Courtesy of Herzog August Bibliothek, Wolfenbüttel: K 2.6.

Braun's figural world map was not the only contemporary cartographical image which sought to depict Habsburg dominion in such a creative fashion. A sixteenth-century cartographical fad portrayed Europe in the form of a maiden (*Europa in forma virginis* or *Regina Europa*).[34] In these depictions, Europe's head was located in the Iberian Peninsula, while her heart was located in Austria or Bohemia, thus representing the two traditional seats of the Habsburg branches. First created by Johann Putsch (1516–1542) in 1537 during the height of Charles V's reign, the map grew in popularity and was widely imitated. From the 1570s it was reproduced in some editions of Sebastian Münster's famous *Cosmographia*. Although executed without regard for cartographical accuracy, Putsch's *Europa regina* provided a figural representation of Europe emphasizing the extent and power of worldly political authority, and may well have provoked de Gourmont's cosmopolitan statement in his *Congnois toy toy-mesme*.

Christian knights on the shining path

If de Gourmont's *Congnois toy toy-mesme* was intended to demonstrate the folly of fleeting worldly political power by contrasting it with the eternal heavenly *imperium*, a very different representation of the struggles of the true Christian on the path to heavenly citizenship were manifested in the so-called 'Christian Knight Map' (Fig. 3.6), created by the Dutch cartographer Jodocus Hondius (1563–1612). The complete Latin title of this print indicates that it possessed two distinct aims: first, to present an accurate cartographical image of the world, and second, to provoke the 'student devoted to piety' to reflect on the metaphorical toils of the Christian Knight as a mirror of their own.[35]

As Rodney Shirley has observed, this accomplished map used a projection based on the work of Gerardus Mercator (1512–1594), and represented state of the art cartography, incorporating the latest geographical discoveries in the Indies and elsewhere. But for our purposes the map is noteworthy for the drama depicted at the foot of the image, which portrays the struggles of the Christian Knight against anthropomorphic representations of sin, death, the flesh and, finally, the world; a woman clad in garish robes crowned by the *orbis cruciger*. The world is thus represented twice in the image: first as a participant in the allegorical battle waged by the Christian knight, and second as the cartographical projection itself. The centrality of the knight is emphasized by his subtle placement in the image's foreground; his sword and halo are the only features of the figurative battle to protrude beyond the coasts of the southern continent onto the cartographical projection. The presence of shadows beneath the figures furthermore indicates that the observer was intended to understand the southern continent itself as a stage for the drama.

Experts have ventured several interpretations of this dramatic imagery. One scholar has suggested that the knight's battle was intended to represent the contemporary conflict between Catholic Spain and the Protestant Netherlands, and that the various evil figures were 'symbolically identified with Catholicism and the Spanish foe'.[36] Others have seen in the knight the visage of the French King Henri IV (1553–1610).[37] Adopting a wider lens, Joanne Woolway Grenfell has argued that the map attempts to assimilate new geographical territory, especially in the new world, with Christian morality.[38] A closer examination reveals its enmeshment in concerns broader than confessional conflict,

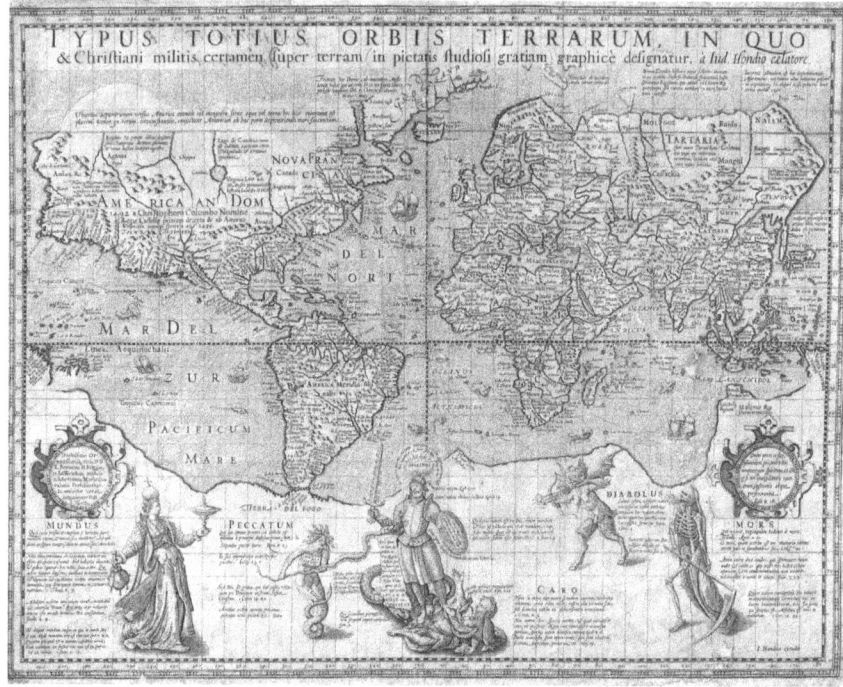

Figure 3.6 Jodocus Hondius, 'Typus totius orbis terrarum' (c. 1596). Engraving, 370 × 480 mm. From a private collection.

political intrigue or even geographical discovery. The figural and scriptural references in the image refer to the narrative of the Christian as *homo viator*, whose life is led as a journey to its ultimate repose in the Heavenly Jerusalem.[39] This reading is reinforced by the identification of the source of the figures that appear on Hondius's map. For these derive from an earlier engraving executed by the Antwerp printmaker Jeronimus Wierix (1553–1619) following a lost design by the Flemish painter Maerten de Vos (1532–1603), titled *Spirituale Christiani Militis Certamen* (c. 1590).

Through its inclusion of several biblical passages, the image reveals cosmopolitan concerns easily overlooked in Hondius's map; for it indicates that the goal of the Christian Knight is to discover the narrow path to the heavenly city and eternal life, where his name is inscribed in the rolls of heaven. Beside the Knight is 1 John 4–5: 'For whatever is born of God overcomes the world. And this is the victory that has overcome the world – our faith,'

Figure 3.7 Jeronimus Wierix, 'Spirituale Christiani Militis Certamen' (c. 1590). Engraving, 300 × 390 mm. © Trustees of the British Museum.

a passage which underlines the struggles of the *homo viator*. To his left is a broad path strewn with games, dice, foibles and distractions, with a warning that 'wide is the gate and broad is the way that leadeth to destruction'. While this path terminates at the feet of *Mundus*, a narrower trail leads up Mt. Zion towards the Heavenly Jerusalem. Beside this appears Matthew 7:14: 'Because strait *is* the gate, and narrow *is* the way, which leadeth unto life, and few there be that find it.' Emphatically confirming the cosmopolitan context is Hebrews 12:22–24 – the passage invoked by Erasmus in his landmark declaration that he was a 'citizen of the world' – which is reproduced beside the holy city:

> But you have come to Mount Zion and to the city of the living God, the heavenly Jerusalem, and to innumerable angels in festal gathering, and to the assembly of the firstborn who are enrolled in heaven, and to God the judge of all, and to the spirits of the righteous made perfect, and to Jesus, the

mediator of a new covenant, and to the sprinkled blood that speaks a better word than the blood of Abel.

The message of the print could hardly be clearer. And if we now turn back to Hondius's map, its relationship to contemporary cosmopolitan discourse becomes apparent. The Christian Knight depicted there is the *homo viator*, the peregrinating everyman, seeking the place where he holds his heavenly citizenship. In Hondius's map, the featureless southern continent becomes a stage, the cartographical projection a theatrical backdrop, and the world a theatre, in which the knight's struggles to reach his true heavenly home of the Christian Cosmopolis are played out.

Geographies of strangerhood

The appearance of cosmopolitan vocabulary and associated concepts in abstruse prophetic declarations, apocalyptic diatribes, manuals of statesmanship and cartographical imagery indicates its polyvalent appeal to Europeans. One of the constants in this literature was the metaphor of the human as a stranger, pilgrim or exile from the city of the world; imagery that could be found in Stoic, Jewish and Christian traditions. Intimately tied to a sense of place, the metaphor expressed the idea of pilgrimage with reference to geography.

Among authors of religious devotional literature, a genre of Christian writing which aimed at granting comfort and solace to its readers, this geography of strangerhood possessed particularly powerful appeal.[40] One of the most noteworthy evocations of this motif occurs in Jan Amos Comenius's devotional novel *Labyrinth of the World and the Paradise of the Heart* (1627).[41] Influenced by Augustine's *City of God*, the narrative traces the movements of our protagonist, named Pilgrim, who is searching for knowledge in the labyrinthine 'city of the world'.[42] Early we learn from Pilgrim's guide, Searchall, that the city is ruled by Queen Wisdom, whom some call 'queen Vanity'.[43] Desiring enlightenment, Pilgrim is disappointed to find only disappointment as he explores the city. In the marketplace he witnesses the hypocrisy of merchants; his encounter with alchemists reveals the depths of human self-deception. Even the churches he finds filled with 'barren priests', who speak with 'tongue[s] full of piety, the eyes full of wantonness'.⁴⁴ Disillusioned, Pilgrim heeds a voice telling him to leave the city and 'return to the place whence you came, to the home of your heart'.⁴⁵ He duly returns home, where he realizes that no wisdom can be found in worldly things. It is only by rejecting the city of the world that Pilgrim is free to accept the spiritual, internal, city of God.⁴⁶

While the geographical aspect of Comenius's *Labyrinth* is inherent in its themes of exile and strangerhood, a later and arguably more influential exploration of the same ideas is provided by the English Puritan John Bunyan (1628–1688).⁴⁷ Imprisoned in 1660 for religious non-conformism, Bunyan experienced a spiritual awakening in his prison cell, during which Hebrews 12:22–24 – a passage already familiar to us from Wierix's *Spirituale Christiani Militis Certamen* – burst suddenly into his mind.⁴⁸ Inspired, he immediately began work on *The Pilgrim's Progress* (1678).⁴⁹ This influential book describes the journey of the character Christian, who must depart the 'City of Destruction' (Isaiah 19:18) and make his way to the 'Celestiall City' atop Mount Zion (cf. Hebrews 12:22). Like Comenius's Pilgrim, the hero's journey is impeded by a variety of obstacles; one, the aptly named Mr Worldly Wiseman, who, like Christian, struggles with the burden of his sins, but seeks absolution in the temporal world. Eventually, Christian finds his way to House of Paradise, where he is equipped with the armour of God (Ephesians 6:10–18) and becomes a Christian Soldier. Transformed, Christian and his new companion Hopeful defeat Apollyon, cross the Enchanted Ground and the River of Death and finally arrive at their destination. The symbolism in this story is as transparent now as it was to its first readers, particularly when considered in the context of the narrative traditions, both Christian and classical, of citizenship, strangerhood, sojourning and an eternal home among the Gods.

In the works of Comenius and Bunyan, the city of the world was Babylon, an ephemeral and imperfect polity, which contrasted with the eternal and perfect Heavenly Jerusalem. But their allegories also make clear that this perfect city exists only in the spirit, and thus in no place at all. It is unsurprising, then, to discover a close nexus between this vision of a perfect society, and the genre of utopian writing; even if scholars have recently been keener to examine these utopias against largely secular backgrounds of natural philosophy, travel and political order.⁵⁰ The foundations of utopian writing were laid by the

Englishman Thomas More (1478–1535) in his *Utopia* (1516), which described an ideal island state, located somewhere in the New World, impressed by Christian traditions and humanist learning. In the sixteenth and seventeenth centuries, a variety of other authors touched on these themes, inspired not only by concerns biblical and devotional, but also by the expanding knowledge won by voyages of discovery. Indeed, the connections between utopian and cartographical imaginations were recognized by Abraham Ortelius, who around 1595 issued a chart of More's *Utopia* embodying tensions between the utopian 'no place' and cartographical fiction (Fig. 3.8). At the very least, Ortelius's map chimes with narratives concerning the home of the true Christian in heaven, as the observer is informed that this non-existent nation 'offers a happy life more than any other place'.⁵¹

Figure 3.8 Abraham Ortelius, 'Vtopiae typus, ex Narratione Raphaelis Hythlodæi' (1595). Engraving, 380 × 475 mm. Coll. Charles Vreeken Fund, King Baudouin Foundation, entrusted to the Museum Plantin-Moretus, Antwerpen (Belgium). © Michael Wuyts & Bart Huysmans.

One utopia that employed the cosmopolitan vocabulary to stunning effect is *Alector, ou le coq* (1560), a brilliant renaissance novel by Barthélemy Aneau (c. 1510–1561). Aneau was a jurist, poet and leading figure in Lyon's humanist scene; and an enthusiast of utopian writing.[52] In 1559 he issued a French revision of More's *Utopia*, and in his posthumously published *Juris Prudentia* (1564), he praised More's book as a showcase for the precepts of divine law.[53] Aneau's *Alector* relates the adventures of the eponymous princely hero, as told by his father Franc-Gal. At a symbolic level the novel concerns France, but as Jenny Meyer has argued insightfully, it contains substantial geographical allusions as well as elements of 'mirror for princes' literature.[54] Its central conceit turns on the now familiar trope of the *homo viator* vanquishing worldly sin and achieving heavenly citizenship. The tale begins *in media res*, with the eponymous Alector on trial in the 'city of Orbe' (i.e. the city of the world), charged with the murder of his fiancé. In the course of the trial, he is accused of being a vagabond, a stranger, a spy, a 'violator of hospitality' (*violateur d'hospitalité*) and a disruptor of the peace.[55] Defending himself from these charges, Alector claims that he is not an 'unknown stranger' but – recalling Cicero's tale of Socrates – a 'worldling and citizen of the world' (*mais mondain et citoyen du monde*).[56] By the end of the novel Alector and his father – who spends the majority of the tale searching for his son while mounted on a winged hippopotamus – are united in Orbe. There, Alector defeats Sin, who had been menacing the metropolis in the guise of a voracious serpent, proving that he is prepared to live in harmony with divine law. Finally, both men are accepted as patricians and citizens of the world (*reçoit pour citoyens et Patrices de la ville d'Orbe*).[57]

Although frequently analysed as a piece of Renaissance romance fiction, the tale straddles genres of devotional and utopian writing, and the conceit of Aneau's *Alector* was inspired by concerns both humanist and Christian.[58] If we briefly examine other early modern utopias, we also encounter cosmopolitan tropes. In Johann Valentin Andreae's *Christianopolis* (1619) – a work examined in greater detail in the next chapter – we encounter the protagonist Peregrinus (Stranger) washed up on the shores of the island of Capharsalama, where he encounters a society living in harmony with God's divine laws. Similarly, Tomasso Campanella's *The City of the Sun* (c. 1602), a paean to Spanish imperial pretensions and universal monarchy, begins with a Genoese sea captain who had 'wandered the whole earth' lost on the equatorial African coast.[59] From thence he is led to the City of the Sun, where he learns of the harmonious and scientific life led by its inhabitants, who serve God 'under the sign of the sun, which is the symbol and visage of God from whom comes light and warmth and every other thing'.[60] To Andreae and Campanella, the stranger, or pilgrim, was central to demonstrating the godly character of the city that each figure ultimately encountered, as well as reflecting the hardships suffered by Christians in their journeys through life towards these fictive destinations.

But the most influential melding of Christian and cosmopolitan themes in a utopia was *The New Atlantis* (1627), an unfinished work by the English polymath Francis Bacon (1561–1626).[61] A subject of considerable debate, scholarly opinion is seemingly irrevocably divided between scholars who see Bacon's use of religious concepts in the text as manipulative and disingenuous, and those who understand these expressions as sincere reflections of his beliefs.[62] An analysis of the text strongly suggests that the latter position is more accurate.

Bacon's tale begins when European explorers are wrecked on an uncharted island in the Pacific Ocean. There, they are stunned to discover a city called Bensalem, which was inhabited by a Christian community. This community claims to have received Jesus's teachings when an 'ark' prepared by St. Bartholomew washed up on their beaches only a few years after Christ's crucifixion. This ark 'contained all the canonical books of the Old and New Testament ... and the Apocalypse itself, and some other books of the New Testament, which were not at that time written'.[63] The miraculous presence of not-yet-written biblical books suggests that Bensalem possessed a prophetic link to God, while John's *Revelation* ('the Apocalypse itself') indicates the apocalyptic character of the narrative. Shortly thereafter, the reader learns that the arrival of divine scripture occasioned further miracles, such as the ability of all islanders to be able to read and understand the books in their own languages, like the apostles at Pentecost (Acts 2:1–41). As Bacon puts it: 'For there being at that time, in this land, Hebrews, Persians, and Indians, besides the natives, everyone read upon the book and letter, as if they had been written in his own language. And thus was this land saved from infidelity ... through the apostolical and miraculous evangelism of St. Bartholomew.'[64]

With its melting pot of cultures, peoples, languages, and religions, Bacon apparently intended Bensalem to be understood by readers as a microcosm of the whole world. As such, the circumstances he relates subtly remind readers of Matthew 24:14, which prophesied that 'the end shall come' only when the 'gospel of the kingdom shall be preached in all the world for a witness unto all nations'.[65] As the political philosopher Howard White has pointed out, Bensalem could therefore be seen as a preview of the future harmony to be enjoyed by Christians in the apocalyptic New Jerusalem, the city in which divine law is united with divine right at the end of time.[66] The name Bensalem, which derives from the Hebrew 'son of peace', might indicate that the city was 'the inheritor of Jerusalem's renown'. If correct, this means that the city described by Bacon was the community of the faithful in the apocalyptic Heavenly Jerusalem.[67]

Upon landing at the island, the pilgrims are conducted to the aptly named 'Strangers' House' in Bensalem, where they find themselves 'between death and life … beyond both the old world and the new'.[68] There they learn of the history of Bensalem, and of the secret wisdom possessed by its inhabitants, instituted in 'Salomon's House'.[69] This institution was named after a local ruler whose name, and reputation, was remarkably similar to that of the prodigiously wise King Solomon of scripture. Salomon's House comprised a body of men 'dedicated to the study of the Works and Creatures of God'.[70] As Richard Serjeantson has pointed out, the pure Christianity of the Bensalemites allowed them a pure knowledge of nature, creating in them 'consummate natural theologians'.[71] At the conclusion of the narrative, the narrator is given permission by the father of Salomon's House to disseminate news of the community of Bensalem to the world at large; 'God blesse this Relation, which I have made. I give thee leave to Publish it, for the Good of other Nations, For wee here are in GODS bosome, a Land unknowne.'[72] This passage draws directly on Augustine's *City of God* by portraying Bensalem itself as a pilgrim city, unknown to all but its true citizens, wherever they might be found across the world. It is only in the pilgrim city that knowledge of the world stands in harmony with divine law and the will of God; both a true utopia, and a true cosmopolis.

Conclusions

The cosmopolitan vocabulary and concepts of strangerhood, pilgrimage and heavenly citizenship it designated, appeared in a variety of early modern works concerning knowledges geographical and cartographical. The cosmopolitan imaginary of the sixteenth and seventeenth centuries was intimately connected to space. The cosmopolis, the city of the world, could be conceived of as everywhere or nowhere. Its citizens could be everyone, or no one. Against this backdrop, it is only natural that expanding geographical knowledge, represented in works cartographical and cosmographical, would become a location where ideas of the cosmopolitan could be explored. Additionally, such ideas could be combined with metaphors of exile, strangerhood and pilgrimage in devotional works, and even in books issued in the utopian genre. The geographical component of the early modern cosmopolitan imaginary was significant, because it expanded the variety of works in which readers and observers alike could encounter the cosmopolitan vocabulary. This exposure to novel expressions of world citizenship would prove crucial to provoking further engagement with both the language and the ideas of the cosmopolitan. A final example, that of the Anglo-Prussian intelligencer Samuel Hartlib (c. 1600–1662), can help illustrate something of the ubiquity and influence of these geographical expressions.

From 1628 Hartlib had lived in exile in London having departed Elbing (Elbląg) in Royal Prussia on account of military unrest. In England, he busied himself with a series of projects proposing the 'Advancement of Universal Learning and the Publick Good' that he hoped would occasion 'the advancement of the Kingdom of Jesus Christ [. . .] which shall come out of Sion by a Gospel-Reformation of this Age and Common-wealth'.[73] His concerns were thus Christian and cosmopolitan. Hartlib hoped that his life's work – which ranged from the creation of a practical 'office of address' to the publication of millenarian prophecies – would inspire the 'building up of the walls of Jerusalem in the mindes of Believers' so that the Temple of Heaven could 'com[e] down from the New Heaven upon the New Earth'.[74] In this fashion his concerns were not far divorced from those of Postel or Dee. Yet while Hartlib considered himself a 'conduit pipe' of wisdom, and a providential tool of God, he appears to have never believed himself to be a prophet or a messianic figure.

In 1651, while walking through London, Hartlib found a fitting motto for himself displayed 'in the window before the Councel-Chamber at Guildhall':

Mundus Mare, Vita Navis, Quisque navigatio
Mors Portas, Patria Cælum, Fidelis intrat.[75]

The world is a sea, our life a ship, we are navigators,
death is the door the faithful enter to our heavenly Fatherland.

While Hartlib saw this statement as a fitting designation for himself and his endeavours, the motto had originally appeared in a very different context, on a 1635 sepulchral monument of Sir Thomas Gorges and the Marchioness of Northampton in Salisbury Cathedral.[76] This episode suggests something of the ubiquity of cosmopolitan expressions in England by 1650, as well as the potential appeal of geographical metaphors in its use.

Prevalent in all of these conceptions is the multivalence of the cosmopolitan ideal. Authors, cartographers, mapmakers and printmakers were inspired by Christian concerns and tropes of antique literature in composing their cosmopolitan visions of cartographical fools, treatises of navigation and descriptions of ideal communities. This eclecticism mirrors the diversity of cosmopolitan expressions in the literature of antiquity. In the next chapter, however, we turn to examine a tradition of cosmopolitan thought which built on the metaphorical tropes of the vanity of the world, and which flourished among Christian thinkers who deliberately inverted the positive associations of the cosmopolitan vocabulary.

4

The cosmopolitan inversion

Babylon is fallen, is fallen ... that great city, which reigneth over the kings of the earth.

Revelation 14:8, 17:18

A Citizen of the World ... is every where at home, because he is indeed at home no where.

Clement Ellis, *The Gentle Sinner* (1660)

In his 1619 utopian romance *De reipublicæ Christianopolitanæ descriptio*, a work better known as *Christianopolis*, the Lutheran pastor Johann Valentin Andreae (1586–1654) of Württemberg in the Holy Roman Empire recounted the adventures of a protagonist known only as Peregrinus (Stranger), afloat and lost at sea:

> While I was wandering about the whole world as a stranger, patiently enduring many tyrannies, sophists and hypocrites, not yet having found the man for whom I was searching anxiously, I decided once again to attempt the Academic Ocean, even though it had very often been hostile to me. So I boarded the ship of Fantasy with many others and left behind the well-known ports, exposing life and limb to the thousand dangers of a desire for knowledge.[1]

The journey was peaceful, until suddenly the winds of envy and false accusation began to gather. Battered by waves, the ship finally broke apart, throwing Peregrinus into the ocean, his life seemingly over. But by divine providence, he was carried by the ocean's currents to an island, 'the merest patch of turf', which he came to learn was named Capharsalama, a name derived from the Hebrew for 'village of peace'. Recalling Bacon's *New Atlantis* and the imagery of Revelation 21:2, the island and its city were described by Andreae as a place where 'heaven had married the earth'.[2] Peregrinus soon met a guide who conducted him through the well-ordered city, where he discovered beautiful buildings and clean streets. In the heart of the city he admired Capharsalama's ecumenical creed, which highlighted the community's reliance on Godly ideals. Ultimately Peregrinus was forced to depart 'that blessed City of God' and return to the mundane world.[3] Before his departure, he received a warning from the city's chancellor: 'Be careful, my brother, that you do not fall under the spell of the world and become a stranger to us.'[4] Andreae's message was clear. If Peregrinus was to inherit his place as a citizen in the New Jerusalem, it was necessary for him to shun the world, and to remember his calling to his heavenly home.

This theme had first emerged in Andreae's works around 1615, in which year he issued several pamphlets employing the metaphor of the godly stranger as its central motif. One of these, an anonymously printed drama titled *De Christiani Cosmoxeni Genitura, Judicium* (A judgement on the horoscope of Christian Cosmoxenus) introduced a radical neologism to the cosmopolitan vocabulary. For Andreae, the true heavenly citizen should not be called a *cosmopolitanus*, or citizen of the world, but instead was better named *cosmoxenus*, or stranger to the world, a coinage he derived from the Greek κόσμος (world) and the adjectival ξένος, denoting a foreigner.[5] For the Lutheran Andreae, the cosmopolitan designation reeked of worldliness. He was not the only clergyman who felt compelled to coin a new word to describe the lot of the heavenly citizen. More than forty years later, in 1658, the Anglican clergyman Samuel Crooke (1575–1649) also rejected cosmopolitans as hypocrites and 'worldlings'. Instead, he designated the citizen of the New Jerusalem as *Uranopolitēs* (a citizen of heaven), a term derived from the Greek οὐρανός, the designation for heaven.[6]

The inversion of the positive associations of the cosmopolitan vocabulary by these Protestant clergymen was made possible by two separate traditions. The first was the language of scripture. In Philippians 3:19–20 Paul and Timothy declared of the enemies of Christianity that 'Their end is destruction; their god is the belly; and their glory is in their shame; their minds are set on earthly things, but our citizenship is in heaven (τὸ πολίτευμα ἐν οὐρανοῖς ὑπάρχει).⁷ The other tradition derived from the Stoic literature of antiquity. In Chapter 1, we saw that the works of Cicero and Epictetus used the words κοσμίος or *mundanus* to describe Socrates. In this frame, the Stoic declarations could be read as promotions of sinful worldliness, which contrasted starkly with the virtuous 'citizen of heaven'.

The deliberate inversion of the cosmopolitan vocabulary by Andreae and Crooke provides a compelling example of how normative vocabularies used to appraise and describe the social world can change. As Quentin Skinner has argued, this is a process that typically occurs when the capacities of normative vocabularies are 'altered in direction or intensity' by external circumstances.⁸ These alterations, Skinner suggests, 'usually reflect an underlying attempt to modify existing social perceptions and beliefs'. Their ultimate goal is to promote the suggestion that 'a society should reconsider and perhaps transvalue some of its moral values'.⁹ In this context it is suggestive to note that the cosmopolitan inversions appeared largely, though not exclusively, in works by reform-oriented Protestant clerics in Germany and England. In Catholic countries, the cosmopolitan vocabulary doesn't seem to have enjoyed a strong foothold, a circumstance that might explain why evidence for a similar clarification is lacking.¹⁰ In England, it featured in works of Puritan ministers, for whom the very idea of worldliness provoked a visceral reaction, and who equally occupied a marginal position within the church, at the mercy of state-sponsored Anglicanism. In Germany, the cosmopolitan inversion was also used with reference to contemporary religious polemics, as a means of drawing boundaries between different religious confessions. Yet it could also appear in a devotional context, as an inspiration for Christians to shun the world – or more specifically its worldly ways – and follow the precepts of a Christian life and practice. Although beyond the scope of the present study, the articulation of these positions in England and Germany occurred against the background of the Thirty Years' War, which created a flood of actual exiles from central Europe into neighbouring territories who drew comfort during their displacements from the imagery of the Christian as an exile on earth.¹¹

The present chapter examines the diversity of expressions of this cosmopolitan inversion. It demonstrates that, by the seventeenth century, the vocabulary associated with the cosmopolitan idea, and indeed the term 'cosmopolitan' itself, could be used by Christians not only as a term to designate specialness, prophecy or divine sponsorship, but could also be wielded as a cudgel to denigrate, to attack and to condemn others. This development is significant, because the circulation of negative cosmopolitan discourses led to an untethering of the cosmopolitan vocabulary from dominant Christian discourses of heavenly citizenship, and thus over time made the terminology unpalatable to Christians. In tandem with independent rediscoveries of Stoic cosmopolitan conceptions by scholars, philologists, dramatists and others throughout the sixteenth and seventeenth centuries, this conception contributed to the secularization of cosmopolitan discourse, a matter that we will examine in greater detail over the two subsequent chapters.

Confronting the world

Andreae first employed the word cosmoxenus in his prose drama *De Christiani Cosmoxeni Genitura, Judicium* (A judgement on the horoscope of Christian Cosmoxenus, 1615).[12] The tract was at one level a polemic against contemporary belief in astrologically influenced predestination, a circumstance emphasized by the appearance of Jeremiah 10:11 on the title-page: 'Learn not the way of the heathen, and be not dismayed at the signs of heaven; for the heathen are dismayed at them.' At another level, the book comprised a précis of Andreae's philosophy of Christian life, a life in which the true Christian is a *homo viator* in search of his heavenly home, even though 'his journeys seem laughable to the worldlings (*cosmopolitis*)'.[13] The tale begins by introducing the eponymous protagonist as a lazy, self-loving, irrational creature, prone to anger, pettiness, pride and sin, whose 'father is Adam, his fatherland the world, and his sister flesh'.[14] For Andreae the antithesis of the worldly Adam is Christ, a dichotomy that builds on Philo of Alexandria's claim, examined in Chapter 1, that Adam was the first cosmopolitan.

To overcome his nature, Christian Cosmoxenus must struggle against 'the world, flesh, and Satan' (*Mundus, Caro, Satan*), and ultimately become reborn in Christ, joining the ranks of the 'servants of the kingdom of Christ, soldiers in the holy army, citizens of the heavenly city and inheritors of His eternal legacy'.[15] To do so, he must reject the world and its worldly ways. The sinful Adamic state in which he was born must die within him, and only then can he become a *renatus*, born again.¹⁶ This rebirth means freedom from worldly temptation and the capriciousness of men.¹⁷ In the conclusion to the work's preface, Andreae epitomized the path of his protagonist through the narrative:

> Christian Cosmoxenus, who, though he was born from a background of human weakness and need, is become through obliging and merciful Grace a new and reborn creation, who endures the present for the benefit of that which is to come, for which he strives. On earth he conducts himself not merely as a stranger; he is unfit for the world and indeed dead to it. Shunned like a monster he dwells among the scoffers, and joyously dedicates himself to God, and is thereby with those whose lives lead elsewhere, who possess spiritual and not worldly happiness, whose knowledge is directed not outward, but inward, who desire nothing that the world recognizes as great, magnificent, exalted, famous, sensational, or valuable, but instead are satisfied solely with those things that today are enough for no man, namely those things that are intangible, things upon which one must first believe in and hope for, and things that scoffers deride as illusory.¹⁸

As Richard von Dülmen and Christoph Neeb have noted, from around 1615 the figure of the spiritually reborn Cosmoxenus became an important *Leitmotif* in Andreae's oeuvre.¹⁹ In one work the reborn Christian was portrayed as a Christian Hercules, striving for heaven.²⁰ In *Theca gladii spiritus* (Scabbard of the spiritual sword, 1616) appeared a satirical zodiac for Cosmoxenus predicting his transcendence of the pernicious influence of the stars, and in *Menippus* (1617) Andreae contrasted the heavenly citizen 'Cosmoxenos' with the worldly 'Cosmopolita': while the former attempted to transcend the world, the latter relished its 'filth and iniquity'.²¹

The dichotomy was revisited in several essays included in Andreae's satirical masterwork, *Mythologiæ Christianiæ* (1619). In one of these, Andreae compared the respective homes of Cosmopolita and Cosmoxenus. The home of the former was built on sand, elaborately decorated with magnificent paintings and fixtures. The house of the latter was simple and utilitarian, built on a foundation of the love of Christ and fashioned from the stone of faith. Although Cosmopolita heaped scorn on the simple dwelling of his neighbour, it was only the home of Cosmoxenus that could withstand the fury of God, and ultimately stood for eternity.²² In another essay, Cosmoxenus was urged to take up his sword and to steel himself against the excesses of the world.²³

Finally, in another piece that squares the circle, Andreae condemned the worldly Cosmopolita as monstrous. In this narrative, a group of learned astrologers from European history – among them Joachim of Fiore (c. 1135–1202), Paracelsus (1493–1541), Pico di Mirandola (1463–1494), the Christian cabalist Johann Reuchlin (1455–1522), Heinrich Cornelius Agrippa (1486–1535) and the astronomer Tycho Brahe (1546–1601) – convened to determine the future of a hideous prodigy. Promised rich gifts by the creature's parents for executing their duty, they provided an astrological judgment stating that the prodigy would 'live to be as old as Nestor, as wise as Aristotle, as rich as Crosius, as fortunate as Alexander, as brave as Hercules, and as famous as Augustus'.[24] At this, Cosmoxenus, here named Cosmopolemus (another neologism denoting an 'enemy of the world'), stated that the efforts of the learned would have been better served in helping the proud parents take stock of their own lives, for 'it is impossible for a Basilisk to raise an eagle'.[25] In Andreae's eyes it was not enough to merely shun the world; the true Christian had to become its enemy.

Andreae's Cosmoxenus was conceived as part of a programme of practical Christianity. This programme was decisively influenced by the writings of the reform-oriented Lutheran clergyman Johann Arndt (1555–1621).[26] Arndt is most famous for his *Vier Bücher vom wahren Christenthum* (Four books of true Christianity, 1606–1610), an influential work that combined practical devotional exercises of prayer and penance with meditative reflections on Christian piety. It emphasized the necessity of the rebirth of the true Christian in spirit as a step towards the practice of 'True Christianity'.[27] Andreae's appreciation of Arndt is clear. In 1615 he issued a pamphlet titled *Christianismus genuinus ... Johannis Arndt*, which comprised a summary and defence of Arndt's doctrines. Furthermore, Arndt was the dedicatee of Andreae's *Christianopolis*. In the dedicatory epistle, Andreae wrote: 'This new community of ours owes its origin to you and looks to you with hope, for it is a very small colony taken out of that great Jerusalem that you have built up with such enormous spirit against the wishes of the sophists.'[28] Although Donald R. Dickson, who believed Andreae's tract to be a call for a kind of radical separatism, has pointed out that Arndt 'nowhere recommended ... cloistered retreat from the world', neither did Andreae; for his project of the Cosmoxenus, of which *Christianopolis* was only a part, was not simply about individual transformation or shunning the world.[29] Indeed, Stefania Salvadori has argued forcefully that Andreae intended the *renati* or reborn to become part of a vanguard of social, religious and political innovation, who would ultimately band together to form a cadre of activists dedicated to reforming European society and religion.[30] Andreae's Cosmoxeni were active: they were ideal citizens in the heavenly city, who would seek, by their words and deeds, to realize Christ's kingdom in this world.

The articulation of this reforming programme was the mature manifestation of an impulse that first emerged during Andreae's youth, and arguably gave rise to one of the more mysterious episodes in seventeenth-century history. Around 1608, Andreae, then a young student at the University of Tübingen, came under the influence of a radical chiliast named Tobias Hess (1586–1614), a jurist who was active as a Paracelsian physician in Tübingen.[31] Together the two men authored a document titled 'Fama Fraternitatis' (Fame of the Fraternity).[32] This text, which was perhaps written between 1608 and 1610, but printed anonymously without the knowledge of its authors in 1614, purported to be a statement issued by the Rosicrucian fraternity, a secret society founded by a certain 'C.R.' in the Middle Ages to institute a 'universal and general reformation of the whole wide world'.[33] According to the 'Fama', since its foundation the members of the fraternity had spread themselves about the world, adopting the languages, costumes and mores of the societies that they infiltrated, all the while working diligently on the reformation of religion and the sciences. But over time, the project had gone awry, the doctrines of the Rosicrucians had become corrupted and its members had lost contact with one another. Then, in 1604, the tomb of the brotherhood's founder – which contained the group's original doctrines and comprised a 'compendium of the universe' – had been rediscovered. In a Europe whose religion had been cleansed by Luther's reformation in the light of the Last Days, the work of the Rosicrucian fraternity could be resumed. The 'Fama Fraternitatis' therefore ended with a call for all the learned of Europe to join the Rosicrucian project. The printing of the 'Fama Fraternitatis' in 1614, and its sequel, 'Confessio Fraternitatis' in 1615, duly provoked several hundred responses in both manuscript and print.[34]

However, there was a problem. The fantastic story of the fraternity was an invention; the Rosicrucian society never existed. Furthermore, whatever the intention of its authors, the 'Fama' and 'Confessio', as well as many of the responses to it, attracted the attention of theologians who denounced the fraternity and their reforming mission as heretical. The timing could not have been worse for Johann Valentin Andreae. By the time 'Fama Fraternitatis' found its way into print in 1614, Andreae had taken up a position as a deacon in the Lutheran church in Vaihingen near Stuttgart. It is safe to say that while he continued to believe in the necessity of the further reform of Christian church and life, he was horrified by the veritable Babel of opinion provoked by his manifestos. Immediately following their publication, he set to work refining the programme of reform announced in them. As we have seen, part of this effort involved the creation of the allegorical figure of Christian Cosmoxenus. Additionally, Andreae disavowed the chaos of opinion provoked by the Rosicrucian manifestoes in his *Turris Babel* (Tower of Babel, 1616) and recast the mythical founder of the Rosicrucian fraternity as a literary avatar of Christian Cosmoxenus in his allegorical romance *Die Chymische Hochzeit des Christiani Rosencreutz Anno 1459* (The alchemical wedding of Christian Rosencreutz, 1616).[35]

But his efforts were not only literary. Andreae also attempted to establish a series of learned Christian societies that – unlike the Rosicrucian fraternity – would not remain 'immersed in the dreggs of Earth' but instead 'stirre foward any one aspiring Christian liberty and communion in the way of heaven'.[36] These plans were outlined by Andreae in his *Invitatio fraternitatis Christi* (Invitation to the Fraternity of Christ, 1617) and *Christianae Societatis Imago* (Model of a Christian Society, 1620).[37] Such a society would be established and led by *renati*, dedicated to charity, virtue and wisdom, obeying the 'Rules and Laws of nature' while securing the 'propagation of the kingdom of heaven'.[38] This would be achieved by means of a series of institutions resembling those described in *Christianopolis*.

Under the leadership of a German prince, these institutions would be chaired by a privy council of twelve men of various professions, including 'presidents' of religion and virtue, each of whom would supervise groups of scholars working in triumvirate; the first dedicated to fields of divinity, censorship and philosophy; the second to politics, history and economics, and the last studying medicine, mathematics and philology.[39] Coordinating these results, the privy council would employ this wisdom to steer society towards the kingdom of heaven. If this life was a preface of the eternal heavenly life to come, as Andreae believed, then the mission of the true Cosmoxenus was therefore to create a preview of the true heavenly patria on earth.

Andreae's inversion of the cosmopolitan vocabulary was embedded in a variety of discourses, all of which were critical of worldly ways and human frailty. But these criticisms were tied to a reforming attitude which valued action both individual and corporate. Following the disappointment of his Rosicrucian project, Andreae created the figure of Cosmoxenus, and placed the nexus of worldly reform in the heart and soul of the true Christian. By directing his critique at the individual, rather than society and its institutions, Andreae could avoid the charges of controversy and even heresy that had plagued his Rosicrucian project.[40] Only after elaborating this vision of the true Christian as a foreigner, pilgrim, and even enemy of the world and its ways, did Andreae then attempt to band the *renati* together, and in his later programmatic writings describe a series of learned societies that would work towards the practical reformation of the world.

Cosmopolitan polemics and Protestant identity

While Andreae's later works demonstrated the potential of the cosmopolitan vocabulary to support wide-scale social and religious reform, the controversy surrounding the Rosicrucian fraternity provides an example of how it could be invoked to contest confessional boundaries. While all Protestant authors castigated the claims of the Catholic church to universal dominion – a pretension inherent in the very word 'catholic', which derived from the Greek καθολικός (*katholikos*), meaning 'universal' – the various Protestant confessions were also militantly opposed to one another and their respective claims to be the sole proponents of true doctrine, and thus the sole holders of heavenly citizenship. This view was also promoted by so-called spiritualists and Radical Reformers like Sebastian Franck (1499–1543), Caspar Schwenckfeld von Ossig (1490–1561), Paracelsus and, later, figures like Valentin Weigel (1553–1588) and Jacob Böhme (1575–1624).[41] All of these claimed privileged prophetic access to divine wisdom, which made their teachings more legitimate than those of the 'churches of walls'.[42] Rhetoric concerning the worldliness of rival religious factions, theologians or individuals was thus often crucial to processes of identity building, social discipline and identity differentiation. The cosmopolitan vocabulary fit comfortably within these discourses of difference.

Accordingly, we find instances of the occurrence of the vocabulary in Protestant polemic from the late sixteenth century. In 1574 for example, a controversial pamphlet titled *Le Réveille-matin des François* – a title that might be colloquially rendered as 'France's wake-up call' – was issued in Strasbourg or possibly Basel.[43] Despite being widely attributed to the French alchemist Nicholas Barnaud (*c.* 1539–1604), the tract was likely authored by the jurist Hugues Doneau (1527–1591).[44] Written in the wake of the St. Bartholomew's Day massacre, it was intended as a warning concerning the tyranny of Catholicism, as well as a call to arms for 'Christian soldiers' (*soldats Chrétiens*) to revolt against the French royal family. Simultaneously, the tract was also a cautionary notice to the Polish nobility of the dangers of electing the fanatical Duke of Anjou Henri III (1551–1589), brother of the French king, to the Polish-Lithuanian throne. *Les Réveille-matin des François* was clearly written by a Huguenot, a circumstance indicated not only by its content, but also by the pseudonym under which it was printed: 'Eusebe Philadelphe Cosmopolite', a name that might indicate 'a cosmopolitan esteemer (εὐσέβειν) of Philadelphia'. Again, we meet here with the cosmopolitan designation being used in tandem with Protestant religious polemic, in particular the identification of the persecuted Huguenots with the apocalyptic church of Philadelphia (Revelation 3).

In territories with primarily Protestant cultures, such as England and much of Germany, the cosmopolitan vocabulary was regularly invoked to demarcate doctrinal boundaries, or cast moralizing aspersions on other religious factions. An example is provided by George Goodwin's *Melissa religionis pontificae* (1620). Goodwin was an Anglican vicar in Moreton, Sussex, who used the cosmopolitan vocabulary to lambast the 'Babylonian' Catholic Church.[45] In the eighth satire of this work, Goodwin contrasted the worldly aspirations of the pope, described as 'a Cosmopolite',[46] with the heavenly nature of Christ's kingdom, manifested on earth in the doctrines of the Anglican church:

Christs *Throne* is Heav'nly, Heav'nly things doe muse:
But Papall *Pride*, an earthly *Throne* doth chuse.
Yet, vaine's this *Choice*, which chooseth Earthly things:
For, by such a choice, toward God hee *folly* brings.[47]

For Goodwin, the illegitimacy and worldliness of Catholicism provides *prima facie* evidence of corrupt doctrine. In another discourse concerning the folly of Papal councils, Goodwin condemned the pope as a 'hyperbolicke-Priest' dwelling 'in Gods house', a figure antithetical to the tenets of true Christianity.

Yet the cosmopolitan designation could be turned against anyone, not just the Papacy.[48] This volatility is exemplified in the several-hundred works, both print and manuscript, inspired by Andreae's 'Fama Fraternitatis', the document that told the story of the fictional Rosicrucian fraternity. Although absent from the Rosicrucian manifestos themselves, the cosmopolitan vocabulary was used by several respondents who authored tracts both for and against the brotherhood's reforming agenda. In 1616, the Hamburg scholar, librarian and publicist Joachim Morsius (1593–1644) issued a pamphlet concerning the fraternity under the pseudonym Anastasius Philaretus Cosmopolita, which might be translated as the 'resurrected cosmopolite inclined to do good'. Given that Morsius was an avid reader of the works of Johann Arndt and Andreae, this pseudonym was likely a tip of the cap to the idea of the born-again *renatus*.[49] Emphasizing the apocalyptic nature of the ideas of Christian fraternity and heavenly citizenship, the pamphlet identified Philadelphia as its place of printing (cf. Revelation 3:7–13).[50] The idea of a 'true' Christian community, guaranteed of salvation at the End of Days, was thus emphasized in a manner similar to *Les Réveille-matin des François*. Although the text of the pamphlet consisted of a sincere petition for Morsius to be accepted into the ranks of the Rosicrucian fraternity – which he earnestly, although mistakenly, believed to actually exist – it concluded with a statement offering further insight into his cosmopolitan conception: 'Anastasius Philaretus, who sought the splendour here on earth and found it not; for it may be found only in the celestial spheres, where we gather amongst the souls in Heaven.'[51] In a later pamphlet, issued under the same pseudonym, Morsius argued for freedom of conscience and belief, stating that all worldly churches were enemies of true Christianity, whose doctrines were instead communicated directly to the individual through the inspiration of the Holy Spirit.[52]

Morsius evidently considered the cosmopolitan vocabulary to be compatible with the Rosicrucian reforms, but opponents of the fraternity saw things differently. For example, in 1619, the French philosopher René Descartes (1596–1650) apparently intended to mock the fraternity in his projected

Thesaurus mathematicus, a work he desired to publish under the pseudonym 'Polybius Cosmopolitanus'.[53] The long subtitle of the promised tract indicated that it was to contain 'the true means of solving all the difficulties in the science of mathematics', and would thus 'expose the emptiness' of recent pretensions to universal wisdom. Tellingly, it was to be dedicated 'especially to the distinguished Fraternity of the Rosy Cross in Germany'.[54] Yet Descartes was not the only figure who viewed the fraternity in such a light. In 1621, Valentin Grießmann (d. 1639) a Lutheran pastor of Wählitz near Magdeburg, condemned the Rosicrucians as agents of a 'seditious conspiracy against all good order'.[55] Grießmann was incensed by the fraternity's prophetic claims, especially their declaration of an imminent universal reformation before the Last Judgment. As a staunch defender of the status quo in the Empire, Grießmann was convinced that such predictions would be disappointed by the passage of time itself. Nevertheless, in the meantime, the Rosicrucian 'Cosmopolites and companion pilgrims (*Cosmopoliten und Wallfarts Brüder*) ... wait for that time, when they shall be able to effect the golden Reformation according to their own imaginations'.[56] It was thus important to warn the simple and gullible about their imposture. For the Rosicrucians were 'neither beggars nor in need'. Instead, they claimed to be 'possessors of gold and other riches, a royal treasure greater than any that might be found on earth', a claim that alone revealed the corrupt worldliness of their goals.[57] For Grießmann, all Rosicrucian hopes of chiliastic reformation were thus built on quicksand (*Triebsand*), rather than on the firm foundations of the Lutheran faith. By following the Rosicrucian promise, a person not only risked their worldly reputation, but also their soul.[58]

The gripulous fist of the carnal worldling

Grießmann's attack on Rosicrucian worldliness draws our attention to a genre of anti-cosmopolitan polemic which flourished among those clerics in Britain that Patrick Collinson described memorably as 'the hotter sort of Protestant': the Puritan wing of English Anglicanism.[59] They rejected the idea that the reformation had been completed under Elizabeth I, and argued that Anglicanism retained too many trappings of Catholicism. As such, the character of English religion had to be further 'purified'; a conviction which gave the reformers their name.

The inversion of the cosmopolitan vocabulary was naturally of interest to these Puritans, who largely understood 'citizens of the world' as 'carnall worldlings'.[60] A detailed account of the logic that underwrote the appeal of this link is provided by Samuel Purchas, whom we briefly discussed in the previous chapter. Purchas opened the first volume of his *Hakluytus Posthumus* (1622–1626) with a discourse on cosmopolitan identity. Referring to Philo of Alexandria, he condemned Adam as the first 'worldling', whose expulsion from Eden had occasioned an enormous confusion among the 'commons of mankind'. Adam's choice meant that humanity had since been captives of the devil, trapped 'in so well ordered furniture, and so well furnished order, as the name κοσμὸς and *mundus* import'.[61] For Purchas, Christians could gird their souls by using the 'supernaturall gifts' to obey the 'Charter of Reason' that God had originally given to Adam. Thereby, humanity would finally overcome the devil and be granted dominion over the earth.[62]

Against this background, Purchas castigated those seeking solace in worldly endeavour, riches and wisdom. He ridiculed 'Foolosophers' like Diogenes, Aristotle, Seneca, Socrates and all '*Cynikes, Gymnosophists* and *Stoikes*' who knew not the 'Fear of God' with which true knowledge began (Proverbs 1:7).[63] For Purchas, Socrates's declaration that he was 'κοσμοπολίτης, all places his Countrie' showed that his wisdom had been corrupted by a demonic worldliness.[64] This was unsurprising, for as Purchas argued, following the revelation of Christ, the universe itself was

> not large enough to bee the Mappe of the Christians inheritance, whose are the world, and life, and death, and things present and things to come, all are theirs; the third Heaven and Paradise of God their Patrimonie; the Angels their Gard (are they not all ministring spirits sent forth for their sakes that are heires of salvation?) the Devils, the World, Sinne, Death and Hell their triumph; Paul, Apollo, Cephas, all the Worthies, Elders, Senators & Patres Conscripti of the celestiall Jerusalem, those first-borne, whose names are written in Heaven, their Kindred, Brethren, fellow Citizens, fellow members; Christ himselfe their head, their life; and God their portion, their exceeding great reward, their owne God amongst them, in a tenure like himselfe, eternall and unspeakably glorious.... Christ with his bodie is the Centre, and God the Circumference of this mysticall Corporation.[65]

Purchas's reading of history as the story of man's salvation provided yet another context in which early modern thinkers prised the cosmopolitan vocabulary away from its once positive connotations. For Purchas, true citizens of heaven should shun citizens of the world.

Other English clerics were more modest in their appropriation of the cosmopolitan vocabulary. Let us take for example the case of Thomas Adams (1583–1652). Often identified as a Puritan, Adams attended Cambridge University before being ordained in the diocese of Lincoln in 1604, finally arriving in London in 1619.[66] Throughout his career he issued sermon collections under appealing topical titles like *Mystical Bedlam* (1615) and *The Sacrifice of Thankefulnesse* (1615), publications that have led one literary historian to describe him as 'the Shakespeare of Puritan theologians'.[67] Adams employed the figure of the cosmopolite in several works. His *The Diuells Banquet* (1614) addresses at length the temptations confronting true Christians. For Adams, who was likely influenced by Neostoicism, the task that the Christian faces is not 'being free from lusts, but in brideling them, not in escaping temptation, but in vanquishing it'.[68] In his brief commentary on Galatians 2:19, concerning spiritual rebirth, Adams argued that the true Christian must 'choose between God and Mammon', because 'they command contrary things ... Thus is the world *dead* to us: For since the world is not so precious as the soule; wee leave the world to keepe our soule'. For the faithful, therefore, the 'vanitie of carnall joyes, the varietie of vanities, are as bitter to us, as pleasant to the Cosmopolite or worldling'.[69]

Adams reinforced this position the following year in *England's Sickness* (1615). 'Behold the Cosmopolite,' he wrote,

> He buildes neither Church nor Hospitall (eyther *in cultum Christi*, or *culturam Christiani*, to the service of *Christ*, or comfort of any Christian) ... He minds onely *Horreum suum, & Hordeum suum*, His barne and his Barley. Behold at last he promiseth his *Soule* peace, ease, mirth, security: but when his Chickens were scarse hatch'd ... he heares a fatall voyce confiscating his goods, and himselfe too.[70]

The 'gripulous fist' of this Cosmopolite grasps at worldly goods, but it thereby breeds a soul-destroying disease that corrupts first the individual, and then all of society.[71] For Adams, this worldliness was the chief cause of the 'sickness' of

England's religion. As he recorded in a commentary on the story of Jacob and Esau (Genesis 25–33), it is only a 'besotted Cosmopolite, that refuseth to purchase such spirituall *Friends* by his riches, as may procure him a place in the celestiall habitations'.[72] For Adams, this celestial habitation was not merely the Heavenly Jerusalem, but *Eirenopolis*, the universal city of truth.[73]

By the mid seventeenth century, the subjects of riches, sin and expressions of worldly citizenship seemed inseparable in English clerical literature. In 1628 Sebastian Bennefield (1559–1630), a professor of divinity at the University of Oxford, issued a commentary on Amos, in which he represented the aggregation of worldly wealth as a waypoint on the path to atheism. For Bennefield the rich and affluent behaved 'as if there were no *other life* but *this*', and thus 'in heart … say, *there is no God*'.[74] In 1657 the London minister Thomas Reeves added an anti-clerical dimension to this same argument. He wrote that 'The Devill hath his strongest chains upon rich mens heeles [and] hath an Incorporation of Cosmopolites, an Host of Lucre-worms'. For Reeves 'a man had better anger all the Witches, and Conjurers, provoke all the Centaures, and Minotaures in the world, than to menace this haughty spirited generation'.[75] Yet God's wrath was never far from visiting these 'carnall worldlings'. This much is expressed in *A prospectiue glasse to looke into heauen* (1618), by the Presbyterian clergyman John Vicars (1580–1652).[76] There, he portrayed the true Christian as a Soldier, struggling against worldly temptation on a journey 'from Earth the Stage of instability, to Heav'n the Fortresse of true Constancy'. As such, Vicars encouraged all 'godlesse *Heliogabolites*, You carnall Worldlings, [and] proud Cosmopolites' to indulge themselves in their own inconstancies: 'Goe please your selves in swearing, feasting, fighting, And not what's *just*, but what's your *Lust* delight in.'[77] The title page of Vicars's book was adorned with a passage from Revelation 21:1 'And I saw a New Heaven and a New Earth', which added a distinct apocalyptic urgency to his anti-cosmopolitan polemic.[78] A similar message was delivered almost exactly half a century later by the Puritan minister of Surrey, William Gearing (1625–1690). In his *God's Soveraignty displayed* (1667), a lengthy commentary on Job 9:12, Gearing offered a palliative for those citizens of London whose worldly possessions had been reduced to ashes by the great fire of September 1666.[79] Printed – pointedly, one would imagine – as an appendix to this lachrymose work was a discourse on Hebrews 13:14, titled *No Abiding City in a Perishing World; But Heaven only the continuing City, which we must diligently seek.* Gearing here represented London's destruction as a timely reminder that the pleasures of an earthly city were fleeting, and not to be prized above those of the enduring, heavenly cosmopolis.

Denizens of the heaven polis

In his 1622 work *Axiomatum de consilio politico appendicula*, a collection of political aphorisms, the Tübingen jurist Christoph Besold, a close friend and mentor of Johann Valentin Andreae, included the statement: 'The new man is liberated from the elements and earthly limbo, from the iniquities of the stars: he is not a citizen of the world, but of heaven.'[80] Besold's 'new man' was identical to Andreae's born-again Cosmoxenus. His inclusion of this statement in a collection of political aphorisms is another reminder of the close nexus between political and religious concerns in early modernity. But Besold's work also draws our attention to a concurrent problem faced by Christians; namely the question of the obedience owed by the faithful to heavenly and worldly authorities.

The subject had been hotly debated since the earliest days of the faith, and was addressed by Jesus, Paul, the Gnostics and many others. The interests of states didn't always coincide with those of the true Christian, and the faithful struggled to find a *via media* between religious and secular obligations as they trod the narrow path to heaven. So it continued in early modernity. In his *Hypercritica* (*c.* 1622), the English poet Edmund Bolton (1575–*c*. 1633) echoed John Dee and Marcus Aurelius when he wrote that a Christian had 'a fourfold Duty' in his everyday life: '1. As a Christian Cosmopolite. 2. As a Christian Patriot. 3. As a Christian Subject. 4. As a Christian Paterfamilias.'[81] For Bolton, the worldly obligations of believers remained anchored in their faith. A few years later, Samuel Purchas announced that mankind has a 'threefold tenure' in life; 'A *Microcosmicall* in respect of our selves; a *Cosmopoliticall* in regard of the World; [and] a *Catholicke, Spirituall,* and *Heavenly* in relation to Christ.'[82] For Purchas, these obligations existed extra to '*Politicall* Law and Societie', which he considered 'the last and least of all'.[83] The cosmopolitan vocabulary here firmly designated the worldly obligations of the Christian.

The resonance of such questions in England deepened during the 1640s, when Britain became embroiled in Civil Wars, and clerics linked the fortunes of government to religious rectitude. In his *Logos agonios* (1643), the staunch Royalist Thomas Barton (*c.* 1600–1682) preached a sermon before the king on the 'Christian race'.[84] In it Barton drew up hard and fast boundaries of exclusion that went well beyond the confessional. Drawing on Luke 10:42, he argued that only 'vaine Cosmopolites' did 'stirre up the dust to stifle the Monarchie' in England. Barton called upon these wealthy cosmopolites – evidently identical with the Parliamentarian faction – to save their souls by placing their monies 'into the Kings treasury' to reduce 'the high disparity between the Scepter and the Coulter' and maintain stability across the country. As Barton concluded, this was one way 'to justify Gods most respected' for everyone 'that fears the Lord, and honours the King will be so justified'.[85] While Barton here trod familiar ground with his objections to worldly cosmopolitans, the appraisal of their duty to authority, especially political authority, is new.

Another observer of the uproar caused by the Civil War, and a victim of its whims and wiles, was Samuel Crooke. Crooke was an Anglican vicar of Wrington in Somerset, who baptized the English philosopher John Locke (1632–1704).[86] In 1642, in the wake of the first Civil War, Parliament invited Crooke to join a committee aimed at reform of the Anglican Church. Although he never took up this position, in 1643 he was pressured by Royalists to recant his Parliamentarian commitment. Crooke finally acquiesced to royalist demands, which led to him being accused of hypocrisy in open print. Such accusations must have stung all the more if, as several historians speculate, this recantation was a dissimulation occasioned only by political pressures.[87] Finally, in 1648, Crooke re-joined the reforming party, as part of an effort to introduce Puritan doctrines throughout the Three Kingdoms.

External political pressures rankled Crooke, and his concerns about the interference of worldly politics in religious life duly became the subject of his *TA ΔΙΑΦΕRONTA* (Excellent Things, 1658), an incendiary work published almost a decade after his death.[88] Its seventh chapter concerned 'The politique Hypocrite, or Hypocrite of State', which Crooke defined as 'he whose piety is policy'. Drawing on his own experiences, Crooke argued that just as man's piety is changeable, so too are the interests of state. Therefore a precondition of religious freedom was separation of the doctrines of the Christian church from political influence.⁸⁹ This was a dangerous opinion to state during Oliver Cromwell's (1599–1658) protectorate, where Protestant interest – understood as the mutual support of Protestant states against common enemies – partly defined foreign policy.⁹⁰ Crooke vehemently condemned those figures who used religion 'either as a means of correspondence with neighbour Princes and States; or as a course to reconcile to bring under his Subjects, or as a support to his own State and greatnesse ... Such are least to be trusted in matter of Religion, and little more in matter of State, seeing they dissemble the one, to deceive in the other'.⁹¹ According to Crooke, such figures contrasted with the 'heavenly minded Statist' who supports a reason of state aimed at the propagation of the kingdom of heaven. Invoking Philippians 3:20, he argued that such a Christian Statist

> hath his habitation on earth for a while, and is therefore willing to serve the State wherein he is placed, in any warrantable way of justice and truth, but even then he hath his *conversation in heaven, τὸ πολίτευμα ἐν οὐρανοῖς*; and though it be well with him in this world, and this world be the better for him, yet he is not a man of this world; not *cosmopolites* a Citizen of the world, but, *uranopolites*, a Denizon of heaven.⁹²

As Crooke went on to summarize: 'while the common Statist makes use of Religion as a spade to dig deep, and root himself further in the earth; the true Christian useth it ... to fill him more fully with all the fulnesse of God'.⁹³ As such, whether he was known as Cosmoxenus or Uranopolitanus, it was the duty of the true Christian to keep his mind focussed on his heavenly citizenship, and by means of his devotion to this ideal, to bend to his will the reason of state, if the poleis of heaven and of earth were to merge.

Conclusions

The inversion of the cosmopolitan discourse by Christian authors during the seventeenth century points to the inherent volatility of the cosmopolitan vocabulary. As we have seen, this inversion was hastened by both scripture and external circumstances. Andreae coined *cosmoxenus* and *cosmopolemus* while articulating projects for individual and collective religious reform in the Holy Roman Empire. This can be contrasted with the largely positive usages of the cosmopolitan vocabulary by the Rosicrucian respondent Joachim Morsius, or the anonymous author of *Les Réveille-matin François*. They, like Guillaume Postel and John Dee before them, used cosmopolitan epithets as self-designations to indicate prophetic rectitude in a similar quest for reform.

The inversion of the cosmopolitan vocabulary by Andreae, Crooke and their ilk sought to establish difference rather than promote concord. These differences could be doctrinal – as in the case of Valentin Grießmann or John Vicars – or based on ethical approbation, as in the Puritan polemics of the first half of the seventeenth century. The inversion of the associations of the cosmopolitan vocabulary by reform-oriented Protestants in England and Germany had widespread implications for the cosmopolitan concept itself. By the end of the seventeenth century Christians throughout Europe only occasionally used the cosmopolitan vocabulary to designate concepts like heavenly citizenship. This might profitably be understood as an outcome of the inversion of associations of the normative vocabulary theorized by Skinner. Namely, after the negative connotations of the cosmopolitan terminology had been publicized, 'a whole society may eventually come to alter its attitude towards some fundamental value or practice and alter its normative vocabulary accordingly'.[94] The few known late-century Christian statements on the subject document this alteration. In 1669 the Bohemian statesman Sigismund von Birken (1626–1681) impugned Seneca's maxim that 'the whole world is my fatherland' by stating that 'had the heathens been enlightened by the true godly and messianic doctrine of Christ, they would have instead ... written: We are citizens of heaven (*Himmelsbürger*), and our fatherland is heaven'.[95] Scarcely two decades later, the preacher William Bates (1625–1699) attacked Diogenes's claim to have been a citizen of the world, writing that 'scripture corrects the Language, and teaches us that we are Citizens of Heaven'.[96] By around 1700 many European Christians had seen fit to eschew the cosmopolitan vocabulary and return to the language of scripture to designate their heavenly citizenship. This left the cosmopolitan terminology as the largely exclusive preserve of humanists, Neostoics and natural philosophers. But as we shall see, despite working in largely secular contexts, their visions of world community were often informed by the sacred associations of centuries past.

5

Sharing Diogenes's tub

Believe me, if my rank and station were not what they are, I should enjoy nothing so much as a solitary life, or to have joined Diogenes in his tub.

Michael Sendivogius

In 1656 the London lexicographer Thomas Blount (1618–1679) issued a dictionary documenting 'the hard words of whatsoever language, now used in our refined English tongue'.[1] One of these 'hard words' was 'cosmopolite', and Blount's *Glossographia* became the first vernacular dictionary in any European language to include it.[2] He defined it as: '*Cosmopolite* (from *Cosmos* and *Polites* l[atin] *Cives*) a Citizen of the world; or Cosmopolitan'.[3] Perhaps the most notable thing about this definition is its inscrutability. It provides no interpretation, but merely synonyms. Nevertheless, as we have seen over prior chapters, there was no single way to understand cosmopolitan vocabulary. It was deployed in registers sacred and secular, as an expression of inclusion and of exclusion. A remarkable example of this instability is provided by Francis Bacon. In a 1621 historical work, Bacon castigated a pretender to the English throne as 'a runagate [*sc*. renegade] and citizen of the world'.[4] But, just a few years later, he praised the cosmopolite as a man who is 'gracious and courteous to strangers, [for] it shews he is a citizen of the world, and that his heart is no island cut off from other lands, but a continent that joins to them'.[5] Bacon's indecision is emblematic of tensions that have always been inherent in the cosmopolitan ideal. The present chapter examines meanings attached to the cosmopolitan vocabulary in nominally secular contexts. Yet, as we shall see, these contexts were often informed by sacred traditions or assumptions, even during that time when clerical authors were distancing themselves from the vocabulary.

This chapter follows cultural, intellectual and philosophical moments that historians have often pinpointed as crucial to the emergence of modernity; the rise of a transnational republic of letters, the desacralization of natural law, and the rise of science. The cosmopolitan vocabulary was not a prompt to change in any of these particular fields, but it did bear witness to them. By listening in on these moments, we witness how cosmopolitan terminology became firmly embedded in European consciousness over the sixteenth and seventeenth centuries, even as it was never able to shed entirely its sacred connotations.

The problem of the everyman

What, if anything, did a cosmopolitan owe to the world? We might expect authors influenced by the Cynic tradition to reject their obligations to fellow man and understand the designation as a passive identity. On the other hand, those influenced by the Stoics might have been likely to see themselves entangled in a range of active obligations to patria, society and family. Yet in early modernity, cosmopolitan expressions were often located in a dynamic space between identity and obligation. An example is provided by the Italian humanist Stefano Guazzo (1530–1593), who in a 1560 letter claimed to be a Cynical 'cittadino del Mondo' while outlining his travel plans; 'Now I am in Mantua, I do not know if we shall come to Casale, and I do not want to know, because I do not belong (*non piego*) to one place more than another, and like Diogenes I am very much a citizen of the world.'[6] While the reference to Diogenes signals Guazzo's putative indifference to his future plans and self-sovereignty, his expression of them in a letter to a friend is simultaneously a manifestation of his recognition of his social obligations.

Nevertheless, a reasonable division to make among the statements of early modernity is that between passive and active conceptions of the cosmopolitan, both of which could be informed by Cynic and Stoic sentiments. The most prominent example of the passive understanding of the cosmopolitan vocabulary is as a designation for the 'everyman'. In 1568 the Polish statesman Grimaldus, whom we have already met in Chapter 2, expressed that: 'Among all creatures contayned within the circle of the earth, that which we call man, is the chiefest and of most reputation. For he alone, of all other living things of what nature so ever, is made not onely an inhabitant and Citizen of the world, but also a Lorde and Prince therein.'[7] A different, though equally egalitarian understanding of the cosmopolitan appears in the *Deux dialogues* (1578) of Henri Estienne (1528/31–1598). This work aimed to defend the French language from its pervasive 'Italianization' by Florentine courtiers of Queen Catherine of Medici (1519–1589). In one passage, Estienne declared that anyone using 'courtly jargon' on the streets of Paris was 'in danger of being laughed at by the cosmopolitans (*cosmopolitains*), who neither live nor speak like courtiers, and yet know how to live and how to talk'.[8] Similarly, in 1677 the English poet Simon Ford (*c*. 1619–1699) wrote that, whatever hardships one faced, one could take solace from their basic humanity: 'When stripp'd of all, whilst living; whilst a man; Th' art still a Cosmopolitan!'[9] While all of these expressions suggest that all men could be cosmopolitans, they indicate that not all men were treated equal. The cosmopolitan, in other words, was enmeshed in class and social status, and treated accordingly.

Naturally not everyone wished to be associated with a vulgar *cosmopolitain* everyman. The Reformed controversialist Jérôme Bolsec (d. 1585) counselled that the identity of the Cosmopolite was not one vested in mere passive identity, but in action.[10] Others described the cosmopolitan as one who exercised cardinal virtues, such as wisdom (*prudentia*), or who displayed desirable attributes, such as honesty. The English poet John Lyly (1553–1606) included in his *The Anatomy of Wit* (1578) a letter by the character Euphues to Botonio, who had suffered a sentence of banishment for an unspecified crime. Consoling his correspondent, Euphues remarked that Socrates considered himself a 'Citizen of the World', a sentiment which he then compared to Plato: '*Plato* would never accompt him banished that had the Sunne, Fire, Aire, Water, & Earth, that he had before, where he felt the Winters blast and the Summers blaze, wher[e] the same Sunne & the same Moone shined, whereby he noted that every place was a countrey to a wise man, and all partes a pallaice to a quiet minde.'[11] For Lyly, the virtuous wise man thus deserved praise above all others. The French legal scholar and sceptic, Pierre Charron (1541–1603), espoused a similar position in his essay *De la sagesse* (1601), where he wrote that '[a]n honest man is a citizen of the world, free, cheerfull, and content in all places, alwaies within himselfe, in his owne quarter, and ever one and the same, though his case or scabberd be removed and caried hither and thither'.[12]

Unsurprisingly, the cosmopolitan vocabulary soon appeared in literature on the *honnête homme*, a genre of aspirational writing that promoted ethical, moral and courtly conduct as a fillip to its readers' prospects.[13] In a German translation of one such manual by Nicolas Faret (c. 1596–1646), the *honnête homme* was described as 'the virtue-loving man of the world' (*der ehrliebende Welt-Mann*).[14] In a 1680 example of the genre from England, William de Britaine praised 'the cosmopolite' as one possessing an ethical 'Aversion to any thing that is unkind, that I look upon an Injury done to another, as done to myself'.[15] Within this literature, it was the active exercise of the virtues which separated the cosmopolitan from his vulgar counterparts. As the libertine Cyrano de Bergerac (1619–1655) summarized in a letter that sought to defend Cardinal de Richelieu (1585–1642) of being a foreigner, and thus no true servant to the French crown: 'To that I answer . . . that an honest man is neither a French man, a Dutch man, nor a Spaniard; he is a Cosmopolite, a Citizen of the world, and his Country is every where: but I grant that the Cardinall is a stranger; are we not the more obliged to him that he will leave his domestick Gods, to defend ours?'[16] De Bergerac praised, in other words, Richelieu's patriotism and honesty as a marker of his cosmopolitan status. Nevertheless, from this discussion it is clear that early modern thinkers could not agree on one of the most fundamental aspects of the cosmopolitan identity. Was everyone a cosmopolitan? Or only a privileged elite?

Such questions also occupied the literary *salons* of early modern France.[17] The cosmopolitan vocabulary also appeared there as for example in a 1634 *salon* arranged by Théophraste Renaudot (1586–1653) in Paris.[18] Weighing into the *querelle des femmes*, one attendee dared to extend the cosmopolitan identity to women;

> For as they are mistaken who impute some Vice or Virtue to . . . Man or Woman, who are Citizens of the whole world; either of whom taken in general hath nothing in themselves but what is very decorous, Good and perfect, and consequently very noble . . . If there be any defect, it proceeds from the individual person, and ought no more to be attributed to the Sex then to the Species.[19]

Welcome as this view may be, it hardly helped resolve the fundamental problem; for the debates about whether a cosmopolitan was an elite member of society, or if everyone was a cosmopolitan, were conducted only among the wealthiest and most learned of contemporaries.

Useful knowledge in the republic of letters

One of the most remarkable cultural and intellectual changes of the sixteenth and early seventeenth centuries was the gradual transformation of curiosity from a vice to virtue.[20] As Peter Harrison has argued, this change is 'part of a larger story in which moral sensibilities delimit the sphere of legitimate knowledge'.[21] Part and parcel of this change in perception of legitimate knowledge – which tended to revolve around categories of utility, political, economic and otherwise – was a change in perception of scholars themselves. Early in the sixteenth century, the scholar, hidden away in a cloister or a university, could be regarded with some degree of suspicion. The German polymath Heinrich Cornelius Agrippa's *On the Vanity of Arts and Sciences* (1530) portrayed all knowledge unsupported by divine insight as insufficient, while in German-speaking lands, the proverb 'the learned are perverted' (*die Gelehrten die Verkehrten*) flourished.[22] Be that as it may, by the late sixteenth century, scholars were gradually rehabilitating their reputations, both by elaborating programmes of long-term research that could be undertaken as a collective endeavour, as well as by linking the fruits of their scholarship to the reason of state. As Vera Keller has shown, the enmeshment of bodies politic and epistemic prompted nascent notions of progress that simultaneously carved out a distinctive place for knowledge makers within a variety of different spheres.[23] The cosmopolitan vocabulary was employed in several of these endeavours.

One expression of these convictions, which coalesced in the course of the sixteenth century, was the 'republic of letters'. This imagined epistolary community linked moral character with the production of useful information in a globe-spanning network of scholarly exchange and endeavour.[24] The conceptual groundwork was laid by figures like Marsilio Ficino (1433–1499), who contributed to the revival of the Ciceronian concept of *humanitas*, and was given further voice by Pietro Pomponazzi (1462–1525), who conceived of the existence of 'an autonomous elite of philosophers dedicated to the solidarity of mankind'.²⁵ Ernst Cassirer has claimed that the universal animating principle of these Renaissance visions was Greek and Roman Stoicism, which made the humanistic vision otherwise unthinkable.²⁶ But the enduring rationale of such a virtual republic of learning was articulated by the Belgian humanist Justus Lipsius (1547–1606). Lipsius is known foremost as a Neostoic, a philosophical school that united ancient Stoicism with Christian ideals to help mankind conquer the Passions and devote themselves more fully to God.²⁷ Lipsius's influential *Politica* linked this philosophy to *ratio status*, establishing a nexus between learned production of 'useful knowledge' and the interests of the early modern state.²⁸

One of Lipsius's most influential works, *Epistola de Peregrinatione Italica* (1578), explicitly drew on Stoic cosmopolitan conceptions.²⁹ Writing in praise of the *peregrinatio academica*, Lipsius described the existence of a learned and morally superior 'nobility', united by their common pursuit of learning and their abhorrence of the Passions.³⁰ The interests of this elite were universal because they coincided with the interests of humanity at large. As such their endeavours assumed a moral valence as a supporting pillar of contemporary order. According to Lipsius, the supernal quest of this elite to manifest the virtues contrasted with the foibles of the everyman, which reflected national temperaments and vices. It was only through the pursuit of study among different nations and peoples that such virtues could be instilled. Lipsius described this cohort of the learned elite further in his *Physiologia stoicorum* (1604), describing them as a group that promoted the virtue of fortitude as they mediated between God and the world.³¹ The debt to Epictetus and other Stoics in Lipsius's thought is clear, even if he grounded his expectations in a thoroughly Christian framework.

Lipsius's works were publicized in England by, among others, Sir John Stradling (1593–1637). In 1599 he issued an adaptation of Lipsius's *Epistola* which laid out the core Neostoic concepts of Lipsian thought, and connecting them with the cosmopolitan vocabulary. In his preface, Stradling wrote that all great figures in history – from Jesus through to the 'profane philosophers' – believed it 'a great straine and dishonour to the libertie which nature hath given them (to be *Cosmopolites*, that is Cytizens of the whole world) and yet to bee restrained within the narrowe precincts of a little countrie'. As such, it was the duty of the great and good of the present to set off on their own peregrinations, 'to profite and inrich themselves with experience, and true wisdome'. In true Lipsian fashion, however, such journeys were not merely to be undertaken for personal benefit, but also for that of his 'owne proper and naturall countri[e]'.[32] The Neostoic or Lipsian cosmopolitan thus gathered useful knowledge from throughout the world not merely for his own edification, but also that of his state.

Naturally, thinkers outside the Lipsian School also linked academic peregrination to an elite cosmopolitan identity, even if they remained unconvinced of the need for the political utility of what was learned. One of these was the sceptical French philosopher Michel de Montaigne (1533–1592), who wrote against the backdrop of the bloody wars of religion in France.[33] In his landmark essay 'On the Education of Children', Montaigne lauded the philosophers of antiquity for their desire to learn more about the world, for there 'is a marvelous cleerenesse, or as I may terme it an enlightning of man's judgement drawn from the commerce of men, and by frequenting abroad in the world'. Montaigne believed that Socrates embraced 'all the world for his native Citie, and extended his acquaintance, his societie, and affections to all man-kind: and not as we do, that looke no further than our feet'.[34] Socrates's 'citizen of the world' was especially praiseworthy, and a model for the literate European elite of Montaigne's own time, for such a position transcended 'these intestine and civill broiles of ours'.[35] In other words, the cosmopolitan elite were a cadre of figures – wealthy and privileged enough to undertake academic travel – whose very existence contributed to the good of mankind.

Not all of Montaigne's readers were satisfied with this position. An example is provided by *Comédie du Cosmopolite* (1605), a farce composed by the Swiss playwright Pierre de l'Eussa (fl. 1588–1604). The protagonist, named Cosmopolite, had spent his life travelling the world and learning at the feet of the great and the good. But instead of finding satisfaction with the globe and its people, his encounters prompted only disgust. He judged Native Americans to be 'slaves of the devil', the Turks were little more than gluttonous 'swine' and the Tatars were blood-drinking savages.[36] The only place Cosmopolite truly felt at home was in his Swiss patria, where a 'divine harmony' reigned. Although it lampoons patriotism, the play also questions Montaigne's notion that a Cosmopolite's encounters with other cultures would foster a transcendent benevolence; indeed, in this case, encounters with other cultures only deepened difference. For the playwright, a learned and moral Cosmopolite was better off judging what he found before him according to the precepts of divine wisdom, rather than seeking new revelations abroad. De l'Eussa's amusing critique suggests that the locations for honing such judgments could conceivably be anywhere. The humanist sceptic Gabriel Naudé seems to have agreed. In his *Advis pour dresser une bibliothèque* (1627), he wrote that one 'might with reason name himself *Cosmopolitan*, or Habitant of the *Universe*' on account of owning a well-stocked library, through which 'he might know all, see all, and be ignorant of nothing'.[37] While this position mitigated the importance of travel central to Montaigne's idea of the cosmopolitan, Naudé's position that the knowledge won through reading comprised 'fruitful entertainment, and most agreeable divertissement' chimed entirely with the sceptical position.

This position was reinforced in the works of François de La Mothe Le Vayer (1588–1672), sometime tutor to Louis XIV (1638–1715) and member of the French Academy.[38] While La Mothe Le Vayer was politically active, his epistemic and civil scepticism led him to reject the idea that knowledge must be 'socially useful'.[39] This position was articulated with reference to the cosmopolitan vocabulary in his dialogue 'On private life'.[40] Here La Mothe Le Vayer declared that '*Cosmopolites*, or Citizens of the World' did not belong to 'the bodies of particular *Estates*' but were instead inhabitants of the 'City of the Universe'.[41] Employing the imagery of the world theatre, the 'Kings, Princes, and great Monarchs are so many Actors', who 'seem onely to play for the content and satisfaction' of philosophers and cosmopolites.[42] Following Pythagoras, La Mothe Le Vayer declared that a philosopher must devote himself to informing humanity 'of the marvellous things of the *Almighty*, and of *Nature*, being the witnesses, interpreters, and admirers of them'.[43] The sentiment is close to Montaigne's. But like the Neostoic position, it is also clear that La Mothe Le Vayer's understanding of the cosmopolitan united concerns both sacred and secular. Nevertheless, his formulation that 'the Philosophers we are talking about are called Cosmopolites' (*les Philosophes dont nous parlons sont appelez Cosmopolites*) would become of crucial importance to the eighteenth-century *Philosophes*.[44]

While the sceptical movement flourished in France, Neostoicism maintained a firm presence in the cosmopolitan literature of the seventeenth century, particularly after the conclusion of the Thirty Years' War in 1648 and the British Civil Wars in 1649. The admixture of Christian and secular elements remained prominent. In his drama *A German Diet* (1653), the Anglo-Welsh historian James Howell (1594–1666) had Duke Friedrich of Württemberg (1557–1608) – the ruler mercilessly lampooned in Shakespeare's *The Merry Wives of Windsor* – declare that it was the duty of the cosmopolitan 'to convert every good thing they see into wholesome juice and blood, and for the future benefit of their own Country'.[45] This was particularly the case if the reason of state – understood by Howell as the pursuit of a common Christian interest by all nations – resulted in a political and philosophical 'Ballance'.[46] A slightly different emphasis was made in the next year by the lexicographer Thomas Blount, with whom we opened this chapter. He appropriated sceptical and Neostoic thought to argue that 'Terrestriall Cosmopolites' could create an enduring peace among polities by recognizing their obligations within natural law established by the heavenly 'upper sphere'.[47] If these tenets were followed, earth would be no longer governed by Passions, but ruled by a union of 'constant souls' impervious to all disorder, a world where 'tranquility eternally triumphes'.[48] There is a touch here of both Lipsius's constant cosmopolitan, and the transcendent philosopher of Montaigne and La Mothe Le Vayer.

This survey makes clear that there were considerable differences in the conception of cosmopolitan identity and obligation, even among those Europeans who valued learning as its marker. Informed by a ground-stock of motifs from classical and Christian antiquity, some associated the vocabulary with a broad-ranging philosophical identity that reached beyond any particular national boundary, while others saw the cosmopolitan rooted firmly in specific polities. Important to all, however, was the idea that scholars and philosophers could and should band together. The borders of these virtual 'republics of letters' were defined not by political boundaries, but by the virtues of wisdom, curiosity, and moral and ethical discrimination. The virtual community of the learned moral elite, as leaders and arbiters of humanity's development, played key roles in the maintenance of a divine order, and divine law.

From divine law to natural law

One of the key elements of antique discourse on the cosmopolitan was its relationship to an abstract universal law. A foundational doctrine of the Greek

Stoic tradition – initially developed by Zeno of Citium (d. 264 BCE), expanded by Cleanthes of Assos (331–232 BCE), and epitomized in the works of Chrysippus of Soli (279–206 BCE) – was that an individual should live in concord with the moral law of nature.[49] This could be variously conceived of as a natural law, a moral law, or indeed a divine law, which established basic principles by which an individual should conduct their life, with their obligations balanced against those of their fellow community members.[50] Cicero discussed this law in his *De legibus*, while Plutarch saw the citizen of the world as one 'driven forth by divine decrees and laws' from his heavenly abode.[51] Arius Didymus, on the other hand, emphasized that the citizens of the world were linked by reason, 'which is the natural law'.

For communities bound by religious obligations, the idea was slightly different. An example is the Hebrews. There, Philo of Alexandria linked natural law with the *Logos* and to the lawgiver Moses, and thereby understood the Hebrews as inheritors and arbiters of divine law. For Philo, contravention of this law could mean the loss of the cosmopolitan status: a matter best demonstrated by the sad fate of the first cosmopolitan, Adam, who was expelled from paradise on account of his rebellion. For Philo, the status of the Hebrews as the Chosen people was assured by the covenant (cf. Exodus 34:28). As Anthony D. Smith has recently shown in detail, this devolution was later appropriated by numerous peoples – both by religions as well as nations – all of whom claimed guardianship of divine authority and, subsequently, claims to the mediation of divine law.[52] As such, mythologies of chosenness bound religious with moral concerns, and could be used to justify abuses of putatively universal law. The wars of religion in the sixteenth and seventeenth centuries – Montaigne's 'intestine and civill broiles' – were arguably an inevitable result of such appropriations, where the warring factions all remained convinced of their divine sponsorship.[53]

In the sixteenth and seventeenth centuries, discourse on the devolution of divine law to specific peoples or polities sometimes appeared in conjunction with the cosmopolitan vocabulary. As we have seen in Chapter 2, both Guillaume Postel and John Dee used it when propping up their imperial fantasies. However, it also appeared elsewhere, even in juridical works. In his verse-form *Juris Prudentia* (1554), the French humanist Barthélemy Aneau praised the 'wise cosmopolitans' (*sapientes cosmopolitæ*) who maintained divine law throughout the ancient world.[54] Aneau's major concern was to trace the devolution of divine law initially invested in Adam and Moses – which he claimed was also maintained by ancient legislators among the Hebrews, the Gymnosophists of India, the Magi of Persia and others – until it ultimately came to contemporary Europe via Christian statesmanship. Reminiscent of Postel's patriotism, Aneau argued that the noble art of divine jurisprudence was, however, maintained only among the French.[55] Reflecting as it did the moral and 'legal' basis for French sovereignty, Aneau's work contributed towards strengthening the nexus between divine right and earthly power, even if in a primarily rhetorical mode.

Comparable ideas appear in the works of the Anglican divine Richard Hooker (*c.* 1554–1600), especially his *Of the Lawes of Ecclesiastical Polity* (1594).[56] For Hooker, civil society is composed of individuals whose chief desire is, like Socrates, 'to have a kind of society and fellowship even with all mankind'. This fellowship 'appeareth by the wonderful delight men have, some to visit foreign countries, some to discover nations not heard of in former ages, we all to know the affairs and dealings of other people, yea to be in league or amity with them'. Recalling Plutarch, and the words of the Polish statesman Grimaldus, Hooker wrote that this desire existed because 'nature doth presume that how many men there are in the world, so many gods as it were there are, or at leastwise such they should be towards men'. This was why ecclesiastical bodies had to regulate the 'Laws of Nations', Hooker argued, for, without them, worldly authorities were apt to lose sight of divine influence.[57]

Some juridical discourses used the cosmopolitan vocabulary to gird readings of divine law that posited a nexus between subject and *patria*. An example is provided by the English jurist Charles Gibbon (fl. 1589–1604), who in 1604 contrasted the differing cosmopolitan identities of Diogenes and Paul to theorize an individual's duty to a *patria*:

> One demanding of Diogenes what countrie man he was, said, he was *Civis mundi*, a citizen of the world: Paul said he was no citizen but a sojourner in the world; yet commonly we account that our Countrie where we have our birth, bringing up, and abode, and therefore it is called our Nation *à natu*, because it is as it were *natale solum*, our native countrie: but more properly it is called our countrie *à patriae*, which is derived of *pater*, to signifie that in both kinds our Countrie is the father and the mother of us all. And this should make us regard our native countrie, as our naturall parents.[58]

Gibbon's position on duty – again a mélange of sacred and secular conceptions – was somewhat typical of juridical opinion at this time. But the relationship between subject and *patria* was reformulated after the Thirty Years' War (1618–1648), a disastrous conflagration which prompted European jurists to conceptualize new approaches to governance and the obligations of citizens.[59] As Ian Hunter and Robert von Friedeburg have argued, a crucial part of this reconceptualization involved the establishment of a rational theory of law as a touchstone for relations between polities.[60] From 1648 the jargon of natural law began to trump that of divine law in the affairs of state.[61] This new *ius publicum universale* rejected competing narratives of the devolution of divine law – in the past a fillip, or even spur, for religious conflict – and established in its place the universal sovereignty of all states.[62]

Hand in hand with this reconceptualization was a perceived need for jurists to rethink the rights and obligations of the individual in relation to these states, a move that would eventually dissolve the ruler–subject dichotomy largely derived from the notion of *patria*. Crucial to this initiative was the German jurist Samuel von Pufendorf (1632–1694), who in 1661 was appointed to the chair of natural law (*ius gentilem*) at the University of Heidelberg, the first professorial chair of its kind in Europe. In 1663 Pufendorf supervised an important dissertation by Andreas von Ulcken (1645–1688), *De obligatione adversus patriam* (Concerning obligations against the patria). Here, the scholars dissolved the idea of a *patria* that commanded obedience on account of being a 'father' to the individual – compare the abeyance demanded by Gibbon's 'native countrie' – and asserted in its stead a *patria iuris*. Under this scheme, citizens (*cives*) owed obligations to a state (*civitas*) under a fixed regime of laws.[63] Thus an individual would be subject to the laws of his own state when at home, and to a foreign state when abroad. The establishment of such a principle would result, Pufendorf believed, in the creation of a society of citizens without vested or irrational interests, and allow the free movement of persons and capital. Pufendorf and Ulcken saw a utility in the classical Stoic idea of the wise man 'who considers himself a citizen of the world' as a concept informing *patria iuris*.

The attractiveness of the natural law positions was undeniable in light of the extravagant bloodshed of the first half of the century, even to thinkers working in largely sacred contexts. Indeed, reconsiderations of divine law were often prompted by juridical advances in natural law. An unusual example of this is

Conjectura cabalistica (1654), an abstruse work of occult science authored by the Cambridge philosopher Henry More (1614–1687). This book subverted narratives of the devolution of divine law to any one nation by arguing that Jesus of Nazareth had established a *lex aeterna* for the benefit of humanity in general, akin to the new natural law. 'It is a truth and life that is the safety of all Nations,' wrote More, 'and the earnest expectation of the ends of the Earth; *Christ the same yesterday, to day, and for ever*, whose dominion and Law neither time nor place doth exclude.'[64] More was no statesman, let alone a jurist, and his chief task in *Conjectura* was to demonstrate the unbroken existence of a *prisca theologia*, or ancient theology, passed on through various rites and traditions in different religions, but which found its perfection in reformed Christianity. Nevertheless, his conclusions were similar to those of his juridical contemporaries. Natural (or divine) law provided a constant for all peoples, and its appropriation by a specific nation – such as the Hebrews – would only lead to abuses and injustices.

Although the cosmopolitan vocabulary featured in tracts concerning the transformation of natural law and divine law in the early modern period, this vocabulary was not a driving force in the formulation or expression of these changes. Nevertheless, the vocabulary was a witness to the crucial emergence of a secular register of legal regulation of state and individual obligations. What emerges from the evolution of natural law ideas, however, is the impression, once more, that their expression would be impossible without an engagement with the sacred ideas of the past.

Science, secret wisdom and universal panaceas

In his monumental *The Legitimacy of the Modern Age*, the German philosopher Hans Blumenberg (1920–1996) pointed to the 'scientific revolution' of the seventeenth century as one of the turning points in the creation of the secular modern age, encouraging mankind to adopt responsibility for its own future.[65] While the accuracy and applicability of the term 'scientific revolution' remains hotly contested, scholars of cosmopolitanism have recently also viewed early-modern natural philosophy as a key location for the birth of new mores of international cooperation and communication.[66] At first glance, this seems justified. For example, the 1686 publication of Anthonius Everaerts's *Historia naturalis* under the pseudonym 'Cosmopolita', provides a reassuring linkage of the cosmopolitan vocabulary to the method and magisterium of scientific enquiry, where knowledge is produced for the benefit of all mankind.[67]

However, if we take a closer look at the cosmopolitan vocabulary as it was used by early-modern natural philosophers, a different story emerges. This is not a story where cosmopolitan ideas anchor the enterprise of a secular natural philosophy. Indeed, perhaps against expectations, we witness the cosmopolitan vocabulary being used in contexts sacred and secular, within cultures not of scientific certainties, but of 'doubt, desire, and probabilism'.[68] In other words, when early modern natural philosophers used the cosmopolitan vocabulary, they often did so to designate ideas very different from the 'cosmopolitanism' associated by scholars with early modern science.

One area of natural philosophical endeavour in which the cosmopolitan vocabulary appeared was medicine. Medicine, after all, was a pursuit dedicated to the health of the public as well as the individual. Thus in the 1620s the Frankfurt physician Johann Peter Lotich (1598–1669) invoked the terminology in the Stoic sense of the cosmopolitan everyman when he wrote that his medicines could cure all 'mortals and cosmopolites'.[69] The Rosicrucian *Fama Fraternitatis* (1614), which we examined in the previous chapter, on the other hand, portrayed the fictional fraternity as physicians who would cross the globe to 'cure the ill and do so without charge' (*krancken zu curiren und diß alles umbsonst*), as part of an apocalyptic universal reformation that would ameliorate the world.[70]

One respondent to the Rosicrucian message with whom the medical aspect of their message resonated was the Holstein physician Michael Maier (1586–1622).[71] In the 1610s, Maier spent several years in England, where he met the pathetic Francis Anthony (1550–1623), a physician embroiled in controversy prompted by his creation of potable gold, a powerful emetic which, Anthony claimed, cured all infirmities. While several physicians rejected Anthony's claims, Maier was so convinced of the elixir's potency that he defended it in print in *Apologia veritatis illucescentis* (1616), which appeared under Anthony's name.[72] The prefatory epistle declared that:

> As no man is created solely for his owne particular, but for the profit and good of others; (for nature hath made, and charitie commanded a vicinitie

and neighbourhood betwixt all men) so this being materially a kinde of universall Medicine: it ought not to be restrained from the publike tender of profit to all men. Socrates being demanded what Countriman he was, answered, not only an Athenian but a Cosmopolitane, a Cittizen of that great Commonwealth, the whole world. So ought every good Physition in the publike profession of his facultie, not to burie his talent in the soyle of one Countrey, but to remember, that the very Character of his calling doth challenge the fruits of his function for all the world, so far as possible capacitie extendeth; specially of this neerest communitie in Christendome.[73]

Based largely on Matthew 5:15–16, the Stoic and Christian sentiments in this passage are readily apparent. They were echoed by others. In 1657 for example, James Howell – author of the Neostoic drama *A German Diet* (1653), which we discussed above – praised the Welsh politician Walter Rumsey's (1584–1660) advocacy for the healthful nature of coffee and tobacco; 'for he who findes out any thing conducing to humane health, is the best Cosmopolite, the best among the Citizens of the World; health being the most precious jewel of Nature, without which we cannot well discharge our duties to God or man'.[74] While the application of scholarly learning and knowledge was stridently debated within the wider Republic of Letters, the application of helpful medical knowledge was not.

Michael Maier's reputation endures to this day, though not because of his defence for the lethal 'cures' of an obscure English physician. Instead, it is assured through his alchemical works, among them *Atalanta Fugiens* (1617), a captivating multimedia portrayal of the quest for the philosophers' stone told in prose, poetry, engravings and music.[75] Although Pierre Bourdieu excluded alchemy from a place in the scientific revolution on account of its secretive nature, Margaret C. Jacob, among others, has identified alchemical practice as 'one of the keys to understanding the emergence of the cosmopolitan'.[76] Furthermore, as Pamela Smith has shown in her account of the mercantilist and alchemist Johann Joachim Becher (1635–1682), there can be little doubt that alchemical enterprise played roles in the emergence of international commerce and technological exchange in the late seventeenth century.[77] There is indeed a comparatively frequent occurrence of cosmopolitan vocabulary in alchemical books. But if we examine these sources carefully, we find that the senses in which the terminology appeared have little to do with secular and commercial contexts ascribed to them by modern scholars.

In the rhetoric of many alchemical writings, the success of laboratory processes were attributable to secret knowledge bestowed by God. Access to this knowledge was tinged by prophecy. This position was sometimes justified with reference to supposedly ancient texts attributed to the legendary father of the alchemical art, Hermes Trismegistus. While Hermes was widely believed to have predated Moses, Florian Ebeling has demonstrated that the Hermetic corpus, which was largely a pseudepigraphic product of late antiquity, was influenced by Platonism, Neoplatonism, Stoicism and Christianity.[78] In the pseudepigraphic *Tabula Smaragdina* (*c.* fifth-century CE), one of the most influential hermetic writings, reference is made to an adept working under 'mother earth' and 'father sun' to create a substance that mediates between 'heaven and earth'. We have already seen shades of hermetic influence in the works of Postel and Dee, both of whose imperial fantasies were based on claims to prophetic knowledge.

Perhaps the most prominent occurrence of the cosmopolitan vocabulary in alchemy is by Michael Sendivogius (Michał Sędziwój, 1566–1636).[79] In 1604 Sendivogius, a Polish alchemist, physician and sometime councillor to Emperor Rudolf II in Prague, issued his *De lapide Philosophorum tractatus duodecim* (Twelve Tracts on the Philosophers' Stone), one of the most influential alchemical works of early modernity. Printed anonymously, an unusual passage towards the conclusion of the book declared that:

> If you ask who I am: I am a Cosmopolitan [*cosmopolita sum*]. If you know me, and wish to be good and honorable men, keep my name a secret. If you do not know me, forbear to enquire after my name, for I shall make public nothing more than appears in this writing. Believe me, if my rank and station were not what they are, I should enjoy nothing so much as a solitary life, or to have joined Diogenes in his tub. For I behold this world full of vanity, greed, cruelty, venality, and iniquity; and I rejoice in the prospect of the glorious life to come [cf. Hebrews 11:14].[80]

This statement draws on Christian imagery and Greek Cynicism to emphasize secrecy as a core component of the cosmopolitan identity. Perhaps surprisingly, there is nary a hint of Stoic influence on Sendivogius's position.[81]

There can be little doubt that discourses of secrecy inherently belonged to the social place of alchemical practice, if not cosmopolitan ideas more generally.[82] There was good reason for this. Practitioners who claimed to be able to transmute base metals into gold were occasionally imprisoned by ruthless rulers, who sought to exploit alchemical 'trade secrets' for their own gain.[83] Just such a narrative became attached to Sendivogius in 1646, if not before, when Pierre de Noyers (1608–1693), a secretary to the Polish queen, gossiped that Sendivogius's works had been authored by 'Cosmopolita', an anonymous adept who was thought to be an Englishman, and whom Sendivogius had once ventured to have rescued from imprisonment in order to protect his secrets.[84] While this rumour may have been prompted simply by the publication of French and Dutch editions of Sendivogius's works under the pseudonym 'Cosmopolite' in 1620s, the figure of the prophetic alchemical cosmopolite would reappear throughout the seventeenth century.[85] In the spring of 1651, the Bermudan alchemist George Starkey (1628–1665) informed the English natural philosopher Robert Boyle (1627–1691) that he possessed a special elixir created by a certain 'adept'.[86] Shortly thereafter, he told another correspondent of 'a certain young friend' who possessed 'chrysopoetic and argyropoetic' elixirs, and began to circulate manuscripts putatively authored by him.[87] In a preface to George Ripley's *The Marrow of Alchemy* (1654–1655), Starkey finally identified the adept as 'Eirenaeus Philoponos Philalethes', who, although an Englishman, 'His present place in which he doth abide I know not, for the world he walks about, Of which he is a citizen.'[88] This claim was evidently an elaborate smoke-screen to protect Starkey himself from calumny, but it soon merged with grander claims. In Starkey's posthumous *Introitus Apertus* (1667), he claimed that his alchemical work heralded the coming of Elias Artista, recognized in the Paracelsian tradition as a natural-philosophical messiah who would 'prepare the royal way of the Lord' to the Heavenly Jerusalem.[89] Starkey would achieve this by creating a 'gift of God' (*donum dei*), a universal medicine that would cure all illnesses and eliminate the need for money, that 'filthy lucre' used by the Antichrist to corrupt the world. Starkey's mission, alas, was cut short by his death in 1665.

Apart from the common thread of secrecy, what is apparent in these chymical accounts is their relation of the cosmopolitan idea to fictions of identity, as well as to prophetic scenarios of an imminent reformation. It is therefore unsurprising to see the cosmopolitan identity appropriated by others claiming prophetic insight at the margins of natural philosophy. An example is Giordano Bruno (1548–1600), a defrocked Dominican friar who wandered

Europe in search of truths religious and natural philosophical.[90] While most historians reject the idea of Bruno as a martyr for science, recent archival spadework by Alberto Martinez has indicated that Bruno's cosmological convictions were 'the principal accusation leading to his execution'.[91] Bruno invoked the cosmopolitan vocabulary in two distinct ways. First, to portray himself as a figure privy to hidden truths and, second, to claim – like Postel before him – that he was a maligned *homo viator*. This appropriation of the vocabulary was to some extent justified by his wandering life. After spending time in Italy, France and Germany, in the 1580s Bruno found himself in England, where he promoted a worldview informed by Neoplatonism and pre-Socratic thought. Disappointed by his experiences at Oxford – where he was snubbed by the university's Aristotelians – in 1584 Bruno used the cosmopolitan vocabulary when condemning his frosty reception: 'I declare two things: first, that one must not kill a foreign doctor, because he attempts those cures that native doctors do not attempt, second, I say, that for the true philosopher every land is his country.'[92] Bruno's frustration is palpable here.

Bruno voiced similar frustrations in his allegorical *Expulsion of the Triumphant Beast* (1584). Since the beginning of time, this titular beast – who is identical with the Devil – had distorted man's sense of reason, impeding his ability to grasp truth. It is only by expelling the beast from this world that man will be able to grasp his destiny and place in the universe. Yet those prepared to challenge the status quo and confront the beast risked persecution and condemnation by the world at large:

> Come! Come! We see how this man, as a citizen and servant of the world (*cittadino e domestico del mondo*), a child of Father Sun and Mother Earth, because he loves the world too much, must be hated, censured, persecuted, and extinguished by it. But, in the meantime, may he not be idle or badly employed while awaiting his death, his transmigration, his change.[93]

Although Bruno's relationship with Christianity has been disputed, this statement is reminiscent of Philippians 3:20, which depicts *homo viator* journeying towards eternal repose in the heavenly Jerusalem. Yet Bruno's words are also tinctured by Postel, and his declaration that he is 'a child of

Father Sun and Mother Earth' chimes not only with ancient Stoics, but also with the *Tabula Smaragdina* of Hermes Trismegistus. A more eclectic cosmopolitan vision would be difficult to find.

Similar in some respects to Bruno is the case of the Bohemian chymist, Rosicrucian respondent and adventurer Andreas Haberweschel von Habernfeld (1587–c. 1659).[94] In 1640 Haberweschel felt compelled to attack René Descartes's mechanistic philosophy under the pseudonym 'Mercurius Cosmopolita', or the 'Hermes of the cosmopolis'.[95] In this work, Mercurius is portrayed as a son of nature and agent of divine authority. Where Descartes in his *Discourse on Method* impugned the utility of 'false sciences' like magic, alchemy and astrology, Haberweschel defended them as vouchers of God's favour.[96] Again, the cosmopolitan identity was here invoked in defence of decidedly Christian ideas and Hermetic ideas, arrayed in this instance not against ancient Aristotelianism, as in Bruno's case, but against the new sciences.

Nevertheless, even for representatives of these new sciences, presumptuousness concerning both the will of God and vanity of knowledge – natural philosophical or otherwise – had to be guarded against vigilantly. Bruno learnt this lesson at the stake in 1600. But it could also be taught in other ways. Thus in his *Occasional Reflections* (1665) the 'sceptical chymist' Robert Boyle – who himself pursued the philosophers' stone – declared:

> I take it to be as true of the Intellectual, as the Material World, that it profits not a Man if he gain the whole World, and lose his own Soul (Matthew 16:26). Whatsoever therefore Philosophers do tell us, of a wise Man, that he is nowhere banish'd, because he is a Citizen of the World; I must think a Christian everywhere in Exile, because he is a Citizen of the Heavenly Jerusalem, and but a Stranger and a Sojourner here.[97]

Although often inspired by the legacy of classical antiquity in the Cynic and Stoic schools, the cosmopolitan discourse of seventeenth-century natural philosophers remained bound to concerns sacred. If the reputation of natural philosophers for pushing forward modern cosmopolitan mores must be maintained, as asserted by recent scholarship, then we must acknowledge that sacred conceptions of world community played key roles in fostering the emergence of a secular modern science.

Conclusions

Europe changed a great deal over the course of the seventeenth century, and with it changed the possible associations of the cosmopolitan vocabulary. In the prior chapter we saw how some Christian authors retreated from the terminology over the course of the seventeenth century, a product of the inversion of positive connotations related to 'heavenly citizenship' with antithetical associations of 'worldliness'. In this chapter, we have witnessed the flourishing of the vocabulary in other contexts; humanistic, legal and natural philosophical. When viewed by scholars searching for the roots of nominally secular ideals of modern cosmopolitanism, the expressions examined in this chapter might initially seem to lay the bedrock of 'modern' secular cosmopolitan doctrine. But, as we have seen, there was rarely any consensus among users of the vocabulary about its precise meaning. Frequently cosmopolitan conceptions were tinged by ideas and associations sacred, even in works dedicated to nominally secular fields. In other words, the cosmopolitan ideal was far from homogenous during this period. It would not be until the beginning of the eighteenth century that a group of thinkers would deliberately attempt to shape the cosmopolitan vocabulary, and bend it to their will. This would occasion the emergence, for the first time in history, of a meta-discourse concerning the meaning and significance of the cosmopolitan vocabulary and the ideals it designated, and the emergence of a putative 'cosmopolitanism', for the first time in history. This is the subject of our next chapter.

6

Heavenly cities of the eighteenth-century philosophers

Modern philosophy wants to make us all cosmopolitans.

Jean-Marie-Bernard Clément

The eighteenth century witnessed a variety of stunning social and cultural changes which laid the foundations of secular modernity.[1] It saw the cessation of witchcraft prosecutions, the discovery of the definitive proofs of heliocentrism and the institutionalization of experimental natural philosophy. It benefitted from the genius of Isaac Newton (1643–1727), Gottfried Wilhelm Leibniz (1646–1716), Immanuel Kant (1724–1804) and the French *philosophes*, to say nothing of the postulation of the new idea of 'rights of man', and the invention of the steam engine. It has been described as an age of enlightenment, an age of reason and a time of disenchantment, and the rise of secularism. For some scholars, cosmopolitan expressions occupy a vaunted place in the conceptual and philosophical armoury of the period; a fuel for the secular engines of the age. Peter Gay, for example, saw the Enlightenment as unthinkable without cosmopolitanism.[2] For Kwame Anthony Appiah, the cosmopolitan idea 'underwrote some of the great moral achievements of the Enlightenment, including the 1789 "Declaration of the Rights of Man" and Immanuel Kant's work proposing a "league of nations"'.[3] To Jeremy Adler 'cosmopolitanism was the apex and indeed the glory of Enlightenment philosophy, encompassing liberty, equality, fraternity, and all our human rights'.[4] For Paul Hazard, the eighteenth century was nothing less than 'the age of cosmopolites and of cosmopolitanism'.[5] For these scholars, the cosmopolitanism of the Enlightenment revived 'ancient ideas about cosmopolites', forging them into an essentially homogenous secular ideal that played a crucial role in the birth of modernity.[6]

Recently, however, scholars have challenged both the nature of a secular 'age of reason', as well as the roles of that cosmopolitan ideals played in it. In several insightful contributions, David Sorkin has convincingly argued that the Enlightenment was, at is core, religious in nature.[7] This line of research has been advanced by Anton Matytsin, Dan Edelstein and Jeffrey Burson, who have documented some of the stranger mystical, sceptical and religious roots of eighteenth-century culture.[8] In the area of the cosmopolitan, the careful scholarly work of researchers like Andrea Albrecht, Luca Scuccimarra, Gerd van den Heuvel and Pauline Kleingeld have challenged the notion of a homogenous eighteenth-century cosmopolitanism, by documenting the diverse array of concepts designated by the cosmopolitan vocabulary in the eighteenth century.[9]

The present chapter builds on these two strands of scholarship, and examines the sacred and secular registers of the cosmopolitan vocabulary used in the eighteenth century. While, in this sense, the cosmopolitan discourse of the period echoed that of prior centuries, it also gave rise to something entirely new: 'cosmopolitanism' itself. For it was in this century that Europeans began to reflect consciously on historical usages of the cosmopolitan vocabulary, and began to sift and weigh them. If the early-modern usages that we have surveyed in this volume can be said to represent the primary discourse of the cosmopolitan, then these eighteenth-century reflections upon their meaning represent a cosmopolitan meta-discourse. This prompted the emergence of an abstract cosmopolita*nism*, or in other words, a conception of the cosmopolitan as 'a system of theory or practice' (*OED*). The emergence of this meta-discourse is documented in European lexical works, which defined the cosmopolitan vocabulary for readers by interpreting historical statements. It continued with the appropriation of terms like 'cosmopolite' by the French *philosophes*, who, inspired by the likes of Montaigne and La Mothe Le Vayer, sought to bend the vocabulary to their will and to define it as a near-synonym of 'philosopher'. By 1770, an anonymous work reflecting on the abstract obligations of the cosmopolitan was issued under the title *Le Cosmopolisme*.[10] Yet, as in prior centuries, the vocabulary and its meanings remained contested. On the eve of the French Revolution, the French author Jean-Marie-Bernard Clément complained that 'modern philosophy wants to make us all cosmopolitans'.[11] What emerges in the course of the eighteenth century is, perhaps against expectation, not the story of a decisive break with the sacred and secular cosmopolitan readings of the past, but rather their continuation. Even Immanuel Kant, that most vaunted of secular cosmopolitan thinkers, owed significant debts to sacred metaphysics in articulating his vision of world community.

The lexical tradition

If the eighteenth century witnessed the birth of cosmopolitanism, it got off to an inauspicious start. Around 1700 there appears to have been something of a lull in the usage, and perhaps the appeal, of cosmopolitan vocabulary throughout Europe. In his survey of the career of the terminology in France, the philologist Paul Hazard could locate barely a handful of references from this time.[12] In Germany, where the vocabulary had never been particularly prevalent, it appears to have been employed sparingly.[13] In England in 1699 it was used in a tract condemning Deism, and again in a medical work of 1700 equating health with heavenly citizenship.[14] In 1711, the essayist and politician Joseph Addison (1672–1719) invoked Diogenes – or Socrates – while promoting the idea of free commerce and providing a vivid account of walking the floor of London's Royal Exchange.[15]

This calm after the comparative storm of the seventeenth century may initially seem puzzling, particularly because, as Margaret C. Jacob has pointed out, it was at precisely this time that social and cultural circumstances made 'modern' cosmopolitan mores possible.[16] Nevertheless, there are historical explanations for this lull. In Britain the terminology was largely the preserve of Puritans anxious to distance themselves from the worldly evils of other confessions. But when their rights were guaranteed following the passing of the *Toleration Act* (1689), anti-cosmopolitan polemic receded. In France, the terminology had been employed largely by a generation of sceptical and libertine intellectuals, many of whom had died by the mid-seventeenth century. Elsewhere in Europe, the cosmopolitan vocabulary had never been widely used.

Nevertheless, the terminology was present; it slumbered on shelves, in homes, libraries and bookstores, in books written in Greek, Latin, Italian, French, Dutch, German, Spanish and English, waiting to be rediscovered and reinterpreted. At any moment, one of these works could be plucked from its dusty abode, setting a 'raw' cosmopolitan vocabulary before a variety of literate publics.[17] Every historical usage of the words offered new possibilities for readers to (re)interpret the vocabulary afresh, to reproduce old interpretations, or to develop new ones entirely. The initial job of interpreting these historical statements fell to those harbingers of Enlightenment intellectual culture, the many dictionaries and encyclopaedias that appeared in print in the early eighteenth century. These lexica are of crucial importance to the history of cosmopolitan discourse, for they occasioned directly the emergence of a meta-discourse on the subject of cosmopolitanism, and have coloured the views of later historians on the subject.

Today, readers assume – reasonably so – that a dictionary will reflect the common usage of a word in a given context. But this was not always the case. The dictionaries of Thomas Blount – whom we encountered in the previous chapter as the first European to include 'Cosmopolite' in a vernacular dictionary – have been praised for introducing 'a consciousness of language as a living, growing organism, changing from year to year'.[18] As such, Blount's works are consulted by historians tracing evolutions in the meaning of words for insights into historical cultures; an approach enshrined in dictionaries like the *Oxford English Dictionary* and the Grimms' *Deutsches Wörterbuch*. But early-modern dictionaries didn't always reflect the language as it was used. As an example we need look no further than Blount's *Glossographia*, which features the word 'Cosmodelyte', a term defined by Blount as denoting 'one fearful of the world, or a worldly wretch'.[19] This was neither a term used in everyday conversation in early modern England, nor one employed in abstruse academic discussion; it was a 'ghost word', a neologism deliberately inserted by Blount to trap plagiarists.[20] Posterity has failed to realize this, and even today Blount's 'Cosmodelyte' stubbornly reappears in English dictionaries and lexica.[21] There are two points to be made here. The first is that pre-modern dictionaries did not always reflect the language as it was spoken. The second is that these dictionaries were lexically promiscuous. Both of these factors impacted substantially on cosmopolitan discourse and meta-discourse in the eighteenth century, and have also informed scholarly conclusions about the nature of contemporary cosmopolitan ideas.

Despite the fact that French authors had used the words *cosmopolite* and *cosmopolitain* since the 1550s, neither appeared in a French dictionary before

1721. In that year, the second edition of the influential *Dictionnaire universel* was issued in Paris. It contained the following entry:

> COSMOPOLITAIN, AINE. singular, masculine and feminine. *Cosmopolita, Cosmopolitanus*. The word is sometimes used in jest, to designate a man who has no fixed abode, or a man who is nowhere a stranger. It derives from κόσμος, the world, and πόλις, city, and signifies a man for whom the world is his city or fatherland. An ancient philosopher, upon being asked from whence he came, responded: I am a *Cosmopolitain*. The unknown author of an excellent alchemical tract, titled *Lumen Chymicum*, gave himself the name *Cosmopolitain*. Some say *Cosmopolite*, but just as one says Neapolitan and Constantinopolitan, and not Neapolite and Constantinopolite, by analogy one should say *Cosmopolitain*.[22]

This entry is surprisingly substantial. It states that both men and women could be called *Cosmopolitain*, albeit sometimes in jest (*en badinant*). The reader is provided with a short notice concerning its derivation from Greek, which is held to indicate a man who considers the whole world his city or his fatherland. There is a brief reference to the well-known declarations of Diogenes or Socrates, and also to Michael Sendivogius's *Lumen Chymicum*, which, as we have seen, was published under a cosmopolitan pseudonym. Finally, the entry shows that its author was aware of the use of the alternative form *Cosmopolite* – possibly by Guillaume Postel, François de La Mothe Le Vayer, or others – although this variant is not preferred.

Here then is a substantial lexical engagement with the cosmopolitan vocabulary and the various concepts associated with it in early modernity; an evaluation of what is significant and what is not, and a step further towards the creation of a discursive space for a meta-discourse of cosmopolitanism. Indeed, the 1721 edition of the *Dictionnaire* is arguably the most influential eighteenth-century statement on the cosmopolitan, for in France and England it furnished the basis of similar entries for other lexica. The most prominent example of this international reception can be found in England. In 1728 the lexicographer Ephraim Chambers (1680–1740) adapted the *Dictionnaire* entry in his *Cyclopædia, or, An Universal Dictionary of Arts and Sciences* (1728), one of the most influential reference works of the Enlightenment. This entry read:

> COSMOPOLITAN, or COSMOPOLITE, a Term sometimes used to signify a Person who has no fix'd living, or Place of abode; or a Man who is a Stranger

nowhere ... One of the antient Philosophers being interrogated what Countryman he was; answer'd he was a *Cosmopolitan*, i.e., an Inhabitor or Citizen of the World.[23]

Chambers's adaptation simplified its source a great deal; it omitted a feminine form, dropped any reference to it being used in jest, and left out entirely its alchemical valence. But most importantly, Chambers's entry didn't document the cosmopolitan vocabulary as it was actually used in England. The case was similar in Germany, where, in the entry for 'Cosmopolitain' in a French–German dictionary of 1737, the linguist Johann Leonard Frisch (1666–1743) maintained the *Dictionnaire*'s reference to a jocular employment of the term, but omitted its alchemical history.[24] Like Chambers, Frisch failed to register historical German usages of the cosmopolitan vocabulary. A modern observer consulting the works of Frisch, Chambers and the *Dictionnaire universel* might therefore be forgiven for concluding that, in the period before 1730, an essentially homogenous conception of the cosmopolitan existed throughout France, Germany and England. As we have seen in prior chapters, this could not be further from the reality.

But more significant than the *Dictionnaire*'s international reception was that which it experienced in France itself. For, in the *Encyclopédie, ou dictionnaire raisonné des sciences* (1751) the entry was adapted by the art critic and journalist Denis Diderot (1713–1784), as the basis of his entry for 'Cosmopolitain'.[25] The *Encyclopédie* is widely recognized as a foundational text of the Enlightenment, and the most significant statement of the ethos of the *philosophes*. Robert Darnton has described it as the 'supreme work' of the period, while Daniel Rosenberg has suggested that its import is 'difficult to overestimate'.[26] Diderot's entry read:

> COSMOPOLITAN, or COSMOPOLITE, (Gram. and Philosoph.) This name is sometimes used in jest, to signify a man who has no fixed abode, or a man who is nowhere a stranger. It derives from κόσμος, world, and πόλις, city. When an ancient philosopher was asked from whence he came, he replied: 'I am a cosmopolitan, that is, a citizen of the universe.' 'I prefer,' said another, 'my family to myself, my country to my family, and the human race to my country.' See also *Philosophe*.[27]

While based substantially on the *Dictionnaire*, an examination of this definition indicates that it was the result of deliberate and calculated reflection on historical and contemporary usages of the cosmopolitan vocabulary. As such, it differs from the earlier appropriations of Chambers and Frisch. This can be established, first, from those aspects of the *Dictionnaire* entry that Diderot chose to omit from the *Encyclopédie*. While there are several – such as the elimination of the genders, and the discussion of the relative merits of *cosmopolitain* versus *cosmopolite* – the most glaring of these is the reference to the alchemical resonance of the cosmopolitan vocabulary in Sendivogius's *Novem Lumen Chymicum*. Diderot himself was no admirer of the 'great art' of alchemy.[28] Indeed, he likely witnessed alchemical experiments in the laboratory of his school-master Guillaume François Rouelle (1703–1770), a self-professed adept. The journalist, who found superstition 'more offensive to God than atheism', believed that alchemy needlessly sheathed chemistry in mystical obscurantism.[29] It was perhaps on these grounds that he struck the reference to Sendivogius from the *Encyclopédie*. Its omission indicates that Diderot was familiar with at least one seventeenth-century usage of the cosmopolitan vocabulary, which he chose deliberately to exclude.

The second aspect of Diderot's reflection on historical usages of the cosmopolitan vocabulary is apparent in his additions to the *Dictionnaire*. The first is his expansion of the statement of the 'ancient philosopher' to include the clause 'c'est-à-dire *citoyen de l'univers*'. In the eighteenth century, the formulation 'citizen of the universe' was rare.[30] But one work in which it had appeared was a 1733 refutation of Pyrrhonism by the Swiss philosopher Jean-Pierre de Crousaz (1663–1750). In this work de Crousaz castigated an unnamed *Pyrrhonien* for claiming 'I am a philosopher, I am a citizen of the universe in general.'[31] De Crousaz's unnamed *Pyrrhonien*, it appears, was none other than François de La Mothe Le Vayer, who in a 1630 dialogue declared that 'Philosophers are called cosmopolitans,' and that they reside with the Gods in 'the City of the Universe.'[32] Here we have Diderot's word *Cosmopolite* rubbing shoulders with the identity of the philosopher *and* citizenship of the universe. It seems likely, then, that this addition was inspired, directly or indirectly, by La Mothe Le Vayer.

Diderot also added a more contemporary reference. This was through his inclusion of a maxim by 'another' philosopher who, as the entry indicates, preferred 'the human race to my country'. As Thomas Schlereth has pointed out, this philosopher was the French jurist Montesquieu (1689–1755), who in a then-unpublished letter declared: 'If I know of anything advantageous to my family but not to my country, I should try to forget it. If I knew of anything advantageous to my country that was prejudicial to Europe and to the human race, I should look upon it as a crime.'³³ For Diderot, Montesquieu's adage apparently clarified, advanced, or was synonymous with, the position adopted by the ancient philosopher, and by La Mothe Le Vayer.

While it has been vaunted as a rediscovery of ancient philosophical ideas, as one historian has recently asserted, Diderot's foundational cosmopolitan statement in the *Encyclopédie* is instead product of careful reflection on historical usages of the cosmopolitan vocabulary in sources classical, early modern and contemporary. Important for this narrative is the fact that Diderot's entry was not merely intended to define the word *Cosmopolite*, it was part of a broader attempt to link the word to a grander vision of the place of the cosmopolitan in contemporary France. This is signalled at the end of the entry, where Diderot provides the reader with a telling cross-reference to another entry in the *Encyclopédie*: '*Voyez* Philosophe'.

The *philosophes* and the birth of cosmopolitanism

In contemporary France the word *philosophe* was used not only to designate historical philosophers like Plato or Aristotle; it also described a cadre of well-known public intellectuals.³⁴ Yet as A.N. Whitehead reminds us, 'the *philosophes* were not philosophers'.³⁵ By profession they were authors, economists, journalists, art critics and politicians. Among those most closely associated with the movement were Jean-Jacques Rousseau (1712–1778), Voltaire (1694–1778), the Scots philosopher David Hume (1711–1776), the Prussian writer and jurist Anarchasis Cloots (1755–1794), Diderot, Montesquieu and many others. The group was heterogeneous in terms of nationality, background, education – and interests – although most were united to some extent by Deist commitments. As Dena Goodman has pointed out, the *philosophe* was in several senses the conceptual end point of an idea whose rise we have already witnessed; the humanistic and Neostoic ideals of a moral and learned elite whose duty it was to guide humanity by means of reason.³⁶ Late in the seventeenth century, the French sceptical philosopher Pierre Bayle (1647–1706) gave a name to this movement, calling it the *res publica literaria*.³⁷

The *Encyclopédie*'s lengthy entry for 'Philosophe' was not written by Diderot, but probably by his sometime collaborator César Chesneau du Marsais (1676–1756). The text which furnished the basis for the entry has a strange history.[38] A version had been circulating as a scribal publication among Frenchmen sympathetic to philosophical deism since the 1720s. Two decades later, it was printed anonymously in Bernard de Fontenelle's *Nouvelles Libertés de penser* (1743), before it was included in the *Encyclopedié*. A close reading of this entry shows that du Marsais's 'philosophe' was clearly intended to be identical to Diderot's 'cosmopolite'. According to the entry, the *philosophe*'s identity is defined by 'the philosophical spirit, [which] is a spirit of observation and accuracy, [and] which relates everything to its true principles'.[39] Du Marsais makes clear that the *philosophe* exercises these abilities within a web of civil obligations that creates of him 'a divinity on earth'. In an earlier chapter we have seen that this formulation first appeared in Cicero, and was repeated by Laurentius Grimaldus, Richard Hooker and La Mothe Le Vayer. The former figures reconciled Cicero's sentiment with Christian notions of life as exile from heaven.[40] Du Marsais was clearly aware of this Christian cosmopolitan tradition, for he explicitly excluded it from this new philosophical identity:

> Our philosopher does not find himself in exile in this world; he does not at all believe himself to be in enemy territory; he wants to enjoy like a wise housekeeper the goods that nature offers him; he wishes to find pleasure with others: and in order to do so, he must give it: thus he seeks to get along with those with whom he lives by chance or his own choice; and he finds at the same time those who suit him: he is an honorable (*hônnete*) man who wishes to please and to make himself useful.[41]

The *philosophe* is thus a person who is both in the world and intimately concerned with and by it, who wants to be hospitable, of use and of help to his fellow men. His allegiance is to them and not to a supernatural authority. He is not the subject of God, but rather a custodian or 'housekeeper' of nature, and a promoter of natural law. The statement is thus a pointed rejection of the Christian *homo viator*. In addition to establishing the ostensibly secular nature of the cosmopolitan identity among the *philosophes*, this statement also provides clear evidence that, like Diderot, du Marsais was familiar with Christian cosmopolitan discourse of centuries past. Furthermore, these sacred conceptions helped to shape and define the ideal of the *philosophe*.

The *philosophe* was also no ancient Stoic or Lipsian Neo-Stoic. Indeed, for du Marsais, a 'true philosopher', and thus true cosmopolite, pursued a reflective philosophy that appreciated humanity in all its flawed glory, including a moderate embracing of the passions:

> The *philosophe* is an honourable man who acts in everything according to reason, and who joins to a spirit of reflection and precision, morals and sociable qualities. [...] From this idea it is easy to conclude how far removed the insensitive sage of the stoics is from the perfection of our *philosophe*: such a *philosophe* is a man, and their sage was nothing but a phantom. Humanity would make them blush, and our *philosophe* glories in it; they wished foolishly to deny the passions, and to raise us above our nature by means of a chimerical insensitivity: as to our *philosophe*, he makes no claim to the chimerical honour of destroying the passions, because that is impossible; but he works at not being dominated by them, at benefitting from them, and at making reasonable use of them, because that is possible, and because reason directs him to do so.[42]

These two passages make clear that like Diderot, du Marsais and other French *philosophes* were intimately aware of historical usages of cosmopolitan vocabulary. In fashioning their intellectual identity, they associated cosmopolitan identity with a flexible creed informed by, but rejecting, Stoic, Christian and Neo-Stoic traditions. Meta-discursive reflection on disparate cosmopolitan statements of history had finally given rise to a distinct philosophical ideal, which we might well describe as 'cosmopolitanism'.

The attractiveness of this new cosmopolitanism articulated by Diderot and du Marsais was made quickly evident by the adoption of the cosmopolitan vocabulary and its sentiments by other Enlightenment thinkers. In 1760, Charles Palissot de Montenoy's (1730–1814) pointed comedy *Les Philosophes* contained the line 'the true sage is a cosmopolite'.[43] When the Scot David Hume arrived in Paris in 1763, he was compared to Diderot by the German philosopher Friedrich Melchior von Grimm (1723–1807), for 'the *philosophes* belong less to their own country than to the universe that they enlighten'.[44] Hume admired Paris so much that, in a letter to a Scottish friend, he appropriated the language of his intellectual circles to declare: 'I am a citizen of the world, but if I were to adopt any country, it could be that in which I live at present.'[45] Several years later, Diderot squared the circle in an epistle to Hume:

'My dear David, you belong to all the nations of the earth and you never ask a man for his place of birth. I flatter myself that I am like you, a citizen of the great city of the world.'[46] After being popularized in Diderot's *Salons* (1765), the vocabulary soon spread beyond the immediate networks of *philosophes*. In 1770 the Parisian jurist Joseph-Honoré Remí (1738–1782) issued a work in which he defined cosmopolitanism (*le cosmopolisme*) as a philosophy of life 'consisting of the virtues pursued by philosophers (*philosophes*)'.[47] For Remí, the essence of this cosmopolitanism consisted in the creation of a globe-spanning sense of fraternity. But as Remí well recognized, the ideal itself had historical roots:

> This happy sentiment, which nature inspires in individuals of the same kind, a sacred instinct that the legislator of the Christians wished to make a merit to man by establishing him in virtue, and placing him at the head of his immortal Code: the Fraternity, degraded by the fanaticism of zeal and by the maxims of intolerance, has only now begun, since the Renaissance of letters, to recover its rights. It owes its glory to the efforts of the Cosmopolitans. Returned by them to Europe, under the name of benevolence and humanity, this virtue may be announced to our nephews as the daughter of misfortune and philosophy.[48]

As should be clear, this passage explicitly acknowledges the impossibility of the Enlightenment expression of cosmopolitanism without the efforts of those 'cosmopolitans' who had emerged since the Renaissance. Perhaps Remí had in mind the likes of French sceptics like Montaigne and La Mothe Le Vayer. The precise identity of these patriots is less significant than the fact that Remí's cosmopolitanism, too, was inflected by sixteenth- and seventeenth-century cosmopolitan discourse, to say nothing of that of antiquity.

Dissenting voices

The efforts of the *philosophes* meant that, by the 1760s, the cosmopolitan vocabulary was being used relatively intensively in Europe for the first time since the mid-seventeenth century. Indeed, if we accept Diderot's suggestion that the word 'cosmopolite' was synonymous with 'philosophe', then we are dealing with a veritable deluge of cosmopolitan discourse, and meta-discourse, in this period. The vocabulary not only appeared in works by *philosophes* and their readers, but also inspired scholarly journals like the *Journal étranger*, which emphasized the internationality of the 'new' deistic philosophical endeavour, even as it adopted for its title the trope of heavenly citizenship.[49]

Despite this, understandings of cosmopolitanism remained heterogeneous. Not all were content with accepting the attempts by *philosophes* to appropriate the terminology. One of their most prominent critics was the Swiss novelist Jean-Jacques Rousseau.[50] Most historians who have examined Rousseau's cosmopolitan stance have done so through the lens of his patriotic commitments, which are seemingly antithetical to any cosmopolitan view.[51] Here, I am more concerned with documenting Rousseau's evolving understanding of the cosmopolitan vocabulary, for this offers insight into his critique of the *philosophes*, and contemporary society, more broadly. Hailing from Geneva, Rousseau had been friends with Diderot since the 1740s, when both lived in Paris in near penury. Initially linked by a shared philosophical outlook, both men worked hard to climb the ranks of the city's intellectual elite. Later, when Diderot began his editorship of the *Encyclopédie*, he commissioned Rousseau to contribute several hundred articles. As such, it is unsurprising to see Rousseau employ the cosmopolitan vocabulary throughout his early works, in manners similar to Diderot and other *philosophes*. For example, in his *Discours sur l'origine de l'inégalité* (Discourse on the origins of inequality, 1755) he wrote of ancient society that:

> Civil law having become the common rule of the citizens, the law of nature took place only between the various societies, where, under the name of the law of nations, it was tempered by some tacit agreement to render the commerce possible. And to supply the natural commiseration, which, losing from society to society almost all the strength it had from man to man, now resides only in a few great cosmopolitan souls, which cross the imaginary barriers that separate the peoples, following the example of the Sovereign Being who created them, embrace the whole human race in their benevolence.[52]

In this passage – which recalls Barthélemy Aneau's praise of the anonymous upholders of divine law in his *Juris Prudentia* (1554) – Rousseau makes clear that the cosmopolitan is a rare soul, a mediator of natural law, and representative of a deistic 'Sovereign Being' who could embrace the 'human race' in his benevolent endeavours, all the while crossing 'imaginary barriers'. When he made this statement, Rousseau likely thought of himself and fellow thinkers like Diderot and Montesquieu as among the 'few great cosmopolitan souls'; modern arbiters of this cosmopolitan ethos.

All the rest were, it seems, pretenders to the cosmopolitan title. When composing his statement, Rousseau may have had in mind someone like Louis-Charles Fougeret de Monbron (1706–1760), a minor Parisian *littérateur* whose autobiography, *Le Cosmopolite ou le citoyen du monde* (1750) described his globetrotting adventures in self-aggrandizing and occasionally lascivious detail.[53] Rousseau despised this slothful individualism masquerading as cosmopolitanism, which was hardly a life lived according to or in promotion of 'divine law'. For Rousseau, the cosmopolitan identity was active, duty-bound and, importantly, ephemeral; if the duties of the cosmopolitan were not fulfilled, the identity itself would lapse.

In 1757 Rousseau experienced something of a philosophical crisis. He departed Paris, which was then gripped by enlightenment fervour, to wander the countryside and reconnect with the traditions and experiences of his youth.[54] In his absence from the metropolis, Rousseau gradually came to despise the self-serving narratives of Paris's urban elite, among them Diderot and other self-proclaimed cosmopolites. This much is clear from his influential *Letter to d'Alembert* (1758), a work that praised the rustic wisdom of country-folk above that of their urban, and urbane, counterparts. Rousseau's absence from the metropole intensified his scepticism concerning claimants to cosmopolitan identity. Several years later, Rousseau issued *Émile* (1762), a controversial *Bildungsroman* that became a work of foundational importance in post-revolutionary France. In it he warned readers to 'beware of those cosmopolites who go to great lengths in their books to discover duties they disdain to fulfil around them'.[55] Although this passage has been read by some scholars as evidence of Rousseau's 'anti-cosmopolitanism', approaching the statement in context makes clear that it was an expression of a critique of hypocritical cosmopolitans expressed in prior works, like his *Discourse on Inequality* (1755). Rousseau's statement does not indicate that he was opposed to the ethical and moral duties of the cosmopolitan *per se*, but only that some cosmopolites – or *philosophes*, to borrow the lingo of the *Encyclopédie* – had no right to use the title.[56] The critique in *Émile* was almost certainly directed against Rousseau's former friends in Paris, like Diderot and Montesquieu, from whom Rousseau had become estranged, both personally and philosophically. In Rousseau's eyes, these cosmopolites had succumbed to hubris. Coddled by the cloistered group-think of Paris's elite, they no longer sought to serve humanity with their ideas. Instead, they had become false cosmopolitans who pretended 'to love the whole world in order to have the right to love no one'. For Rousseau, who valued love of patria as much as the love of distant peoples, the obligation of humans came down to the golden rule: 'the essential thing is to be good to the people with whom one lives'.[57] The cosmopolites swanning about Paris did neither. For Rousseau they were neither true cosmopolites nor true *philosophes*.

There were other objections raised to cosmopolitan ideals in this period. In 1786, the Weimar privy councillor Ernst August Anton von Göchhausen (1740–1824) issued his controversial 'Disclosure of the system of the republic of the cosmopolitans'.[58] As Andrea Albrecht has shown, Göchhausen's cosmopolitans were a motley crew of *philosophes*, Jesuits, Freemasons and even the Bavarian Illuminati, all of whom he viewed as engaged in an antichristian conspiracy against good national order.[59] For Göchhausen, these Cosmopolites were 'Confreres and fellow-members' to 'Turks, Jews, Hottentots, and cannibals ... or in other words, citizens of the world in the same meaning as our new *philosophes*' (*Aufklärer*).[60] While echoing Valentin Grießmann's seventeenth-century fears of a Rosicrucian conspiracy, Göchhausen's connection of Enlightenment cosmopolites to a 'system' of secret societies anticipated some of the wilder conspiracy theories that soon emerged in Europe.[61] In 1788, on the eve of the French Revolution, Jean-Marie-Bernard Clément (1742–1812) complained of Diderot and others that 'modern philosophy wants to make us all cosmopolitans, and wants us to understand the love of our *patria* as small-minded. The *philosophe* has all men as fellow citizens: he loves with equal humanity those he never encounters, like the Lapp and the orang-utan, and considers his countrymen, whom he encounters every day, to be strangers'.[62] In addition to being a call for loving one's own *patria*, this objection is notable foremost for its critique of *philosophes*' attempts to appropriate the cosmopolitan vocabulary, and could be understood as evidence of their partial success. Inspired by very different circumstances, these critiques contested *philosophes*' claims that the cosmopolite belonged to a benevolent elite tasked with guiding humanity. They felt that the cosmopolites achieved the opposite, by doing little more than setting the man of reason on the same level as an ape.

The critiques of world community offered by Rousseau, Clément and Göchhausen mirror the rise of nationalist sentiment in Europe. As David A. Bell has shown, these ideas were particularly widespread in France, where new ideas of nation-building, which saw unity among citizens as a crucial priority, quickly butted against cosmopolitan ideals.[63] A striking early manifestation of this tension appeared in the fourth edition of the *Dictionnaire de l'Académie française* (1762), which defined the word 'Cosmopolite' as 'one who does not recognise his *patria*. A cosmopolite is not a good citizen'.[64] While this definition demonstrates, to a certain extent, the success of the *philosophes*' attempts to co-opt the cosmopolitan vocabulary, it also shows why the terminology remained a lightning rod for controversy during the French Revolution. While Paul Hazard suggested that cosmopolitan terminology possessed little valence during this period, Charles van den Heuvel has recently shown that understandings of the terms waxed and waned with the fortunes of the revolution.[65] Before late 1792 there was a latent suspicion of the aims and goals of 'cosmopolites' – however this designation may have been understood – a view encouraged by the usage of the vocabulary by the revolutionary Jacobins, who considered themselves to be 'Fellow-citizens of the world' (*concitoyens du monde*, cf. Ephesians 2:19) and thus members of a 'fraternity of humanity'.[66] But a reversal of fortune loomed. As J.M. Roberts has shown, it was the Jacobins' self-confessed openness to the world – together with their involvement in actual political intrigues – which prompted accusations of colluding with foreign powers and secret societies to seize political power.[67] The spectre haunting this narrative is philosophical cosmopolitanism. On 26 September 1792, shortly after the abolition of the monarchy, eighteen European luminaries were honoured by the revolutionary regime with the title 'Citoyens du monde'. Among them was the Prussian *philosophe*, Anarcharsis Cloots. This honorary title was bestowed only shortly after the beginning of the September Massacres in Paris, which were prompted by xenophobic fears that foreign armies were about to invade France. Shortly thereafter, polemic against real or imagined enemies of the patria and 'cosmopolitan pretenders' (*charlatans cosmopolites*) – to borrow Robespierre's memorable formulation – appeared in print.⁶⁸ The repercussions were immense. On 24 March 1794, Cloots was guillotined on the Place de la Révolution as a traitor to the revolutionary movement: a martyr, in some senses, for the cosmopolitan cause. Despite the best efforts of Diderot and the *philosophes* to shed the cosmopolitan vocabulary's unsavoury early-modern associations, their efforts to appropriate and homogenize the discourse never transcended the volatility inherent in the ideal.

Perpetual peace

While the *philosophes* – and their enemies – played crucial roles in the emergence of cosmopolitan meta-discourse, there can be little doubt that, for historians and philosophers alike, the towering figure of eighteenth-century cosmopolitanism is the Königsberg philosopher Immanuel Kant. There are several conceptual features of Kant's cosmopolitan expressions that have seemingly ensured their appeal to modern observers. For example, Kant discussed the cosmopolitan as a manifestation of hospitality. While hospitality has been a feature of cosmopolitan thought since at least Barthélemy Aneau, its centrality has been emphasized by the Algerian-French philosopher Jacques Derrida (1930–2004) in his writings on the cosmopolitan.⁶⁹ Another appealing aspect of Kant's cosmopolitan expressions is that they were explicitly international in outlook. As we have seen throughout this volume, this was not always a feature of early-modern cosmopolitan discourse. Indeed, Kant largely eschewed the idea of the cosmopolitan as a privileged identity, and conceived of it instead as a feature common to all mankind; albeit with several important exceptions. When Martha C. Nussbaum revivified debate about the philosophical place of cosmopolitanism in the west in 1994, it was Kant that she chose as an emblematic representative of cosmopolitan thought.⁷⁰ Yet as Galin Tihanov has argued, Kant's vaunted place in the modern cosmopolitan pantheon relies at least partially on his vision being one of 'cosmopolitan world order'. That is to say, Kant provided an early formulation of obligations of the individual within a global, and thus 'modern', intellectual landscape, expressed in a way that made it immediately reconcilable with thinkers in a political order reeling from the collapse of communism.⁷¹

Be that as it may, Kant's cosmopolitanism is not unproblematic, and his talismanic status as the first of the modern cosmopolitans makes him an interesting case study of tensions inherent in eighteenth-century cosmopolitan discourses. This is particularly because, as in the case of the French *philosophes*, his thought was so heavily influenced by early-modern ideas, and evolved over time. As Pauline Kleingeld has pointed out, Kant used the cosmopolitan vocabulary throughout his *oeuvre* to signify different things at different times.[72] In his 'Universal history from a cosmopolitan perspective' (1784), for example, Kant employed the terminology adjectivally, when describing a citizen of the world's view of human endeavour. Conversely, in his essay 'On Theory and Practice' (1793), Kant argued that a universal tendency to misanthropy might be countered by considering international rights from a 'cosmopolitan point of view', by which he meant a 'universal philanthropy'. This was an expression of the concept of the brotherhood of man, thoroughly consonant with religious and secular conceptions of world citizenship encountered in prior chapters.

Two years later, Kant's major statement on the cosmopolitan appeared in a very different register in his influential 'Perpetual Peace: A philosophical sketch' (1795). Inspired by Enlightenment ideas, and written against the background of disintegration of the French Revolution and the rise of Prussian aggression, this essay provided a guide to ensuring lasting equanimity between states. While projects for ensuring a lasting peace had been articulated by European thinkers for more than a century, Kant's essay is of interest because of its third article, which declared that 'the cosmopolitan right (*Weltbürgerrecht*), shall be restricted to conditions of universal hospitality'.[73] In essence, this article demanded that foreigners be treated hospitably, and not as enemies merely because they were strangers. There are echoes here of Pufendorf's natural citizens, in addition to a powerful ethical compulsion recalling ideas of the cosmopolitan everyman. For Kant, the humane treatment of strangers was consonant with a 'right of nature' akin to natural law, under which 'distant continents may enter into peaceful relations with each other. These may at last become publicly regulated by law, and thus the human race may be always brought nearer to a Cosmopolitical Constitution'.[74] For Kant, this advance was essential, for

> the social relations between the various Peoples of the world, in narrower or wider circles, have now advanced everywhere so far that a violation of Right

in one place of the earth, is felt all over it. Hence the idea of a Cosmopolitical Right of the whole Human Race, is no phantastic or overstrained mode of representing Right, but is a necessary completion of the unwritten Code which carries national and international Right to a consummation in the Public Right of Mankind. Thus the whole system leads to the conclusion of a Perpetual Peace among the Nations.[75]

While Kant's conception of a cosmopolitical right would have been impossible without the widespread changes to European legal regimes in the wake of the Thirty Years' War, what leaps out from his statement is his appreciation of such a right existing within a web of global relations. This is one sense in which Kant's views appear immediately more 'modern' within our globalized world, particularly when compared with cosmopolitan expressions of his contemporaries.

The influence of Kant's 'Perpetual Peace' on modern conceptions of the cosmopolitan has been tremendous. The philosopher Francis Cheneval has argued that the essay, with its promise of a legal cosmopolitan guarantee, was the apex of Kant's intellectual development, and a model for super-national thinking at the origins of modernity.[76] Nussbaum saw Kant as the postulator of a cosmopolitan philosophy that countered the crude universalisms of other Enlightenment theorists of world community.[77] But as Pauline Kleingeld and Georg Cavallar have argued, the cosmopolitan positions articulated in Kant's work are best studied in the context of his philosophical project as a whole.[78] And when Kant's 'Perpetual Peace' is read alongside his other contemporary works, the Protestant vision at the core of his cosmopolitanism – and therefore his debt to early modern thought – becomes clear. For example, although 'Perpetual Peace' was written on the heels of *Religion within the Boundaries of Mere Reason* (1793) and was followed by the essay 'The End of All Things' (1794), both of these works demonstrate that the Königsberg philosopher understood humans as 'temporal though supersensible beings'. As such, Kant understood earthly existence as a presage to an eternal reality. The philosopher's vision of worldly perpetual peace sprung from his belief that moral reason and faith, and therefore natural religion, would help create a world religion adhering to a Christian 'pure religious faith' that would eventually encompass the globe, creating a 'visible Kingdom of God on earth'.[79] Like many contemporary deists, Kant recognized the corruptibility of institutionalized religions, and saw tensions between morality, reason and religion. I am inclined to agree with Cavallar's controversial stance that Kant's religion 'is universal since it is valid for every human being', and 'is identical with the authentic Christian religion'.[80] As such, the 'the exact correspondence of happiness with morality' – arguably the basis of his vision of the cosmopolitan right expressed in 'Perpetual Peace' – can only be guaranteed in the heavenly kingdom, or a kingdom consonant with it.[81] Even as it echoed ancient doctrines, this scenario is reminiscent of the imperial visions of a Dee, Postel or even the fictional Rosicrucian fraternity.

Kant's status as an emblem of modernity has meant that these topics are the subject of considerable debate by scholars, some of whom argue that Kant's conception of religion occupies a fundamentally distinct philosophical sphere from the religious commitments of his predecessors.[82] Whatever the status of these debates, it is apparent that Kant's statements on the cosmopolitan were informed by both Christian and secular commitments, even if later generations have favoured overwhelmingly secular readings. Perhaps the apex of Kant's melding of secular and religious influences was his postulation of a 'philosophical chiliasm', which aimed at the realization of the highest worldly good through a state of 'perpetual peace based on a federation of nations united in a world republic'.[83] This striking juxtaposition of seemingly incommensurable opposites not only recalls Campanella, but suggests that Kant's thought should not be reduced from its complex whole, in which he acknowledged God's presence as critical to the fate of moral humanity, and philosophical visions of its fulfilment.[84]

Yet even if we reject out of hand the presence of religious ideas of world community in Kant's cosmopolitan expressions, and accept furthermore that these are essentially secular and 'modern' in their outlook, there remains a sting in the tail. As this study has demonstrated, the cosmopolitan designation, whether understood positively or negatively, has always been used to establish difference. Who defines the cosmos defines its citizens, and thus the preconditions for inclusion, or exclusion, from the world community. In his 'Perpetual Peace' Kant indicated that the rights of cosmopolitan law applied to all rational beings. However, recent scholarship on Kant's racial theory indicates that this did not include all of humankind. Indeed, as Mark Larrimore, Raphaël Lagier and others have pointed out, Kant draws a distinction throughout his *oeuvre* between 'human beings' and 'rational beings'.[85] So it was in 'Perpetual Peace', in which Kant expressed doubts about the moral capability of 'Indians', 'Negroes' and 'Americans' to occupy the category of 'rational beings'. As Kleingeld put it, Kant's 'moral cosmopolitanism is profoundly inconsistent with his defense of a white supremacist racial hierarchy'.[86]

A curious paradox thus emerges, for in this perspective, Kant's 'modern' cosmopolitan vision suddenly compares less than favourably with the apocalyptic scenarios posited in early modernity. Let us take, for example, the imperial fantasies of Guillaume Postel. As we have seen in Chapter 2, Postel's cosmopolitan vision stipulated that citizenship in the heavenly city was open to any person; the sole precondition being that they first convert to Christianity. For Postel, this possibility would be offered to the world's people first by means of missionary activity. Yet if this missionary activity failed, the Frenchman detailed military plans to invade and conquer foreign polities, in order to force their people to convert on pain of death. All this in the name of establishing the cosmopolis. As distasteful as Postel's scenario may be to modern secular observers, his cosmopolitan ideal at least allowed the world's non-believers a choice to secure their heavenly citizenship. The same cannot be said for Kant, whose vision excluded all whom he did not consider 'rational'.

Conclusions

In 1932 the American historian Carl L. Becker argued that the philosophy of the Enlightenment period did not represent a decisive break with the thought of the medieval and early modern periods, but rather continuity. This led him to declare that 'the *Philosophes* demolished the Heavenly City of St. Augustine only to rebuild it with more up-to-date materials'.[87] While Becker's thesis has been subject to substantial – and warranted – criticism, the statement provides a provocative lens through which to examine Enlightenment cosmopolitan visions of the city of the world. The present chapter has gone beyond Becker's argument, demonstrating concretely that the cosmopolitanism of the *philosophes*, and indeed of Kant, was indebted to the beliefs and commitments of early modernity. The word 'cosmopolitan' and its variants did not appear *ex nihilo* in the minds of eighteenth-century thinkers. They found it in early modern lexica, in editions of classical authors of antiquity, or in the writings of Lipsius, La Mothe Le Vayer, Montaigne or even Sendivogius. The reflection of figures like Diderot, Rousseau, Remí, Kant and others on these historical usages, together with the growing lexical encapsulation of the cosmopolitan vocabulary, were necessary preconditions in the emergence of a meta-discourse which paved the way for expressions of cosmopolitanism as a distinctive philosophical, ethical or moral commitment. This occurred because of, not despite, the cosmopolitan discourses of early modernity.

Epilogue

'Cosmopolitanism,' argued Frank Ejby Poulsen recently, 'does not exist and it never has'. This confronting statement was inspired by Poulsen's conviction that 'there has never been any successful philosophy combining universally agreed upon principles respecting local particularities'.[1] But the statement is true in another sense, for as Thomas Schlereth has observed, cosmopolitanism is foremost an intellectual ideal. It is therefore a thing that is inherently unrealizable: something perpetually imagined, reimagined and strived towards, but always receding beyond the horizon of possibility.[2] While cosmopolitanism might never have existed in the sense articulated by Poulsen, the ideal, like any other, nevertheless has a history. This history resides in how thinkers have thought about, conceived of, and defined the cosmopolitan.

Based on a survey of usages of the cosmopolitan vocabulary between 1500 and 1800, the present study has shown that there has never existed a single, universally accepted conception of cosmopolitanism. Instead, there has always flourished a host of competing claims to world citizenship and its meanings, expressed in registers both sacred and secular. In antiquity, the cosmopolitan vocabulary was employed by Cynics, Stoics, Hebrews and Christians alike, who employed it to designate very different concepts. From ideas of self-sovereignty implicit in Diogenes's foundational aphorism, to collective covenental identity expressed in the works of Philo of Alexandria, cosmopolitan terminology provided an appealing and flexible vocabulary to a variety of observers and for a variety of concepts. Following the decline of the Roman Empire and the rise of Latinate Christianity after the fifth century, the terminology disappeared from usage for centuries, until it was rediscovered in Europe around the beginning of the sixteenth century. When it did re-emerge, it retained the diversity of associations that prevailed in antiquity.

In early modernity, European thinkers from a variety of nations, languages and backgrounds collected, collated and compared the cosmopolitan expressions of antiquity. Mulling over ancient texts, they revised old associations and articulated new connections. Gradually, over the course of the seventeenth century, some Protestants turned their backs on this cosmopolitan vocabulary, and some actually inverted its once positive associations with heavenly citizenship, associating it instead with carnal worldliness. Partially as a result of this, the vocabulary gradually became the almost exclusive preserve of thinkers who, although they remained influenced by Christian conceptions of the cosmopolitan, nevertheless employed the vocabulary in a variety of nominally secular contexts, from law to science to philosophy.

But even within these secular registers, the meanings and associations of the cosmopolitan vocabulary remained plural and contested. In the eighteenth century, the *philosophes*, most notably, attempted to bend the vocabulary to their will. By engaging with and reflecting on the usages of their forebears, they consciously rejected the sacred associations of centuries prior, and attempted through the *Encyclopédie* and other works to appropriate the word *cosmopolite* as a synonym for a secular 'philosopher'. While their detractors contested this, the reflections of Diderot and his fellow *philosophes* on historical usages of the cosmopolitan vocabulary mark a landmark moment, for they opened the door for the creation of a meta-discourse of the cosmopolitan. 'Cosmopolitanism', in a conceptual sense, emerged for the first time in history.

Despite its importance, this history of how we have thought about and defined the cosmopolitan has been largely overlooked. It has, in other words, been lost. In search of the roots of secular 'modern' cosmopolitanism, scholars have instead hastily connected the philosophical pronouncements of Greek and Roman antiquity with the Enlightenments of the eighteenth century, thereby reifying, or constructing, a peculiar and insubstantial narrative genealogy of the cosmopolitan. They have ignored the fact that this narrative was one first proffered by the *philosophes* themselves, who very carefully shaped and edited their own conclusions. This genealogy has been defended, at least once, with feeble reference to a reductionist – and faintly ridiculous – principle that defining the cosmopolitan is itself a thing 'un-cosmopolitan' in nature.[3] As such, the gloriously messy and complex history of how early modern thinkers conceived of the cosmopolitan has remained 'lost' and virtually unknown.

Yet the implications of this history are not merely historical. If cosmopolitanism 'needs a mid-life crisis', as Richard Miller has recently claimed, then the material for a reconsideration of the ideal, its significance and its possibilities, is offered by this study.[4] While much modern discourse on cosmopolitanism is mired in disputes about its relationship to patriotism, morality, ethics, global citizenship, equality, democracy, egalitarianism and other matters, history demonstrates that this has not always been the case. By understanding and engaging with the diversity of historical cosmopolitan expressions, we are better equipped to analyse and contextualize the cosmopolitanisms of the present.

These modern cosmopolitanisms are conceived in senses both positive and negative, precisely as they have always been. On the one hand there are the soaring moral and ethical visions of civilizational unity propounded by philosophers like Kwame Anthony Appiah and Martha C. Nussbaum. Inspiring in their nature and inclusive in their vision, they are nevertheless defined by a kind of unreachability of the type already identified by Schlereth.[5] On the other hand, there are more exclusive visions. In an address to the Conservative Party Conference in October 2016, former British Prime Minister Theresa May declared that 'if you believe you're a citizen of the world, you're a citizen of nowhere', as part of her justification for Britain's proposed exit from the European Union. It was a warning, she said, to global elites, for businesses and individuals to face their obligations – financial and patriotic – to Britain.[6] In August 2017 Steve Miller, policy advisor to US president Donald Trump, accused a journalist of possessing a 'cosmopolitan bias' when he was confronted about plans to curb immigrant intakes. In a wash of moral outrage, commentators saw in both episodes anti-Semitic echoes of dismissals of Jews as 'rootless cosmopolitans' by twentieth-century totalitarian regimes.[7] In this view, the cosmopolitan vocabulary itself appears to have assumed a kind of charged, sacred status, a moral weight borne by untested assumptions about its historical, and potential, meanings, and their legitimacy.

But while the statements of Miller and May inspired scorn and condemnation, the register of their comments is, as we now know, anything but new. May's words, for example, echo Diderot's condemnation of Paris's 'false cosmopolites', to say nothing of their resonance with the words of seventeenth-century Puritan ministers, who located citizenship in the heavenly Jerusalem and scorned so-called 'citizens of the world'. Miller's comments, on the other hand, were anticipated in the struggle over the obligations to *patria* theorized in antiquity, debated by proponents of natural law in the seventeenth century, and contested by Kant and the *philosophes* in the eighteenth century. While the contexts are ever-changing, the tensions perceived by modern observers in these uses of the cosmopolitan vocabulary have always been present; they are part of the very fabric of the cosmopolitan ideal. Seen in this new light, the opinions of May and Miller seem more explicable as inevitable corollaries to the philosophical and academic cosmopolitanisms of Nussbaum and Appiah. The present volume reveals the problematic and diverse DNA of such modern visions of world community, be they inclusive or exclusive, sacred or secular, good or bad. They have their roots in the expressions of early modern thinkers, who reinterpreted the statements of the philosophers of antiquity, and who were reinterpreted in turn by influential eighteenth-century figures. These competing conceptions of the cosmopolitan ideal made the very imagination of modern cosmopolitanism possible in the first place, even if its inherent tensions have never been resolved.

Notes

Chapter 1

1 Erasmus, *Collected Works of Erasmus. Volume 9. The Correspondence, 1522 to 1523*, R.A.B. Mynors, trans. James M. Estes, annotations (Toronto: University of Toronto Press, 1989), 184.

2 C.R. Thompson, 'Erasmus as Internationalist and Cosmopolitan', *Archiv für Reformationsgeschichte* 46 (1955): 167–195; Stan van Hooft and Wim Vandekerckhove, eds., *Questioning Cosmopolitanism* (New York: Springer, 2010), xv: 'Erasmus [and others] ... draw on cosmopolitanism to advocate world peace through religious tolerance and a society of states'. Compare Jan Papy, 'Erasmus, Europe, and Cosmopolitanism: The Humanist Image and Message in His Letters', in *Erasmo da Roterodam e la cultura europea. Atti dell'Incontro di Studi nel V centenario della laurea di Erasmo all'Università di Torino*, Pietro B. Rossi, ed. (Florence: SISMEL-Edizioni del Galluzzo, 2008), 27–42.

3 Traced in exemplary fashion by Bruce Mansfield, *Erasmus in the Twentieth Century* (Toronto: University of Toronto Press, 2003); Jessica L. Wolfe, 'The Cosmopolitanism of *The Adages*: The Classical and Christian Legacies of Erasmus' Hermeneutics of Accommodation', in *Cosmopolitanism and the Middle Ages*, John M. Ganim and Shayne Aaron Legassie, eds. (New York: Springer, 2013), 207–230.

4 See for example James Tracy, *The Politics of Erasmus: A Pacifist Intellectual and His Political Milieu* (Toronto: University of Toronto Press, 1978).

5 Erasmus to Zwingli, *c.* 3 September 1522, in Erasmus, *Collected Works*, vol. 9, 184. In a letter of 1 February 1523 to Marcus Laurinus, Erasmus related of Zwingli the rather different explanation: 'I responded I wished to be a citizen of the whole world, and not of one town in it' (*respondi me velle civem esse totius mundi, non unius oppidi*). See Erasmus, *Collected Works*, vol. 9, 384. Some years later, inspired by Cicero, Erasmus included 'civis mundi' in his *Apophthegmatum opus cum primis frugiferum* (Leiden, 1533), part 3, no. 171.

6 Gerd van den Heuvel, 'Cosmopolite, Cosmopoli(ti)sme', in *Handbuch politisch-sozialer Grundbegriffe in Frankreich 1680–1820. Heft 6*, Rolf Reichardt et al., eds. (Munich: Oldenbourg, 1986), 41–55 at 35.

7   Adrian Marino, 'Literature and Ideology in the Republic of Letters', in *Aesthetics and the Literature of Ideas. Essays in Honor of A. Owen Aldridge*, François Jost, Melvin J. Friedman, eds. (Newark: University of Delaware Press, 1990), 214–224 at 217; Willem Frijhof, 'Conceptual History, Social History and Cultural History: The Test of "Cosmopolitanism"', in *History of Concepts: Comparative Perspectives*, Iain Hampsher-Monk, Karin Tilmans and Frank van Vree, eds. (Amsterdam: Amsterdam University Press, 1998), 103–114.

8   This sense of this passage is lost in the translation of Cornelis Augustijn, *Erasmus: His Life, Work and Influence*, J.C. Grayson, trans. (Toronto: University of Toronto Press, 1991), 183, who rendered it as: 'I wish to be a citizen of the world, to belong to everyone or rather be alien to everyone.'

9   Margaret C. Jacob, *Strangers Nowhere in the World: The Rise of Cosmopolitanism in Early Modern Europe* (Philadelphia: University of Pennsylvania Press, 2006), 5.

10 This is the position adopted by Thomas J. Schlereth, *The Cosmopolitan Ideal in Enlightenment Thought: Its Form and Function in the Ideas of Franklin, Hume, and Voltaire, 1694–1790* (Notre Dame and London: The University of Notre Dame Press, 1977).

11 An alternative formulation that I have also employed in this work is 'cosmopolitan terminology'.

12 Tamara T. Chin, 'What is Imperial Cosmopolitanism? Revisiting *Kosmopolitēs* and Mundanus', in *Cosmopolitanism and Empire*, Myles Lavan, Richard E. Payne and John Weisweiler, eds. (New York: Oxford University Press, 2016), 129–152 at 130.

13 Diogenes Lärtius, *Lives and Opinions of the Greek Philosophers*, 6.63.

14 H.C. Baldry, *The Unity of Mankind in Greek Thought* (Cambridge: Cambridge University Press, 1965), 108.

15 Plato, *The Republic*, P. Shorey, trans. (Cambridge, MA: Loeb Classical Library, 1935), 9:592a–b; M. Schofield, *The Stoic Idea of the City* (Cambridge: Cambridge University Press, 1991); D. Obbink, 'The Stoic Sage in the Cosmic City', in *Topics in Stoic Philosophy*, K. Ierodiakonou, ed. (Oxford: Oxford University Press, 1999), vol. 7, 178–195; A.A. Long, 'The Concept of the Cosmopolitan in Greek and Roman Thought', *Daedelus* 137 (2008): 50–58. Interestingly, no statement of a similar nature is known in Socrates's writings. See Pauline Kleingeld and Eric Brown, 'Cosmopolitanism', *The Stanford Encyclopedia of Philosophy* (Fall 2014 edition), Edward N. Zalta (ed.), https://plato.stanford.edu/archives/fall2014/entries/cosmopolitanism/

16 Cicero, *Tusculan disputations*, 5.108; Epictetus, *Arr. Epict. Diss.*, 2.10.1–4. See further Chin, 'Imperial Cosmopolitanism', 131. On Epictetus, see Theodore Scaltsas and Andrew S. Mason, eds., *The Philosophy of Epictetus* (Oxford: Oxford University Press, 2010).

17 Philo, *De confusione Linguarum*, 106; Chin, 'Imperial Cosmopolitanism', 135. Further David T. Runia, 'The Idea and the Reality of the City in the Thought of Philo of Alexandria', *Journal of the History of Ideas* 61 (2000): 361–379.
18 Cited in Benjamin Dunning, *Aliens and Sojourners: Self as Other in Early Christianity* (Philadelphia: University of Pennsylvania Press, 2009), 43–44. The Qumran scrolls '11Q18 New Jerusalem' and 'The New Jerusalem' are possibly related to this same tradition; see Michael Chyutin, 'The New Jerusalem: Ideal City', *Dead Sea Discoveries* 1 (1994): 71–97.
19 Dunning, *Aliens and Sojourners*; Troels Engberg-Pedersen, *Paul and the Stoics* (Louisville: Knox, 2000); Troels Engberg-Pedersen, *Cosmology and Self in the Apostle Paul: The Material Spirit* (Oxford: Oxford University Press, 2010); Abraham J. Malherbe, *Paul and the Popular Philosophers* (Minneapolis: Fortress Press, 1989); Johannes Roldanus, 'Références patristiques au "chrétien-étranger" dans les trois premiers siècles', *Cahiers de Biblia Patristica* 1 (1987): 27–52; Reinhard Feldmeier, *Die Christen als Fremde: Die Metapher der Fremde in der antiken Welt, im Urchristentum und im 1. Petrusbrief* (Tübingen: Mohr-Siebeck, 1992). A diffuse evocation of this theme is provided by Julia Kristeva, *Strangers to Ourselves* (Columbia: Columbia University Press, 1991).
20 See the edition of the text in John D. Turner, trans. and ed. 'Allogenes the Stranger', in *The Nag Hammadi Scriptures*, Marvin Meyer, ed. (New York: Harper & Collins, 2008), 679–700.
21 *Constitutiones Apostolorum,* VII, 39.2 quoted in Francis Xavier Funk, *Disascalia et constitutiones apostolorum* (Paderborn, 1906), 440–441.
22 Ambrose, *Letters*, Mary Melchior Beyenka, trans. (New York: Fathers of the Church, 1954), 133. Ambrose repeated this statement in his commentary on the Canticles. See Ambrose, *Sancti Ambrosii Mediolanensis Episcopi Opera Omnia*, vol. 2 (Milan, 1876), 847.
23 The fate of the conceptual background is traced in Luca Scuccimarra, *I Confini del Mondo. Storia del cosmopolitismo dall'antichità al settecento* (Bologna: Il Mulino, 2006).
24 The notion of heavenly citizenship was discussed during the middle ages, most notably by Dante, albeit without recourse to the cosmopolitan vocabulary. See the discussion in Scuccimarra, *I Confini del Mondo*; Claire E. Honess, *From Florence to the Heavenly City: The Poetry of Citizenship in Dante* (Abingdon & New York: Legenda, 2006): Robert R. Edwards, '"The Metropole and the Mayster-Toun": Cosmopolitanism and Late Medieval Literature', in *Cosmopolitan Geographies: New Locations in Literature and Culture*, Vinay Dharwadker, ed. (New York and London: Routledge, 2001), 33–62; Jelena Erdeljan, *Chosen Places: Constructing New Jerusalems in Slavia Orthodoxa* (Leiden: Brill, 2017).

25 An evocative portrayal of Bracciolini's efforts is provided in Stephen Greenblatt, *The Swerve: How the World Became Modern* (New York: W.W. Norton, 2011).
26 Anthony Grafton, *Defenders of the Text: The Traditions of Scholarship in an Age of Science, 1450–1800* (Cambridge, MA: Harvard University Press, 1994); James Turner, *Philology: The Forgotten Origins of the Humanities* (Princeton: Princeton University Press, 2014).
27 Francisco Maria Grapaldi, *De partibus aedium addita modo* (Parma, 1516), 157. The statement is not in any of the earlier editions, the first of which was issued in 1494.
28 In Philo of Alexandria, *Scriptoris eloquentissimi ac Philosophi summi*, Sigismund Gelen, trans. (Louvain, 1555), the Greek *kosmopolitēs* was translated as *civis mundi*. Ambrose's appropriation of the cosmopolitan vocabulary was discussed in Johann Dadré (Dadraeus, 1550–1617), *Loci commvnes similivm et dissimilivm, ex omni propemodvm antiqvitate*, 3rd ed. (Venice: Zalter & Zanettus, 1583, 1st ed. 1577), 9.
29 These words began to appear in polyglot dictionaries in the 1550s, see for example Antonio de Nebrija, *Dictionarium latino-hispanicum* (Antwerp, 1553), s.v. 'Cosmopolites'. On the vernacularization of humanist vocabulary see Douglas M. Painter, 'Humanist Insights and the Vernacular in Sixteenth-Century France', *History of European Ideas* 16 (1993): 67–73.
30 Kathleen Freeman and Hermann Diels, eds. *Ancilla to the Pre-Socratic Philosophers: A Complete Translation of the Fragments* (Cambridge, MA: Harvard University Press, 1948), 123.
31 Cora E. Lutz, 'Musonius Rufus: The Roman Socrates', *Yale Classical Studies* 10 (1947): 3–150 at 69, citing Rufus's essay 'That Exile is Not an Evil'.
32 Justus Lipsius, *Physiologia Stoicorum libri tres* (Anwerp, 1604), 83–86. See further Chapters 5 and 6.
33 Karl. A.E. Enenkel, ed. *Transformations of the Classics via Early Modern Commentaries* (Leiden: Brill, 2013); Ann Moss, *Renaissance Truth and the Latin Language Turn* (Oxford: Oxford University Press, 2003); Anna Eusterschulte and Günter Frank, eds., *Cicero in der Frühen Neuzeit* (Stuttgart-Bad Cannstatt: frommann-holzboog, 2017).
34 Karen O'Brien, *Narratives of Enlightenment. Cosmopolitan History from Voltaire to Gibbon* (Cambridge: Cambridge University Press, 1997), 2.
35 Reinhart Koselleck, 'Einleitung', in *Geschichtliche Grundbegriffe: Historisches Lexikon zur politisch-sozialen Sprache in Deutschland*, Otto Brunner, Werner Conze and Reinhart Koselleck, eds. (Stuttgart: Ernst Klett Verlag, 1972), vol. 1, xiii–xxvii.
36 Respectively Scuccimarra, *I Confini del Mondo*, 91ff; Lorena Cebolla Sanahuja, *Toward Kantian Cosmopolitanism* (London: Palgrave Macmillan, 2017), 19–82;

Derek Heater, *World Citizenship and Government: Cosmopolitan Ideas in the History of Western Political Thought* (London: Palgrave, 1996), 54; Catherine Needham, 'The Idea of Cosmopolitanism in Eighteenth Century Letters', unpublished M.A. diss., University of Illinois, 1919, 12. Heuvel, 'Cosmopolite, Cosmopoli(ti)sme', 41–55 also considered the period between antiquity and the eighteenth century as an 'introductory' era. See also H.J. Busch and Axel Horstman, 'Kosmopolit/Kosmopolitismus', in *Historisches Wörterbuch der Philosophie*, Joachim Ritter and Karlfried Gründer, eds. 8 vols. (Basel: Schwabe & Co., 1976), vol. 4, 1155–1158.

37 Francis Fukuyama, *The End of History and the Last Man* (New York: Free Press, 1992).

38 Matthew Horsman and Andrew Marshall, *After the Nation-State: Citizens, Tribalism and the New World Disorder* (London: Harper Collins Publishers, 1994). Paradoxes of the arguments raised during this period are discussed in Michael Billig, *Banal Nationalism* (London: Sage, 1995).

39 Eric Hobsbawm, *Nations and Nationalism since 1780* (Cambridge: Cambridge University Press, 1990), 181–182; Samuel P. Huntington, 'The Clash of Civilisations?' *Foreign Affairs* 72/3 (1993): 22–49.

40 Martha C. Nussbaum, 'Patriotism and Cosmopolitanism', *Boston Review*, October–November 1994, 3–6.

41 Some of the immediate reactions prompted by the dispute were collected in Martha C. Nussbaum and J. Cohen, eds., *For the Love of Country: Debating the Limits of Patriotism* (Boston: Beacon Press, 1996). See also the slightly later contributions of Jacques Derrida, *Adieu to Emmanuel Levinas*, P.A. Brault and M. Naas, trans. (Stanford: Stanford University Press, 1999); Jacques Derrida, *On Cosmopolitanism and Forgiveness* (London: Routledge, 2001), and further works cited below.

42 See for example Nan Goodman, *The Puritan Cosmopolis: The Law of Nations and the Early American Imagination* (Oxford: Oxford University Press, 2018); Francien Markx, *E.T.A. Hoffmann, Cosmopolitanism, and the Struggle for German Opera* (Leiden: Brill, 2016); Kwame Anthony Appiah, *Cosmopolitanism: Ethics in a World of Strangers* (New York: Norton, 2006); Patrick Hayden, *Cosmopolitan Global Politics* (Farnham: Ashgate, 2005); Mica Nava, *Visceral Cosmopolitanism: Gender, Culture and the Normalisation of Difference* (Oxford and New York: Berg, 2007); Roland Pierik and Wouter Werner, eds. *Cosmopolitanism in Context: Perspectives from International Law and Political Theory* (Cambridge: University of Cambridge Press, 2010); David Held, *Cosmopolitanism: Ideals, Realities, and Deficits* (Cambridge: Polity Press, 2010); Steven Vertovec and Robin Cohen, eds., *Conceiving Cosmopolitanism: Theory, Context, and Practice* (Oxford: Oxford

University Press, 2002); Peter Coulmas, *Weltbürger: Geschichte einer Menschheitssehnsucht* (Reinbeck: Rowohlt, 1990).

43 Bruce Robbins, 'Actually Existing Cosmopolitanism', in *Cosmopolitics: Thinking and Feeling beyond the Nation*, Bruce Robbins and Pheng Cheoh, eds. (Minneapolis: University of Minnesota Press, 1998), 1–19.

44 See Nussbaum, 'Patriotism and Cosmopolitanism'; Martha C. Nussbaum, 'Kant and Stoic Cosmopolitanism', *Journal of Political Philosophy* 5 (2002): 1–25; Rebecka Lettevall and My Klockar Linder, eds., *The Idea of Kosmopolis. History, Philosophy, and Politics of World Citizenship* (Huddinge: Södertörns Höhskola, 2008); Garrett Wallace Brown, *Grounding Cosmopolitanism: From Kant to the Idea of a Cosmopolitan Constitution* (Edinburgh: Edinburgh University Press 2009).

45 Galin Tihanov, 'Cosmopolitanism in the Discursive Landscape of Modernity: Two Enlightenment Articulations', in *Enlightenment Cosmopolitanism*, David Armstrong and Galin Tihanov, eds. (London: Legenda and Routledge, 2011), 136.

46 Galin Tihanov, 'Whose Cosmopolitanism? Genealogies of Cosmopolitanism', in *Whose Cosmopolitanism? Critical Perspectives, Relationalities and Discontents*, Nina Glick Schiller, Andrew Irving, eds. (Oslo: Berghan Books, 2014), 29. This corresponds with the observation of Margaret C. Jacob, 'Assessing the Cosmopolitan', *Eighteenth-Century Studies* 47/3 (2014): 349, that scholars sometimes have 'a well-intended conviction that everything in the Enlightenment and its origins, from Spinoza to Mozart's operas, endorses or facilitates the arrival of the cosmopolitan'.

47 On cosmopolitan mores see Jacob, *Strangers Nowhere in the World*, 4: 'Even when sources do not invoke the word, this book labels as cosmopolitan social practices that others at the time may not have called by that name'; Margaret C. Jacob, 'The Cosmopolitan as a Lived Category', *Daedelus* 137 (2008): 18–25. Frank Ejby Poulsen, 'Anarchasis Cloots and the Birth of Modern Cosmopolitanism', in *Critique of Cosmopolitan Reason: Timing and Spacing the Concept of World Citizenship*, Rebecka Lettevall and Kristian Petrov, eds. (Bern: Peter Lang, 2014), 87–117 at 88.

48 Pauline Kleingeld, *Kant and Cosmopolitanism: The Philosophical Ideal of World Citizenship* (Cambridge: Cambridge University Press, 2012), 207.

49 A meticulous study of the Enlightenment period is provided by Andrea Albrecht, *Kosmopolitismus. Weltbürgerdiskurse in Literatur, Philosophie und Publizistik um 1800* (Berlin: De Gruyter, 2005).

50 Quentin Skinner, 'Rhetoric and Conceptual Change', *Finnish Yearbook of Political Thought* 3 (1999), 60–73 at 63; Quentin Skinner, 'Language and Social Change', in *Quentin Skinner and his Critics*, James Tully, ed. (Princeton: Princeton University

Press, 1988), 119–133; Quentin Skinner, 'Meaning and Understanding in the History of Ideas', in Quentin Skinner, *Visions of Politics*, 3 vols. (Cambridge: Cambridge University Press, 2002), vol. 1, 57–89.

Chapter 2

1. See for example Paul Hazard, 'Cosmopolite', in *Mélanges d'histoire littéraire générale et comparée offerts à Ferdinand Baldensperger*, 2 vols. (Paris: Champion, 1930), vol. 1, 354–364 at 354–355; Jacob, *Strangers Nowhere in the World*, 5.
2. Guillaume Postel, *De la République des Turcs: & là où l'occasion s'offrera, des meurs & loy de tous Muhamedistes* (Poitiers: de Marnef, 1560).
3. Jacob, *Strangers Nowhere in the World*, 5.
4. Thierry Hentsch, *Imagining the Middle East*, Fred A. Read, trans. (Montréal: Black Rose Books, 1992), 65; Tom Genrich, *Authentic Fictions: Cosmopolitan Writing of the Troisème République* (Bern: Peter Lang, 2004), 21–22.
5. Heuvel, 'Cosmopolite, Cosmopoli(ti)sme', 36.
6. William J. Bouwsma, *Concordia Mundi: The Career and Thought of Guillaume Postel, 1510–1581* (Cambridge, MA: Harvard University Press, 1957), 130.
7. For a grounded discussion of Postel's views concerning women see Yvonne Petry, *Gender, Kabbalah, and the Reformation: The Mystical Theology of Guillaume Postel* (Leiden: Brill, 2004).
8. Anthony Pagden, 'Stoicism, Cosmopolitanism, and the Legacy of European Imperialism', *Constellations* 7/1 (2000), 3–22 at 4.
9. Cited in Ina Baghdiantz McCabe, *Orientalism in Early Modern France: Eurasian Trade, Exoticism, and the Ancien Régime* (Oxford: Berg, 2008), 53. For the 1584 description of Postel see Antoin de Verdier, *Les bibliothèques françoises de la Croix du Maine et Du Verdier Nouvelle Édition* (Paris 1773), vol. 5, 115.
10. Further concerning the characteristics of Postel's thought see Judith Weiss, 'Structure amid the Chaos: The Quadruple Structure in Guillaume Postel's Thought', *The Journal of Religion* 99/3 (2019): 361–382.
11. Postel, *Quatuor librorum de orbis terrae concordia Primus* (Paris 1543), sig. a1v: 'Librorvm argvmenta. Primo, religionis christianæ placita rationibus philosophicis docentur. Secundo, uita educatio moresque Muhamedis legislatoris Arabum eiusque sectatorum traditur, demum Alcoranum à capite ad calcem ex Arabico excutitur & refutatur. Tertio, quid commune totus orbis tam iure humano quam diuino habeat. Quarto, qua arte sine seditione falsæ dedeo dijsue persuasiones ad ueram pertrahi poßint.'

12 Postel, *Le Loy Salique*; Alexandre Y. Haran, *Le lys et le globe. Messianisme dynastique et rêve impérial en France aux xvie et xviie siècles* (Paris: Champ Vallon, 2000), 111–114.
13 Bouwsma, *Concordia mundi*, 68.
14 Bouwsma, *Concordia mundi*, 13.
15 Postel, *Merveilles du monde*, 85v.
16 Postel, Πανδενωσια: *compositio omnium dissidorum* (Basel, 1547).
17 Marion Leathers Kuntz, *Guillaume Postel, Prophet of the Restitution of all Things. His Life and Thought* (The Hague: M. Nijhoff, 1981) 72–74.
18 Reproduced in Ján Kvačala, ed. *Postelliana. Urkundliche Beiträge zur Geschichte der Mystik im Reformationszeitalter* (Juriev, 1915), 48. The translation is from Bouwsma, *Concordia mundi*, 216, with some modifications.
19 Postel, *Le livre de la concorde entre le Coran et les Évangiles* (1553); Bouwsma, *Concordia Mundi*, 214.
20 Postel, *De orbis concordia*, 258: '[…] si [sc. *Koran*] vincet, omnes fient Mussulmani'.
21 Postel, *Les premiers éléments d'Euclide chrestien, pour la raison de la divine et ethernelle verité demonstrer* (Paris, 1579).
22 Postel, *L'histoire memorable des expeditions depuys la deluge faictes par les Gauloys ou Francoys* (Paris, 1552), sig. 74r.
23 Postel, *Description et charte de la terre Saincte, quie est la propriété de Iesus Christ* (No Place: No Printer, [1553]). On its dating I have followed Marcel Destombes, 'Guillaume Postel cartographe', in *Guillaume Postel 1581-1981* (Paris: Guy Trédaniel, 1985), 361–371. Claude de *Guillaume Postel publies en France et leurs editeurs (1538-1579)* (Geneva: Droz, 1992).
24 Postel, *La tierce partie des orientales histoires, ou est exposée la condition, puissance et revenu de l'Empire Turquesque* (Poitiers, 1560).
25 Postel, *La tierce partie*, 87–88; Bouwsma, *Concordia mundi*, 250.
26 François Secret, *Postelliana* (Nieuwkoop: B. de Graaf, 1981), 47–54.
27 In a tract on sacred chronology preserved in Paris, Bibliothèque nationale, MS fr. 2116, fol. 23r, Boulaese called himself 'Galoys Cosmopolite'. On Boulaese see Irena Backus, trans. and ed., *Guillaume Postel et Jean Boulaese. De summopere (1566) et Le Miracle de Laon (1566)* (Geneva: Droz, 1995). Kuntz, *Postel*, 158–162 argued that 'Boulaese' was merely a pseudonym used by Postel.
28 Irena Backus, *Le miracle de Laon. Le déraisonable, le raisonnable, l'apocalyptique et le politique dans les recits du miracle de Laon (1566-1578)* (Geneva: Droz, 1994).
29 Robert John Wilkinson, *The Kabbalistic Scholars of the Antwerp Polyglot Bible* (Leiden: Brill, 2007), 56–57.
30 Jehan Boulaese, *Le Miracle de Laon en Lannoys* (Cambray: Lombard, 1566).
31 Postel, *Des merveilles du monde*, 78r; Bouwsma, *Concordia mundi*, 18.

32 Secret, *Postelliana*, 221. On Postel's self-representation as an ass, see further Kuntz, *Postel*, 132–133 and the nuanced study by Nuccio Ordine, *Giordano Bruno and the Philosophy of the Ass*, Henryk Baranski and Arielle Saiber, trans. (New Haven: Yale University Press, 1996).

33 Postel, *De la République des Turcs*, iv. I thank Peter Cryle for his assistance in translating this passage.

34 Jean-François Maillard, 'Postel le Cosmopolite', in *Documents oubliés sur l'alchimie, la kabbale et Guillaume Postel*. S. Matton et al, eds. (Geneva: Droz 2001), 197–198.

35 Postel, *De originibus*, 57; Guillaume Postel, *Candelabri typici in Mosis tabernaculo ... interpretatio* (No Place, 1547), passim; Postel, *De nativitate mediatoris ultima, nunc futura et toti orbi terrarum in singulis ratione praeditis manifestanda, opus* (No Place, 1547).

36 Postel, *De originibus*, 64–66. William J. Bouwsma, 'Postel and the Significance of Renaissance Cabalism', *Journal of the History of Ideas* 15 (1954): 218–232 suggests that Postel's source for this idea may have been the *Zohar*.

37 Guillaume Postel, 'Aphorismoi ... in operis sui De orbis terrae concordia suppetias ...' Paris BNF, Lat.3401, fol. 18r; Secret, *Postelliana*, 198 points out that 'Goileelmo' may play on the Hebrew לאוג (goel), meaning 'redeemer'.

38 Claude Postel, *Les écrits de Guillaume Postel* (Geneva: Droz, 1992), 39–40; Secret, *Postelliana*, 20.

39 Postel, 'Aphorismoi', in Secret, *Postelliana*, 221.

40 J. Roberts and A.G. Watson, eds. *John Dee's Library Catalogue* (London: The Bibliographical Society, 1990), no. 1623.

41 Roberts and Watson, *Library Catalogue*, nos. 372, 432, 486, 557, 826, 868, 1210, 1619, 1622, 1623, B267, D18.

42 Dee's exemplar is in London, Library of the Royal College of Physicians, shelfmark D 144/14, 21b. The passage is from Postel, *De originibus*, 57.

43 For example David Armitage, *The Ideological Origins of the British Empire* (Cambridge: Cambridge University Press, 2000), 105; David Armitage, 'The Elizabethan Idea of Empire', *Transactions of the Royal Historical Society* 14 (2004): 269–277; Ken MacMillan, 'Discourse on History, Geography, and Law: John Dee and the Limits of the British Empire, 1576–80', *Canadian Journal of History* 36:1 (2001): 1–25.

44 William Sherman, *John Dee: The Politics of Reading and Writing in the English Renaissance* (Amherst: University of Massachusetts Press, 1995), 144; Graham Yewbrey, 'John Dee and the "Sidney Group": Cosmopolitics and Protestant "Activism" in the 1570s'. Unpublished PhD dissertation, University of Hull, 1981. See also Jafe Arnold, 'Esoteric Imperialism: The Solomonic-Theurgic Mystique of John Dee's British Empire', *Endeavour* 43 (2019): 17–24.

45 Glyn Parry, 'John Dee and the Elizabethan British Empire in its European Context', *The Historical Journal* 49, 3 (2006): 643–675; Glyn Parry, *The Arch-Conjuror of England: John Dee* (New Haven: Yale University Press, 2011).
46 Parry, 'Dee and the Elizabethan British Empire', 644.
47 Brian C. Lockey, *Early Modern Catholics, Royalists, and Cosmopolitans: English Transnationalism and the Christian Commonwealth* (London: Ashgate, 2015), 8.
48 Parry, *Arch-Conjuror*, 53. Dee's reference to Genesis 27:28 ('May God give thee of the dew of heaven and of the fat of the earth') in *Monas* reminds one of Postel's other appellation 'Rorispergus Cosmopolites'.
49 I quote from the edition published by C.H. Josten, 'A Translation of John Dee's *Monas hieroglyphica* (Antwerp, 1564), with an Introduction and Annotations', *Ambix* 12 (1964), 84–221, here at 117.
50 Dee, *Monas hieroglyphica*, 201.
51 Dee, *Monas hieroglyphica*, 201, 137.
52 Parry, *Arch-Conjuror*, 181 shows that Dee was as good as his word, for in 1585 he offered his wisdom to Maximilian's son, the Holy Roman Emperor Rudolf II.
53 Dee, *Monas hieroglyphica*, 143.
54 Dee, *Monas hieroglyphica*, 119.
55 Peter J. Forshaw, 'The Early Alchemical Reception of John Dee's *Monas Hieroglyphica*', *Ambix* 52 (2005): 247–269; Andrew Campbell, 'The Reception of John Dee's *Monas hieroglyphica* in Early Modern Italy: The Case of Paulo Antonio Foscarini (c.1552–1616)', *Studies in the History and Philosophy of Science* 43 (2012): 519–529.
56 Parry, *Arch-Conjuror*, 68–69.
57 John Dee, *General and rare memorials pertayning to the perfect arte of navigation: annexed to the paradoxall cumpas, in playne: now first published: 24 yeres, after the first invention thereof* (London, 1577). The original manuscript is preserved in Oxford, Bodleian Library, MS Ashmole 1789, fols. 61r–115v. Dee's other works on this subject include 'Of famous and rich discoveries' (London, British Library, MS Cotton Vitellius C.VII, fols. 26r–269v), which Dee completed in mid-1577. Between November 1577 and July 1578, Dee composed his 'Brytanici Imperii Limites', now extant in BL MS Add. 59681, an authorial copy of 1593 from a lost original. Finally, in early September 1597 Dee authored 'The British sea sovereignty' (BL MS Harley 249, fols. 95–105).
58 Dee, *Memorials*, sig. ε iii^v; sig. ε*ii^r, p.3, etc.
59 Dee, *Memorials*, 54.
60 Sherman, *John Dee*: 144; Lockey, *Early Modern Catholics*, 190.

61 Dee, *Memorials*, sig. ▲1r.
62 Dee quoted in Samuel Purchas, *Hakluytus posthumus or Purchas his Pilgrimes*, 5 vols. (London, 1625), vol. 1, 9; Parry, *Arch-Conjuror*, 112 shows that Dee's angelic magic was central to his philosophical work.
63 Laurentius Grimaldus, *De optimo senatore libri duo* (Venice, 1568); Roberts and Watson, *Dee's Library Catalogue*, no. 417 and the note on p. 88; Anon, *John Dee's Books in the Royal College of Physicians' Library. A Handlist* (London [2016]), 10. On Grimaldus see further Aleksander Stępkowski, ed. *O senatorze doskonałym studia: Prace upamiętniające postać i twórczość Wawrzyńca Goślickiego* (Warsaw: Kancelaria Senatu, 2009).
64 Grimaldus, *De optimo senatore*, sigs. 1v–2r; I have used the anonymous English translation published as Laurentius Grimaldus, *The Counsellor. Exactly pourtraited in two Bookes. Wherin the Offices of Magistrats, The happie life of Subiectes, and the felicitie of Common-weales is pleasantly and pithilie discoursed* (London, 1593), 2–3.
65 Grimaldus, *Counsellor*, 3.
66 Dee, *Memorials*, 64.
67 Dee, *Memorials*, sig. ε*ir–v.
68 Dee, *Memorials*, 10.
69 Dee, *Memorials*, 52–53.
70 London, British Library, MS. Add. 59861. I have consulted John Dee, *The Limits of the British Empire*, Ken MacMillan with Jennifer Abeles, eds. (Westport & London: Praeger, 2004).
71 Dee, *Limits of the British Empire*, 48.
72 Claude Postel, *L'homme prophétique. Science et magie à la Renaissance*. (Paris: Les Belles Lettres, 1999).
73 Prague, National Museum, Ms. VI D 17 (5 C 15 a): 'Diss Buch ... ist dem ... Edvardo Kelleo von Imanii und auf Nue Lüben, Röm. Khay. May. Rathen, von mir Caspar Littman aufm Brüxer Schloss 22. Mai a. 1597 ausgeschriben'. On Kelley see Michael Wilding, 'A Biography of Edward Kelly', in *Mystical Metal of Gold: Essays on Alchemy and Renaissance Culture*, Stanton J. Linden, ed. (New York: AMS Press, 2007), 35–114; Rafał T. Prinke, 'Beyond Patronage: Michael Sendivogius and the Meanings of Success in Alchemy', in *Chymia: Science and Nature in Medieval and Early Modern Europe*, M. López Pérez et al., eds. (Newcastle upon Tyne: Cambridge Scholars, 2010), 175–231 at 180–186; Jennifer M. Rampling, 'John Dee and the Alchemists: Practising and Promoting English Alchemy in the Holy Roman Empire', *Studies in History and Philosophy of Science* 43 (2012): 498–508.
74 John Dee, *A Letter, Containing a moste briefe Discourse Apologeticall, with a plaine Demonstration, and feruent Protestation, for the lawfull, sincere, very faithfull and Christian course, of the Philosophicall studies and exercises, of a certaine studious*

Gentleman (London, 1599, repr. 1605). On the practice of autobibliography see Jürgen Beyer and Leigh T.I. Penman, 'Printed Autobibliographies from the Sixteenth and Seventeenth Centuries', *Documenting the Early Modern Book World: Inventories and Catalogues in Manuscript and Print* in Malcolm Walsby and Natasha Constantinidou, eds., (Leiden: Brill, 2013), 161–184.

75 Dee, *Discourse Apologeticall*, sig. B3v–B4r.
76 For further context on the passage that follows see Peer Schmidt, *Spanische Universalmonarchie oder 'teutsche Libertet.' Das spanische Imperium in der Propaganda des Dreißigjährigen Krieges* (Stuttgart: Franz Steiner Verlag, 2001).
77 Latin editions were printed in 1640; an English translation was issued as Campanella, *His advice to the King of Spain for attaining the universal monarchy of the world* (London, 1654).
78 John Headley, *Tomasso Campanella and the Transformation of the World* (Princeton, NJ: Princeton University Press, 1997), 211–212.
79 Christoph Besold, 'Anhang der Spanischem Monarchi Campanellæ,' in Campanella, *Von der Spannischen Monarchy . . .* (No Place, 1623), 34.
80 Besold, 'Anhang', 48. In addition to the Rosicrucians, Besold may have had in mind Wilhelm Eo Neuheuser, whose vision of a Holy United Roman Empire caused consternation among Lutherans. See Leigh T.I. Penman, *Hope and Heresy: The Problem of Chiliasm in Lutheran Confessional Culture, 1570–1630* (Dordrecht: Springer, 2019), 85–98.
81 On Kuhlmann see Walter Dietze, *Quirinus Kuhlmann. Ketzer und Poet. Versuch einer monographischen Darstellung von Leben und Werk* (Berlin: Rütten & Loening, 1963); Wilhelm Schmidt-Biggemann, 'Salvation through Philology: The Poetical Messianism of Quirinus Kuhlmann (1651–1689)', in *Toward the Millennium: Messianic Expectations from the Bible to Waco*. P. Schäfer and M.R. Cohen, eds. (Leiden: Brill, 1998), 259–298.
82 Jan Amos Comenius, *Lux e tenebris, novis radiis aucta* (No Place [Amsterdam]: No Printer, 1665).
83 Comenius, *Lux e tenebris*, 472–473. On Drábik see Libor Bernát, *Mikuláš Drábik: Vizionár, mystik a kazateľ Jednoty bratskej* (Trenčin: Trenčianske múzeum v Trenčíne, 2017).
84 Quirinus Kuhlmann, *A.Z! Quirin Kuhlman a Christian Jesuelit his Quinary of Slingstones, against the Goliath of all Kindreds, Peoples and Languages* (Paris, 1680), 22.
85 [Quirinus Kuhlmann], *A.Z. Salomon a Kaiserstein Cosmopolita de monarchia jesuelitica ultimo ævo reservata ad politicos aulicosque orbis terrarum* (London, 1682).
86 Dietze, *Quirinus Kuhlmann*, 335–338; Leonard Forster, 'Quirinus Kuhlmann in Moscow 1689: An Unnoticed Account', *Germano-Slavica* 5 (1978): 317–323.

Chapter 3

1 There are many studies dedicated to charting these changes, including Roger Schlesinger, *In the Wake of Columbus: The Impact of the New World on Europe, 1492–1650*, 2nd ed. (New York: Harlan Davidson, 2006); Andrew Gordon and Bernhard Klein, eds. *Literature, Mapping, and the Politics of Space in Early Modern Britain* (Cambridge: Cambridge University Press, 2002); Hans Schelkshorn, 'The Change of Geographical Worldviews and Francisco De Vitoria's Foundation of a Modern Cosmopolitanism', in *Between Creativity and Norm-Making: Tensions in the Early Modern Era* (Leiden: Brill, 2012), 165–188; Frank Lestringant, *Écrire le monde à la Renaissance: quinze études sur Rabelais, Postel, Bodin et la littérature géographique* (Caen: Paradigme, 1993).
2 Guillaume Postel (Paris) to Abraham Ortelius (Antwerp), printed in J.H. Hessels, ed. *Abraham Ortelii . . . Epistolae* (Cambridge 1887), 186–192 (letter no. 81).
3 Nicolas de Nicolay, *Les quatre premiers livres des navigations et peregrinations Orientales* (Lyon 1568), 1. Nicolay's preface was omitted from the English translation, which was instead dedicated to John Dee's sometime patron Sir Philip Sidney. See Nicolay, *The nauigations, peregrinations and voyages, made into Turkie by Nicholas Nicholay* (London 1585).
4 Nicolay, *Navigations et peregrinations Orientales*, 6–7.
5 Jean Bodin, *The Colloquium of the Seven about Secrets of the Sublime*, Marion Leathers Kuntz, ed., trans. and comm. (University Park, PA: Pennsylvania State University Press, 1975).
6 Marion Leathers Kuntz, 'Introduction', in Bodin, *Colloquium of the Seven*, lxi.
7 Hakluyt, *Principal Navigations, Voyages, and Traffiques, and Discoveries of the English Nation* (London, 1598), vol. 1, sig. *2r.
8 Hakluyt, *Principal Navigations*, vol. 1, 6.
9 Barlow's later *Magneticall aduertisements* (London 1616) would further his engagement with the subject of the lodestone.
10 William Barlow, *The nauigators supply Conteining many things of principall importance belonging to nauigation, with the description and vse of diuerse instruments framed chiefly for that purpose; but seruing also for sundry other of cosmography in generall* (London 1597), sigs. b1v–b2r.
11 Barlow, *The nauigators supply*, sig. b2r.
12 Barlow, *The nauigators supply*, sig. b1v.
13 Samuel Purchas, *Purchas his Pilgrimage. Or Relations of the World and the Religions observed in all Ages and Places discovered, from the Creation vnto this Present* (London: Printed by William Stansby for Henrie Featherstone, 1613), sigs.

q1r, q2r. Matthew Dimmock, 'Faith, Form and Faction: Samuel Purchas's *Purchas His Pilgrimage* (1613)', *Renaissance Studies* 28 (2014): 262–278.

14 Richard McCoy, *Alterations of State: Kingship in the English Reformation* (New York: Columbia University Press, 2002).

15 On the garb of early modern Jesters see further H.C. Erik Midelfort, *A History of Madness in Sixteenth-Century Germany* (Stanford: Stanford University Press, 1999), 245–247.

16 Juvenal, *Satires*, xi. See also Purchas, *Hakluytus posthumus*, 6 for an additional invocation of this maxim.

17 Pliny, *Natural History*, ii, 72.

18 Jean-Marc Besse, *Les grandeurs de la terre. Aspects du savoir géographique à la Renaissance* (Lyon: ENS Editions, 2003), 339.

19 Anne S. Chapple, 'Robert Burton's Geography of Melancholy', *Studies in English Literature* 33 (1993): 99–130.

20 Mercedes Maroto Camino, *Producing the Pacific: Maps and Narratives of Spanish Exploration (1567–1606)* (Amsterdam: Rodopi, 2008), 85; David Turnbull, 'Cook and Tupaia, a Tale of Cartographic Méconnaissance?' in *Science and Exploration in the Pacific: European Voyages to the Southern Oceans in the Eighteenth Century*, Margarette Lincoln, ed. (Woodbridge: Boydell, 1998), 119.

21 Peter Whitfield, *The Image of the World: 20 Centuries of World Maps* (London: The British Library, 1994), 78.

22 Rodney Shirley, 'Who was Epichthonius Cosmopolites?', *Map Collector* (March 1982), 39–40 at 40, offered the somewhat impenetrable translation 'everyman indigenous in this world of ours'. Ayesha Ramachandran, 'How to Theorize the "World": An Early Modern Manifesto', *New Literary History* 48 (2017): 655–684 at 655 suggests that the epithet 'juxtaposes … "earthly ones," with *kosmopolites*, "citizen of the world"', but this seems to miss the point entirely. I thank David Pritchard for his advice on interpreting the pseudonym.

23 Rodney Shirley, *The Mapping of the World: Early Printed World Maps, 1472–1750* (London: Holland Press, 1983), 181, no. 158.

24 Cicero, *Tusculan Disputationes*, iv.17.

25 Yona Pinson, *The Fools' Journey: A Myth of Obsession in Northern Renaissance Art* (Turnhout: Brepols, 2008).

26 Lucia Nuti, 'The World Map as an Emblem: Abraham Ortelius and the Stoic Contemplation', *Imago Mundi* 55 (2003): 38–55; Richard Helgerson, 'The Folly of Maps and Modernity', in *Literature, Mapping, and the Politics of Space in Early Modern Britain*, Andrew Gordon and Bernhard Klein, eds. (Cambridge: Cambridge University Press, 2001), 243.

27 Shirley, 'Epichthonius Cosmopolites', 39–40 identifies Oronce Finé (1494–1555) as a possible creator, although the evidence for his assertion is unclear.
28 Philip Benedict, *Graphic History: The Wars, Massacres, and Troubles of Tortorel and Perrissin* (Geneva: Droz, 2007), 66–71.
29 Postel, *Les écrits de Guillaume Postel*; Destombes, 'Guillaume Postel cartographe', 361–371.
30 Ramachandran, 'How to Theorize the "World"', 661–662.
31 See further Cora E. Lutz, 'Democritus and Heraclitus', *The Classical Journal* 49/7 (1954), 309–314; A. Blankert, 'Heraclitus en Democritus: in het bijzonder in de nederlandse kunst van de 17de eeuw', *Nederlands Kunsthistorisch Jaarboek* 18 (1967): 31–124.
32 Denis E. Cosgrove, *Apollo's Eye: A Cartographic Genealogy of the Earth in the Western Imagination* (Baltimore: Johns Hopkins University Press, 2001), 41.
33 Shirley, *Mapping of the World*, 155. See further Michael Wintle, 'Renaissance Maps and the Construction of the Idea of Europe', *Journal of Historical Geography* 25 (1999): 137–165 at 146–147.
34 Elke Anna Werner, 'Triumphierende Europa – Klagende Europa. Zur visuellen Konstruktion europäischer Selbstbilder in der Frühen Neuzeit', in *Europa- Stier und Sternenkranz. Von der Union mit Zeus zum Staatenverbund*. Roland Alexander Ißler and Almut-Barbara Renger, eds. (Göttingen: Vandenhoeck & Ruprecht, 2009), 241–260.
35 Jodocus Hondius, *Typus totius orbis terrarum. In quo & Christiani militis certamen super terram (in pietatis studiosi gratiam) graphicè designatur* [Antwerp? c. 1596].
36 Jeremy Harwood, *To the End of the Earth: 100 Maps that Changed the World* (Cape Town: Stuik Publishing, 2006), 86.
37 Peter Barber, 'The Christian Knight, the Most Christian King and the Rulers of Darkness', *The Map Collector* 52 (1990): 8–13; Francis Carey, ed. *Apocalypse and the Shape of Things to Come* (London: British Museum Press, 1999), 193.
38 Joanne Woolway Grenfell, 'Do Real Knights Need Maps? Charting Moral, Geographical and Representational Uncertainty in Edmund Spenser's *The Faerie Queene*', in *Literature, Mapping, and the Politics of Space in Early Modern Britain*, Andrew Gordon and Bernhard Klein, eds. (Cambridge: Cambridge University Press, 2002), 224–238 at 227.
39 On this trope see further Juergen Hahn, *The Origins of the Baroque Concept of Peregrinatio* (Chapel Hill: University of North Carolina Press, 1973) and Andreas Wang, *Der 'Miles Christianus' im 16. und 17. Jahrhundert und seine mittelalterliche Tradition. Ein Beitrag zum Verhältnis von sprachlicher und graphischer Bildlichkeit* (Frankfurt: Peter Lang, 1975).

40 See further Dieter Breuer, ed. *Frömmigkeit in der frühen Neuzeit: Studien zur religiösen Literatur des 17. Jahrhunderts in Deutschland* (Amsterdam: Rodopi, 1984).
41 The starting point for Comenius researchers remains Milada Blekastad, *Comenius: Versuch eines Umrisses von Leben, Werk und Schicksal des Jan Amos Komenský* (Oslo and Prague: Universitets Forlaget and Academia Praha, 1969).
42 For a discussion of Comenius's sources see Dmitri Čiževsky, 'Comenius' *Labyrinth of the World*: Its Themes and their Sources', *Harvard Slavic Studies* 1 (1970): 85–135. See also Howard Louthan and Andrea Sterk, 'Introduction', in Comenius, *The Labyrinth of the World and the Paradise of the Heart*, Howard Louthan and Andrea Sterk, trans. and eds. (New York: Paulist Press, 1998), 7–45 at 31, 42.
43 Comenius, *Labyrinth of the World*, 66.
44 Comenius, *Labyrinth of the World*, 71–77, 112–117, 125–138.
45 Comenius, *Labyrinth of the World*, 187.
46 Comenius, *Labyrinth of the World*, 222–223.
47 Richard L. Greaves, *Glimpses of Glory: John Bunyan and English Dissent* (Stanford: Stanford University Press, 2002); Nancy Rosenfeld, *John Bunyan's Imaginary Writings in Context* (New York and London: Routledge 2018). On Comenius and Bunyan see Lubomír Balcar, 'Theologické srovnání Komenského "Labyrintu světa's Bunyanovou knihou Pilgrim's Progress"', *Archiv pro Badání o Životě a Spisech J.A. Komenského* 14 (1938): 113–125.
48 John Bunyan, *Grace Abounding to the Chief of Sinners* (London, 1666), 82. See further Brainerd P. Stranahan, 'Bunyan and the Epistle to the Hebrews: His Source for the Idea of Pilgrimage in "The Pilgrim's Progress"', *Studies in Philology* 79/3 (1982): 279–296.
49 John Bunyan, *The Pilgrim's Progress from Earth to Heaven* (London, 1679).
50 See the nuanced study by Marina Leslie, *Renaissance Utopias and the Problem of History* (Ithaca: Cornell University Press, 1998); Chloë Houston, *The Renaissance Utopia: Dialogue, Travel, and the Ideal Society* (London: Routledge, 2014); J.C. Davis, *Utopia and the Ideal Society: A Study of English Utopian Writing, 1516–1700* (Cambridge: Cambridge University Press, 1981).
51 Abraham Ortelius, 'VTOPIÆ TYPVS, EX Narratione Raphaelis Hythlodæi, Descriptione D. Thomas Mori, Delineatione Abrahami Ortelij' [Antwerp: 1595]. Cécile Kruythooft, 'Map of Utopia by Abraham Ortelius', *The Map Collector* 16 (1981): 10–14; Ramachandran, 'How to Theorize the "World"', 662, 664.
52 Brigitte Biot, 'Barthélemy Aneau, lecteur de l'*Utopie*', *Moreana* 121 (1995), 11–28; Brigitte Biot, *Barthélemy Aneau, régent de la Renaissance lyonnaise* (Paris: Champion, 1995). See further the material collected in Aneau, *Alector ou le coq. Histoire fabuleuse*, Marie Madeleine Fontaine, ed. 2 vols. (Geneva: Droz, 1996).

53 Thomas More, *La Republique d'Utopie* [...] *Traduite nouuellement de Latin* (Lyon, Saugrain 1559). Kirsti Sellevold, 'The French Versions of Utopia', in *Thomas More's Utopia in Early Modern Europe: Paratexts and Contexts*, Terence Cave, ed. (Manchester and New York: Manchester University Press, 2008), 77 suggests that *Alector* was written while Aneau laboured on his translation of More.

54 Jenny Meyer, 'Barthélemy Aneau's *Alector ou le coq* and the Paradox of Renaissance Cosmopolitanism', *Renaissance and Reformation* 38 (2015): 5–26 at 7.

55 Barthélemy Aneau, *Alector, Histoire Fabuleuse* (Lyon: Pierre Fradin, 1560), sig. 9r. An English translation was issued as *ΑΛΕΚΤΟΡ: The Cock. Containing the First Part of the Most Excellent and Mytheologicall Historie of the Valorous Squire Alector; Sonne to the Renowned Prince Macrobius Franc-Gal and the Peerelesse Princesse Priscaraxe, Queene of High Tartary*, John Hammon, trans. (London, 1590).

56 Aneau, *Alector*, sigs. 9r–v; Aneau, *ΑΛΕΚΤΟΡ*, 11.

57 Aneau, *Alector*, sig. 148r; Aneau, *ΑΛΕΚΤΟΡ*, 187.

58 See further Sellevold, 'The French Versions of Utopia', 78.

59 Tomasso Campanella, *La Città del Sole: Dialogo Poetico. The City of the Sun: A Poetical Dialogue*, Daniel J. Donno, trans. (Berkeley: University of California Press, 1981), 109. The title recalls the *civitas solis* of the vulgate version of Isaiah 19:18.

60 Campanella, *La Città del Sole*, 109.

61 Francis Bacon, *Nevv Atlantis. A Worke vnfinished.* (London, 1628). I have consulted the edition printed in Bacon, *The Major Works*, Brian Vickers, ed. (Oxford: Oxford University Press, 2008), 457–490.

62 An influential representative of the former position is Howard B. White's landmark study, *Peace among the Willows: The Political Philosophy of Francis Bacon* (The Hague: Martinus Nijhoff, 1968). See further the literature cited in Stephen A. McKnight, *The Religious Foundations of Francis Bacon's Thought* (Columbia: University of Missouri Press, 2006), 10–12.

63 Bacon, *Major Works*, 465.

64 Bacon, *Major Works*, 465.

65 The significance of this theme in Bacon's work is emphasised by Mordechai Feingold, '*And Knowledge Shall Be Increased*: Millenarianism and the Advancement of Learning Revisited', *The Seventeenth Century* 28 (2013): 363–393; J.R. Webb, '"Knowledge Will be Manifold": Daniel 12:4 and the Idea of Intellectual Progress in the Middle Ages', *Speculum* 89/2 (2014): 307–357, especially at 343–349.

66 White, *Peace among the Willows*, 135.

67 White, *Peace among the Willows*, 135–136.

68 Bacon, *Major Works*, 461.

69 Bacon, *Major Works*, 471.
70 Bacon, *Major Works*, 471.
71 Richard Serjeantson, 'Natural Knowledge in the *New Atlantis*', in *Francis Bacon's New Atlantis*, Bronwen Price, ed. (Manchester: Manchester University Press, 2002), 89.
72 Bacon, *Major Works*, 488.
73 Hartlib, '[Dedicatory Epistle]', in [Michael Gühler], *Clavis Apocalyptica* (London, 1651), sigs. *2v–*3r. On this work see further Martin Mulsow, 'Who was the Author of the *Clavis Apocalyptica* of 1651? Millenarianism and Prophecy between Silesian Mysticism and the Hartlib Circle', in *Millenarianism and Messianism in Early Modern European Culture: Continental Millenarians: Protestants, Catholics, Heretics*, ed. J.C. Laursen and R.H. Popkin (Dordrecht: Springer, 2001), 57–75.
74 Hartlib, '[Dedicatory Epistle]', sigs. *3v–*4r. Cf. Feingold, '*And Knowledge Shall Be Increased*', 381–382, who argues that Hartlib never 'yearned for an imminent millennium'.
75 Sheffield, Sheffield University Library, Hartlib Papers, 28/1/15a (Hartlib's Ephemerides for 1649).
76 Peter Sherlock, *Monuments and Memories in Early Modern England* (Aldershot: Ashgate, 2008), 123.

Chapter 4

1 Johann Valentin Andreae, *De reipublicæ Christianopolitanæ descriptio* (Straßburg, 1619). I have used the critical edition Johann Valentin Andreae, *Christianopolis*, Edward H. Thompson, trans. and ed. (Dordrecht: Kluwer, 1999), 155. An edition of the German and Latin texts is also in Johann Valentin Andreae, *Gesammelte Schriften. Band 14. Reipublicae Christianopolitanae descriptio (1619) – Christenburg Das ist: ein schön geistlich Gedicht (1626)*, Frank Böhling and Wilhelm Schmidt-Biggemann, trans. and eds. (Stuttgart: frommann-holzboog, 2017).
2 Andreae, *Christianopolis*, 156.
3 Andreae, *Christianopolis*, 280.
4 Andreae, *Christianopolis*, 283.
5 On Andreae see Richard von Dülmen, *Die Utopie einer christlichen Gesellschaft: Johann Valentin Andreae (1586–1654)* (Stuttgart-Bad Cannstatt, 1978); Martin Brecht, *Johann Valentin Andreae, 1586–1654* (Göttingen: Vandenhoeck & Ruprecht, 2008).

6 Samuel Crook, *TA ΔΙΑΦΕΡΟΝΤΑ, or, Divine characters in two parts: acutely distinguishing the more secret and undiscerned differences between 1. the hypocrite in his best dresse of seeming virtues and formal duties, and the true Christian in his real graces and sincere obedience* (London, 1658).
7 Cf. Psalm 17:14; 'By your hand save me from such people, Lord, from those of this world whose reward is in this life; May what you have stored up for the wicked fill their bellies.'
8 Skinner, 'Rhetoric and Conceptual Change', 65–66.
9 Skinner, 'Rhetoric and Conceptual Change', 65.
10 I have only found one Catholic example, Polycarp de la Rivière (1586–1639), *L'Adieu du Monde, ou Le mépris de ses vaines grandeurs & plaisirs périssables* (Lyon, 1619), 470. In this work the author condemned the 'Cosmopolite' – a word he knew from Diogenes Laertius and Socrates – as being obsessed with worldly vanities and concerns. On the lack of appeal of the cosmopolitan vocabulary to French Protestants, see George Hoffmann, *Reforming French Culture: Satire, Spiritual Alienation, and Connection to Strangers* (Oxford: Oxford University Press, 2017), 123–125.
11 See further Douglas Shantz, 'Homeless Minds: The Migration of Radical Pietists, their Writings, and Ideas in Early Modern Europe', in *Pietism in Germany and North America 1680–1820*, Jonathan Strom, et al., eds. (Farnham: Ashgate, 2009), 85–100; Werner Wilhelm Schnabel, 'Exulantenlieder. Über Konstituierung und Verfestigung von Selbst- und Fremdbildern mit literarischen Mitteln', in *Frühneuzeitliche Stereotype. Zur Produktivität und Restriktivität sozialer Vorstellungsmuster*, Mirosława Czarnecka, and Thomas Borgstedt et al., eds. (Bern: Peter Lang, 2010), 317–353; Alexander Schunka, 'Constantia im Martyrium. Zur Exilliteratur des 17. Jahrhunderts zwischen Humanismus und Barock', in *Frühneuzeitliche Konfessionskulturen*, Thomas Kaufmann, Anselm Schubert and Kaspar von Greyerz, eds. (Gütersloh: Gütersloher Verlagshaus, 2008), 175–200; Johannes Müller, 'Transmigrant Literature: Translating, Publishing, and Printing in Seventeenth-Century Frankfurt's Migrant Circles', *German Studies Review* 40/1 (2017): 1–21.
12 I have consulted the edition edited by Roland Edighoffer and printed in Andreae, *Gesammelte Schriften*, vol. 2, 353–447. Hereafter referred to as *Cosmoxenus*.
13 Andreae, *Cosmoxenus*, 434–436, 440.
14 Andreae, *Cosmoxenus*, 402.
15 Andreae, *Cosmoxenus*, 420: 'Regno Christi subditi, militiaeque sacrae milites, civitatis caelestis cives, aeternorum bonorum haeredes.'
16 Andreae, *Cosmoxenus*, 440.

17 Andreae, *Cosmoxenus*, 444.
18 Andreae, *Cosmoxenus*, 396. This statement was also included by Andreae as one of the opening sentences in his *Theca gladii spiritus* (Straßburg, 1616). I have consulted the edition printed in Andreae, *Gesammelte Schriften: Band 5. Theca Gladii Spiritus*. Frank Böhling, ed. (Stuttgart: frommann-holzboog, 2003), 5.
19 Richard von Dülmen, *Die Utopie einer christlichen Gesellschaft*, 136; Christoph Neeb, *Christlicher Hass wider die Welt. Philosophie und Staatstheorie des Johann Valentin Andreae (1586-1654)* (Frankfurt am Main: Peter Lang, 1999). The trope of the true Christian as cosmoxenus appears in Andreae's *Peregrini in Patria errores* (Straßburg, 1618); *Civis Christianus* (Straßburg, 1619), in addition to the works discussed below. See Roland Edighoffer, '"Errores in Patria" zur Ambivalenz der Schöpfung bei Johann Valentin Andreae', in *Das Erbe des Christian Rosenkreuz. Johann Valentin Andreae 1586-1986 und die Manifeste der Rosenkreuzerbruderschaft 1614-1616*, F.A. Jansen, ed. (Amsterdam: In de Pelikaan, 1988), 48-62.
20 Johann Valentin Andeae, *Hercules Christianae luctis XXIV* (Straßburg, 1615).
21 Andreae, *Theca gladii spiritus* (1616), 118-119; Andreae, *Menippus, sive dialogorvm satyricorum centuria* (Cosmopoli [Straßburg?], 1618), 23-24.
22 Andreae, *Mythologiae Christianiae libri tres* (Straßburg, 1619), 128-129.
23 Andreae, *Mythologiae Christianiae*, 76-77.
24 Andreae, *Mythologiae Christianiae*, 258-259.
25 Andreae, *Mythologiae Christianiae*, 258-259.
26 See for example Martin Brecht, 'Die Aufnahme von Arndts "Vier Bücher vom wahren Christenthum"', in *Frömmigkeit oder Theologie: Johann Arndt und die 'Vier Bücher vom wahren Christenthum'*, Hans Otte and Hans Schneider, eds. (Göttingen: Vandenhoeck & Ruprecht, 2007), 231-262; Donald R. Dickson, *The Tessera of Antilia: Utopian Brotherhoods and Secret Societies in Early Modern Germany* (Leiden: Brill, 1999).
27 For a modern introduction to Arndt and his work see Hermann Geyer, *Verborgene Weisheit. Johann Arndts "Vier Bücher vom Wahren Christentum" als Programm einer spiritualistisch-hermetischen Theologie*, 2 vols. (Berlin: De Gruyter, 2001).
28 Andreae, *Christianopolis*, 145.
29 Dickson, *Tessera of Antilia*, 37.
30 Stefania Salvadori, 'From Spiritual Regeneration to Collective Reformation in the Writings of Christoph Besold and Johann Valentin Andreae', *Aries* 14 (2014): 1-19. An occasionally speculative attempt to flesh out further dimensions of this idea is provided by Neeb, *Christlicher Hass wider die Welt*.
31 On Hess see Carlos Gilly and Pleun van der Kooij, *Fama Fraternitatis. Das Urmanifest der Rosenkreuzer Bruderschafft* (Haarlem: Rozekruis Pers, 1999),

17–26; Martin Brecht, 'Chiliasmus in Württemberg im 17. Jahrhundert', *Pietismus und Neuzeit* 14 (1988), 25–49; José Bouman and Cis van Heertum, *Divine Wisdom, Divine Nature: The Message of the Rosicrucian Manifestoes in the Visual Language of the Seventeenth Century* (Amsterdam: In de Pelikaan, 2016), 25–28.

32 Concerning the manifestos see Gilly and van der Kooij, *Fama Fraternitatis;* Carlos Gilly, *Adam Haslmayr: Der erste Verkünder der Manifeste der Rosenkreuzer* (Amsterdam: In de Pelikaan, 1994). The standard text of the manifestos is published in Andreae, *Gesammelte Schriften*, vol. 3.

33 See further Leigh T.I. Penman, '"Sophistical Fancies and Mear Chimaeras?" Traiano Boccalini's *Ragguagli di Parnaso* and the Rosicrucian Enigma', *Bruniana & Campanelliana* 15/1 (2009): 79–98.

34 An accessible preliminary bibliographical survey is provided in Carlos Gilly, *Cimelia Rhodostaurotica: Die Rozenkreuzer im Spiegel der zwischen 1610 und 1660 entstandenen Handschriften und Drucke*, 2nd ed. (Amsterdam: In de Pelikaan, 1994). Gilly's forthcoming *Bibliographia Rosicruciana* (6 vols.) will provide the definitive survey of the extant works.

35 An argument convincingly propounded by John Warwick Montgomery, *Cross and Crucible: Johann and Valentin Andreae, Phoenix of the Theologians*, 2 vols. (Dordrecht: Kluwer, 1973), and nuanced in Roland Edighoffer, *Rose-Croix et société idéale selon Johann Valentin Andreae*, 2 vols. (Paris: Arma Artis, 1981–1987). See further Carlos Gilly, 'Don Quijote und Rosenkreuz: Die *Chymische Hochzeit* als alchemokritischer Ritterroman', *Recherches Germaniques* 13 (2018): 47–62.

36 [Johann Valentin Andreae], *Christianae Societatis Imago* ([Tübingen?] 1620). I cite from [Andreae], *A Modell of a Christian Society*, John Hall, trans. (Cambridge 1647), 6.

37 These works dedicated to Christian reform are collected in Andreae, *Gesammelte Schriften. Band 6. Schriften zur christlichen Reform*, Frank Böhling, ed., comm. and trans. (Stuttgart-Bad-Cannstatt: frommann-holzboog, 2010). On Andreae's utopian enterprises see further G.H. Turnbull, 'Johann Valentin Andreae's Societas Christiana', *Zeitschrift für Deutsche Philologie* 73 (1954): 407–432; 74 (1955), 151–185; Jan Kvačala, *Johann Valentin Andreä's Antheil an geheimen Gesellschaften* (Jurjew: Matthiessen, 1899); Dülmen, *Die Utopie einer christlichen Gesellschaft*, passim and; Dickson, *Tessera*, 18–88. On the translation and dissemination of Andreae's tracts in England see G.H. Turnbull, 'John Hall's Letters to Samuel Hartlib', *The Review of English Studies* 4, 15 (1953): 221–233 and Dickson, *Tessera of Antilia*, 172–180.

38 Andreae, *A Modell of a Christian Society*, 6, 8, 22.

39 Andreae, *A Modell of a Christian Society*, 12.

40 Salvadori, 'From Spiritual Regeneration', 17–19.

41 On these figures see George Huntston Williams, *The Radical Reformation* (Kirksville, MO: Truman State University Press, 1995); Patrick Marshall Hayden-Roy, *The Inner Word and the Outer Word: A Biography of Sebastian Franck* (Zürich: Peter Lang, 1994); Andrew Weeks, *Valentin Weigel: German Religious Dissenter, Speculative Theorist and Advocate of Tolerance* (Albany: SUNY Press, 2000). The literature on Böhme is vast, though an excellent starting point is provided by Bo Andersson, Lucinda Martin, Leigh T.I. Penman and Andrew Weeks, eds., *The World of Jacob Böhme* (Leiden: Brill, 2018). On Böhme's conception of heavenly citizenship see Leigh T.I. Penman, '*Der Weg zu Christo:* Jacob Böhme and Pilgrimage', in *Grund und Ungrund. Der Kosmos des mystichen Philosophen Jacob Böhme*, Claudia Brink and Lucinda Martin, eds. (Dresden: Sandstein Verlag, 2017), 68–81.

42 For a survey of prophets emerging from the Lutheran tradition see Jürgen Beyer, *Lay Prophets in Lutheran Europe, 1500–1750* (Leiden: Brill, 2017); further Jonathan Green, *Printing and Prophecy: Prognostication and Media Change, 1450–1550* (Ann Arbor: University of Michigan Press, 2011).

43 Eusebe Philadelphe Cosmopolite, *Le Reveille-matin des Francois, et de leurs voisins* (Edinburgh [Basel?], 1574). This edition was printed without diacritical marks. Latin, Dutch and German translations were issued later. A detailed study of this work, its backgrounds and its reception, is an urgent scholarly desideratum.

44 Hoffmann, *Reforming French Culture*, 123, 175; Didier Kahn, 'Between Alchemy and Antitrinitarianism: Nicholas Barnaud (*c.* 1539–1604?)', in *Socinianism and Arminianism: Antitrinitarians, Calvinists and Cultural Exchange in Seventeenth Century Europe*, Martin Mulsow, Jan Rohls, eds. (Leiden: Brill, 2005), 82, 85–86.

45 George Goodwin, *Melissa religionis Pontificae ejusdemque apostrophe* (London, 1620). I have used the English translation printed as Goodwin, *Babels balm: or The honey-combe of Romes religion With a neate draining and straining-out of the rammish honey thereof*, John Vicars, trans. (London, 1624).

46 Goodwin, *Babels balm*, 5.

47 Goodwin, *Babels balm*, 82.

48 Lockey, *Early Modern Catholics, Royalists, and Cosmopolitans*, 53 points to Edmund Campion's identification of his place of origin as 'Cosmopoli' as an implication of the universal dominion of the Catholic Church.

49 Heinrich Schneider, *Joachim Morsius und sein Kreis. Zur Geistesgeschichte des 17. Jahrhunderts* (Lübeck: Quitzlow, 1929), 44–47.

50 [Morsius], *Anastasii Philareti Cosmopolitæ epistola sapientissimæ F.R.C. remissa* (Philadelphia: Christianus Harpocratis, [1618]). Morsius also used the pseudonym in [Morsius], *Magische Propheceyung . . . Paracelsi von Entdeckung seiner 3. Schätzen . . .* (Philadelphia, 1625); [Morsius], *Nuncius Olympicus: Von etzlichen geheimen Bücheren und Schrifften . . .* (Philadelphia, 1626). Morsius may have

learned of the cosmopolitan vocabulary through *Les reveille-matins*, passages of which he copied into his commonplace book in Lübeck, Bibliothek der Hansestadt Lübeck, Ms hist. 4° 25,1,70r–71v; 108r–v.
51 [Morsius], *Epistola sapientissimæ F.R.C.*, 'unpag. Anastasius Philaretus, Qui candorem in terrâ quæsiui, non repperi, inuenturus eum in cœlo, vestrisque Cœlo cognatis mentibus.'
52 [Morsius], *Ein güldener Discurs. Von der Freyheit des Gewissens vnd Glaubens . . .* (No Place: No Printer, 1636). An entry in Morsius's commonplace book in Lübeck, Bibliothek der Hansestadt Lübeck, Ms hist. 4° 25,1, fol. 2r contains a similar sentiment, though expressed more pithily: 'Terra exilium Patria cœleum.'
53 Henri Gouhier, *Les Premières Pensées de Descartes: Contribution à l'histoire de l'Anti-Renaissance* (Paris 1958), 109. Chikara Sasaki, *Descartes's Mathematical Thought* (New York & Dordrecht: Springer, 2003), 110 suggests that the pseudonym was inspired by the Greek historian Polybius Megapolitanus (*c*. 200–*c*. 118 BCE).
54 Sasaki, *Descartes's Mathematical Thought*, 110.
55 Valentin Grießmann, Πρόδρομος εὐμενὴς, καὶ ἀποτρεπτικός *Exhibens enneadem quaestionum generalium De Haeresibus ex orco redivivis: Das ist: Getrewer Eckhart/ Welcher in den ersten Neun gemeinen Fragen/ der Wiedertäufferischen/ Stenckfeldischen/ Weigelianischen/ und Calvino-Photinianischen/ Rosen Creutzerischen Ketzereyen/ im Landen herumbstreichende und streiffende wüste Heer zu fliehen/ und als seelenmörderische Räuberey zu meyden verwarnet* (Gera: Andreas Mamitzsch, 1623), 14.
56 Grießmann, *Getrewer Eckhart*, 67.
57 Grießmann, *Getrewer Eckhart*, 67–68. There is a hint of anti-Catholic polemic here, for 'Wallfarts Brüder' was a phrase typically used to refer to Catholic pilgrimage orders.
58 Grießmann, *Getrewer Eckhart*, 95.
59 Patrick Collinson, *The Religion of Protestants: The Church in English Society, 1559–1625* (Oxford: Oxford University Press, 1979), 243–244.
60 Thomas Thomas, *Dictionarium, summa fide ac diligentissime* (London, 1600), sig. Ce2r defined *Mundanus* as 'Worldly or of the World, a Worlding'.
61 Purchas, *Hakluytus posthumus*, 14, 6.
62 Purchas, *Hakluytus posthumus*, 6.
63 Purchas, *Hakluytus posthumus*, 6, 9–10.
64 Purchas, *Hakluytus posthumus*, 10.
65 Purchas, *Hakluytus posthumus*, 9.
66 J.S. McGee, 'On Misidentifying Puritans: The Case of Thomas Adams', *Albion* 30 (1998): 402–418.
67 John Brown, *The Sermons of Thomas Adams, the Shakespeare of Puritan Theologians*, (London, 1909); William Mulder, 'Style and the Man: Thomas Adams,

Prose Shakespeare of Puritan Divines', *Harvard Theological Review* 48 (1955): 129–152.
68 Adams, *The Diuells Banquet Described in sixe Sermons* (London, 1614), 165.
69 Adams, *The Diuells Banquet*, 166.
70 Adams, *Englands Sicknes, comparatively conferred with Israels, Diuided into two sermons* (London, 1615), 74.
71 Adams, *Englands Sicknes*, 75
72 Adams, *Plaine-Dealing, or, a Precedent of Honestie* (London, 1616), 10, and similarly in Adams, *A Commentary or Exposition upon the Divine Second Epistle General, Written by the Blessed Apostle St. Peter* (London, 1633), 274. See also Thomas Drant, *The divine lanthorne, or, A sermon preached in S. Pauls Church* (London, 1637), 15. On concerns about Epicurean philosophy in England during this period, see Reid Barbour, *English Epicures and Stoics: Ancient Legacies in Early Stuart Culture* (Amherst, MA: University of Massachusetts Press, 1998).
73 Thomas Adams, *Eirenopolis: the citie of peace Surueyed and commended to all Christians* (London 1622).
74 Samuel Bennefield, *A Commentary or Exposition vpon the third Chapter of the Prophecie of AMOS. Deliuered In VXII. Sermons* (London, 1628), 311–312.
75 Thomas Reeve, *God's Plea for Nineveh, or, London's precedent for mercy delivered in certain sermons within the city of London* (London 1657), 80.
76 Julia Gasper, 'Vicars, John (1580–1652)', *ODNB*.
77 John Vicars, *A prospectiue glasse to looke into heauen, or The coelestiall Canaan described Together with the soules sacred soliloquie* (London, 1618), sig. E3r. This work was later plagiarised by the royalist John Heydon, *Eugenius Theodidactus. The prophetical trumpeter sounding an allarum to England illustrating the fate of Great Britain, past, present, and to come* (London, 1655), 137 who substituted the words 'carnall worldlings' with the distinctly anticlerical line 'You drunken Vicars.'
78 Vicars also invoked the terminology to praise the poet Joshua Sylvester (1563–1618) as 'no Lordly great *Cosmopolite* ... [but] A true *Nathaniel, Christian-Israelite*'. See Vicars, 'Sacrum Memoriae ornatissimi Pientissimique ipsius Amici, Magistri Josuæ Sylvester', in Guillaume de Bartas, *Du Bartas his Diuine Weekes and Workes*, Joshua Sylvester, trans. (London, 1641), sig. A6r.
79 William Gearing, *God's Soveraignty displayed* (London 1667).
80 Christoph Besold, *Axiomatum de Consilio Politico Appendicula: quæ ad pietatem inprimis ducit* (Frankfurt/Main & Tübingen: Eberhard Wild, 1622), 74: 'Novus homo, liberatus est ab elementis, & terræ limbo, firmamentique iniquitate: non enim est civis mundi, sed cœli.'
81 Bolton, *Hypercritica, or a Rule of Judgement for Writing or reading our Historys* (London, 1722), 241.

82 Besold, 'Anhang der Spanischem Monarchi Campanellæ', 48.
83 Purchas, *Hakluytus posthumus*, 6–7.
84 Thomas Barton, *ΛΟΓΟΣ ΑΓΩΝΙΟΣ or, a Sermon of the Christian Race, preached before his Majesty at Christ-Church in Oxford, May 9 1643. Whereunto is added an advertisement to his country-men, who being misled disaffect the royall cause* ([London], 1643).
85 Barton, *Christian Race*, 10.
86 Vivienne Larminie, 'Crooke, Samuel (1575–1649), Church of England clergyman and author', *ODNB*; Ian Harris, *The Mind of John Locke: A Study of Political Theory in its Intellectual Setting*. Revised ed. (Cambridge: Cambridge University Press, 1998), 28, 33.
87 Larminie, 'Crooke, Samuel', *ODNB*.
88 Crooke, *TA ΔΙΑΦΕΡΟΝΤΑ*, 61.
89 Crooke, *TA ΔΙΑΦΕΡΟΝΤΑ*, 52.
90 On this subject see further Vera Keller, *Knowledge and the Public Interest, 1575–1725* (Cambridge: Cambridge University Press, 2016); Vera Keller and Leigh T.I. Penman, 'From the Archives of Scientific Diplomacy: Science and Shared Interests of Samuel Hartlib's London and Frederick Clodius's Gottorf', *ISIS* 106 (2015): 17–42.
91 Crooke, *TA ΔΙΑΦΕΡΟΝΤΑ*, 61.
92 Crooke, *TA ΔΙΑΦΕΡΟΝΤΑ*, 61.
93 Crooke, *TA ΔΙΑΦΕΡΟΝΤΑ*, 61.
94 Skinner, 'Rhetoric and Conceptual Change', 66.
95 Sigmund von Birken, *HochFürstlicher Brandenburgischer Ulysses* (Bayreuth, 1669), sigs.): (2r–v.
96 William Bates, *A short description of the blessed place and state of the saints above in a discourse upon the word of Our Blessed Saviour, John XIV, 2* (London, 1687), 83–84.

Chapter 5

1 Thomas Blount, *Glossographia, or A dictionary, interpreting all such hard words, whether Hebrew, Greek, Latin, Italian, Spanish, French, Teutonick, Belgick, British or Saxon; as are now used in our refined English tongue* (London, 1656), sig. L4r.
2 It was soon followed by Elisha Coles, *An English Dictionary: Explaining The difficult Terms that are used in Divinity, Husbandry, Physick, Phylosophy, Law, Navigation, Mathematicks, and other Arts and Sciences* (London, 1677), sig. I1r: '*Cosmopolite, -tan*, a Citizen of the world'.

3 Blount, *Glossographia*, sig. L4r. In Blount, *Glossographia*, 2nd ed. (London, 1661), 90, the etymology was expanded to include 'from *Cosmos, mundus*, and *Polites, Cives*'.
4 Francis Bacon, *The History of the Reign of King Henry VII*, Brian Vickers, ed. (Cambridge: Cambridge University Press, 1998), 133.
5 Francis Bacon, *The Essayes or Counsels, Civill and Morall*, Michael Kiernan, ed. (Oxford: Clarendon Press, 1985), 40. The passage appears in a *c.* 1625 revision of an essay first published in 1612.
6 Stefano Guazzo, *Lettere del Stefano Gvazzo* (Venice, 1590), 228 (Guazzo to Cesare Ceppo, 9 October 1560). On Guazzo see John Leon Lievsay, *Stefano Guazzo and the English Renaissance, 1575–1675* (Chapel Hill: University of North Carolina University Press, 1961).
7 Grimaldus, *The Counsellor*, 2–3.
8 Henri Estienne, *Deux dialogues du nouveau langage françois italianizé* (Paris, 1578), I have used the critical edition edited by P. Ristelhuber (Paris, 1885), vol. 2, 269–270. Six years earlier, Estienne included an entry for κοσμοπολίτης in his *Thesauri linguae Graecae* (Paris, 1572), vol. 2, 389, which likely derived from Epictetus.
9 Simon Ford, *The Fall and Funeral of Northampton, in an elegy, Late Published in Latin [...] Since, made English* (London, 1677), 7.
10 'De cosmopolita unde, aut quis ne quærito sed quæ.' Cited in Max Engamarre, 'La Bible de Jérôme Bolsec. Un témoin de l'émergence de la chronologie historique modern,' in *Esculape et Dionysos: mélanges en l'honneur de Jean Céard*, Jean Dupèbe et al., eds. (Geneva: Droz, 2008), 849.
11 John Lyly, *Euphues. The Anatomy of Wit* (London, 1578), 82v. On Lyly see G.K. Hunter, *John Lyly: The Humanist as Courtier* (Cambridge, MA: Harvard University Press, 1962).
12 I have consulted Pierre Charron, *Of Wisdome three books*, Samson Leonard, trans. (London, 1608), 516.
13 Emmanuel Bury, *Littérature et politesse: l'invention de l'honnête homme (1580–1750)* (Paris: Presses Universitaires de France, 1996). On the cultivation of courtly personae see Norbert Elias, *The Civilising Process: Sociogenetic and Psychogenetic Investigations*, Edmund Jephcott, trans. (Oxford: Blackwell, 2000), 389–436.
14 Nicolas Faret, *L'honneste Homme, Das ist: Der Ehrliebende Welt-Mann/ Oder Die von vielen Leuten gesuchte schöne Kunst/ wie einer an grosser Herren Höfen ... sich beliebet und belobet machen könne* (Leipzig, 1648).
15 William de Britaine, *Human Prudence, or the Art by which a man may raise himself and fortune to grandeur* (London, 1680), 36.
16 Cyrano de Bergerac, *Satyrical characters and handsome descriptions in letters written to severall persons of quality* (London, 1658), 135.

17 Antoine Lilti, *The World of the Salons: Sociability and Worldliness in Eighteenth-Century Paris* (Oxford: Oxford University Press, 2015), and the earlier study by Susan Dalton, *Engendering the Republic of Letters: Reconnecting Public and Private Spheres* (Montreal: McGill-Queen's University Press, 2003).
18 On Renaudot see Howard M. Solomon, *Public Welfare, Science, and Propaganda in Seventeenth-Century France: The Innovations of Théophraste Renaudot* (Princeton: Princeton University Press, 1972); Kathleen Anne Welman, *Making Science Social: The Conferences of Théophraste Renaudot, 1633–1642* (Norman, OK: University of Oklahoma Press, 2003).
19 Théophraste Renaudot, ed. *Recueil général des questions traitées és conférences du Bureau d'adresse* (Paris, 1634); Renaudot, *A general collection of discourses of the virtuosi of France, upon questions of all sorts of philosophy, and other natural knowledge made in the assembly of the Beaux Esprits at Paris, by the most ingenious persons of that nation*, G. Havers, trans. (London, 1664), 157. On the 'woman question' see Dominique de Courcelles, *Des femmes et des livres: France en Espagnes XIVe-XVIIe siècle* (Paris: l'Ecole des Chartes 1999), and Gisela Engel et al., eds., *Geschlechterstreit am Beginn der europäischen Moderne: die Querelle des femmes* (Frankfurt am Main: Helmer, 2004).
20 Philip Ball, *Curiosity: How Science Became Interested in Everything* (Chicago: University of Chicago Press, 2013); Peter Harrison, 'Curiosity, Forbidden Knowledge, and the Reformation of Natural Philosophy in Early Modern England', *Isis* 92 (2001): 265–290.
21 Harrison, 'Curiosity, Forbidden Knowledge, and the Reformation of Natural Philosophy', 289.
22 Carlos Gilly, 'Das Sprichwort "Die Gelehrten die Verkehrten" oder der Verrat der Intellektuellen im Zeitalter der Glaubensspaltung', in *Forme e destinazione del messagio religioso*, A. Rotondò, ed. (Florence: Olschki, 1991): 229–375. See also Erika Rummel, *The Confessionalization of Humanism in Reformation Germany* (Oxford: Oxford University Press, 2000).
23 See Keller, *Knowledge and the Public Interest*.
24 The literature on this subject is vast. See Pascale Casanova, *The World Republic of Letters* (Cambridge, MA: Harvard University Press, 2004); Susan Dalton, *Engendering the Republic of Letters*; Dena Goodman, *The Republic of Letters: A Cultural History of the French Enlightenment* (Cornell: Cornell University Press, 1984).
25 Schlereth, *The Cosmopolitan Ideal*, xxii; Anthony Grafton and Lisa Jardine, *From Humanism to the Humanities: Education and the Liberal Arts in Fifteenth- and Sixteenth-Century Europe* (Cambridge: Cambridge University Press, 1986).
26 Ernst Cassirer, *Individuum und Kosmos, in der Philosophie der Renaissance* (Wiesbaden: Springer, 1927), passim.

27 Further Christopher Brooke, *Philosophic Pride: Stoicism and Political Thought from Lipsius to Rousseau* (Princeton: Princeton University Press, 2012).
28 Keller, *Knowledge and the Public Interest*, 317; Merio Scattola, *Dalla virtù alla scienza: la fondazione e la trasformazione della disciplina politica nell'età moderna* (Milan: Angeli, 2003); Ann Moss, 'The *Politica* of Justus Lipsius and the Commonplace-Book', *Journal of the History of Ideas* 59 (1998): 421–436.
29 I have used the text printed in Justus Lipsius, *Epistolarum selectarum III. Centuriae* (Antwerp, 1601), 41–48.
30 Lipsius, *Epistolarum*, 46–47; Jan Papy, '"Italiam vestram amo supa omnes terras!" Lipsius's Attitude towards Italy and Italian Humanism of the late Sixteenth Century', *Humanistica Lovaniensia* 47 (1998): 245–277.
31 Lipsius, *Physiologia stoicorum libri tres* (Antwerp: Plantin, 1604), 83–86 is a *locus classicus* for early modern thought on the cosmopolitan, discussing at length the Stoic conception of the city of the world by drawing on Cicero, Seneca, Philo of Alexandria and others.
32 Lipsius, *A direction for trauailers*, John Stradling, trans. and ed. (London, 1592), sig. A3r-v.
33 For context see Mark Greengrass, 'Montaigne and the Wars of Religion', in *The Oxford Handbook of Montaigne*, Philippe Desan, ed. (Oxford: Oxford University Press, 2016), 138–157; Philippe Desan, *Montaigne: A Life*, Steven Rendell and Lisa Neal, trans. (Princeton: Princeton University Press, 2017); Warren Boutcher, *The School of Montaigne in Early Modern Europe* (Toronto: University of Toronto Press, 2014).
34 Michel de Montaigne, *Essays*, John Florio, trans. (London, 1603), 74–75. On Montaigne's sources, see Elaine Limbrick, 'Montaigne and Socrates', *Renaissance and Reformation* 9/2 (1973): 46–57.
35 Montaigne, *Essays*, 74.
36 Pierre de l'Eussa, *Comédie du cosmopolite représentée en la ville de Mouldon, le dimanche 14 jour d'octobre 1604, à l'entrée de son nouveau Baillif, magnifique et très honnoré seigneur Hans Rudolph d'Erlach* ([Bern], 1605). See further Christophè Pasche, 'Comédie Jouée a Moudon en 1604', *Revue historique vaudoise* 8 (1900): 367–377.
37 Naudé, *Advis pour dresser une bibliothèque* (Paris, 1627), 23; Naudé, *Instructions concerning erecting of a library*, John Evelyn, trans. (London, 1661), 10–11. See further Bernard Teyssandier, 'L'ethos érudit dans l'*Avis pour dresser une bibliothèque* de Gabriel Naudé', *Littératures Classiques* 66/2 (2008): 115–131.
38 See Daniel R. Brunstetter, 'La Mothe Le Vayer and Political Skepticism', in *Skepticism and Political Thought in the Seventeenth and Eighteenth Centuries*, John

Christian Laursen and Gianni Paganini, eds. (Toronto: University of Toronto Press, 2000), 36–54; Françoise Charles-Daubert, *Les Libertins érudits en France au XVIIe siècle* (Paris: Presses Universitaires de France, 1998); Philippe-Joseph Salazar, 'La Divine Sceptique'. *Ethique et rhétorique au 17eme siècle; autour de La Mothe Le Vayer* (Tübingen: Gunter Narr Verlag, 2000). On scepticism in early modernity, see Richard H. Popkin, *The History of Scepticism from Savonarola to Bayle*, 3rd ed. (Oxford: Oxford University Press, 2003).

39 Keller, *Knowledge and the Public Interest*, 201.
40 François de La Mothe Le Vayer, *Quatre dialogues faits a l'imitation des anciens par Orasius Tubero* (Frankfurt, 1604, i.e. 1630), 173; anonymously translated as *The Great Prerogative of a Private Life* (London, 1678), 99. On the dialogues see Bernard Beugnot, 'La fonction du dialogue chez La Mothe Le Vayer', *Cahiers de l'AIEF* 24 (1972): 31–41.
41 La Mothe Le Vayer, *The Great Prerogative*, 100–101; La Mothe Le Vayer, *Quatre dialogues*, 201. This appears to have been inspired by Epictetus.
42 La Mothe Le Vayer, *The Great Prerogative*, 102.
43 La Mothe Le Vayer, *The Great Prerogative*, 100–101.
44 Keller, *Knowledge and the Public Interest*, 202–203 sets out the case for a specific influence.
45 Howell, *A German diet, or, The ballance of Europe* (London, 1653), 3.
46 Keller and Penman, 'From the Archives of Scientific Diplomacy', 17–42.
47 Thomas Blount, *The Academie of Eloquence. Containing a Compleat English Rhetorique, Exemplified, With Common-Places, and Formes, digested into an easie and Methodical way to speak and write, fluently, according to the mode of the present times* (London, 1654), 170.
48 Blount, *Academie of Eloquence*, 171.
49 E. Brown, 'The Emergence of Natural Law and the Cosmopolis', in *The Cambridge Companion to Ancient Greek Political Thought*, S. Salkever, ed. (Cambridge: Cambridge University Press, 2009), 331–363.
50 Maryanne Cline Horowitz, 'The Stoic Synthesis of the Idea of Natural Law in Man: Four Themes', *Journal of the History of Ideas* 35 (1974): 3–16.
51 Plutarch, *Moralia*, VII, 571.
52 Anthony D. Smith, *Chosen Peoples: Sacred Sources of National Identity* (Oxford: Oxford University Press, 2004).
53 Montaigne, *Essays*, 74.
54 Barthélemy Aneau, *Juris prudentia. A primo et divino sui ortu, ad nobilem Biturigum academiam deducta* (Lyon: ad Signo Sagittarii, 1554), 13–14. This passage draws on Cicero, *De Legibus*, I.23 and Polybius, *The General History of the Wars of the Romans*, James Hampton, trans. (London, 1812), 515.

55 See further Marie Madeleine Fontaine, 'Barthélemy Aneau et la *Jurisprudentia*', in *Esculape et Dionysos: mélanges en l'honneur de Jean Céard* (Geneva: Droz, 2008), 1001-1112.
56 Richard Hooker, *Of the Lawes of Ecclesiastical Politie*, R.W. Church, ed. (Oxford: Oxford University Press, 1868). On Hooker's political thought, see W.D.J. Cargill Thompson, 'The Philosopher of the "Politic Society": Richard Hooker as a Political Thinker', in *Studies in the Reformation: Luther to Hooker*, C.W. Dugmore, ed. (London: Athlone Press, 1980), 131-191; Simon P. Kennedy, 'Richard Hooker as Political Naturalist', *Historical Journal* 62 (2018): 1-18.
57 Hooker, *Of the Lawes of Ecclesiastical Politie*, 65-68.
58 Charles Gibbon, *The order of equalitie Contriued and diuulged as a generall directorie for common sessements* (London, 1604), 14.
59 Robert V. Friedeburg, 'In Defense of Patria: Resisting Magistrates and the Duties of Patriots in the Empire from the 1530s to the 1640s', *Sixteenth Century Journal* 32 (2001): 357-382.
60 Ian Hunter, *The Secularisation of the Confessional State: The Political Thought of Christian Thomasius* (Cambridge: Cambridge University Press, 2007); Robert von Friedeburg, 'The Juridification of Natural Law: Christoph Besold's Claim for a Natural Right to Believe What One Wants', *The Historical Journal* 53/1 (2010): 1-19; Robert von Friedeburg, *Luther's Legacy: The Thirty Years War and the Modern Notion of 'State' in the Empire, 1530s to 1790s* (Oxford: Oxford University Press, 2016).
61 See T.J. Hochstrasser and Peter Schröder, *Early Modern Natural Law Theories: Contexts and Strategies in the Early Enlightenment* (Dordrecht: Kluwer, 2002).
62 For a summary see Merio Scattola, 'Before and After Natural Law: Models of Natural Law in Ancient and Modern Times', in *Early Modern Natural Law Theories: Contexts and Strategies in the Early Enlightenment*, T.J. Hochstrasser & M. Schröder, eds. (Dordrecht: Springer, 2003), 1-30.
63 Samuel von Pufendorf (praes.) Andreas von Ulcken (resp.), *De obligatione adversus patriam* (Heidelberg: Wyngaerden, 1663), 2. On this work see further Horst Dreitzel, 'Zehn Jahre Patria in der politischen Theorie in Deutschland: Prasch, Pufendorf, Leibniz, Becher, 1662 bis 1672', in *Patria und Patrioten vor dem Patriotismus. Pflichten, Rechte, Glauben und die Rekonfigurierung europäischer Gemeinwesen im 17. Jahrhundert* (Wiesbaden: Harrassowitz, 2005), 367-534; Vanda Fiorillo, 'La Patria, come Stato dei padri. La *obligatia ergo patriam* nella teoria politica di Samuel Pufendorf', in *Patria e nazione. Problemi di identità di appartenenza: Problemi di identità e di appartenenza*, Vanda Fiorillo and Gianluca Dioni, eds. (Milan: Franco Angeli, 2013), 111-144.

64 Henry More, *Conjectura cabbalistica or, a conjectural essay of interpreting the minde of Moses* (London, 1653), 97.

65 Hans Blumenberg, *The Legitimacy of the Modern Age*, Robert M. Wallace, trans. (Cambridge: MIT Press, 1983).

66 Jacob, *Strangers Nowhere in the World*, 41–65; Schlereth, *The Cosmopolitan Ideal*; Anna More, 'Cosmopolitanism and Scientific Reason in New Spain: Carlos de Sigüenza y Góngora and the Dispute over the 1680 Comet', in *Science in the Spanish and Portuguese Empires, 1500–1800*, Daniela Bleichmar et al., eds. (Stanford: Stanford University Press, 2009), 115–131.

67 Everaerts, *Cosmopolitae historia naturalis: comprehendens humani corporis atomiam & anatomicam delineationem* (Leiden, 1686).

68 Keller, *Knowledge and the Public Interest*, 10.

69 Johann-Peter Lotichius, *Paradoxon sive de febribus in genere dissertatio theorico-practica* (Frankfurt, 1627), 10.

70 Andreae, 'Fama Fraternitatis', in *Gesammelte Schriften* 2, 148.

71 The best work on Maier is Hereward Tilton, *The Quest for the Phoenix: Spiritual Alchemy and Rosicrucianism in the Work of Count Michael Maier (1569–1622)* (Berlin: Walter de Gruyter, 2003). See further Erik Leibenguth, *Hermetische Poesie des Frühbarock, Die 'Cantilenae intellectuales' Michael Maiers, Edition mit Übersetzung, Kommentar und Bio-Bibliographie* (Tübingen: Max Niemeyer Verlag, 2002).

72 On Maier's claims to have authored the tract on Anthony's behalf see Nils Lenke, Nicolas Roudet and Hereward Tilton, 'Michael Maier: Nine Newly Discovered Letters', *Ambix* 61 (2014): 1–47 at 5–6, 30–31.

73 Francis Anthony [Michael Maier], *The Apologie, or defence of a verity heretofor published concerning a medicine called aurum potabile* (London, 1616), sigs. ¶3v–¶4r; For the Latin edition, see Anthony [Maier], *Apologia veritatis illucescentis, pro auro potabili* (London, 1616), sig. ¶¶¶2r.

74 See Walter Rumsey, *Organon Salutis. An Instrument to cleanse the Stomach, As also divers new Experiments of the virtue of Tobacco and Coffee: How much they conduce to preserve humane health* (London, 1657), sigs. a4v–b1r.

75 Michael Maier, *Atalanta fugiens hoc est emblemata nova de secretis naturae chymica* (Oppenheim 1617). On this work see H.M.E. de Jong, *Michael Maier's Atalanta Fugiens: Sources of an Alchemical Book of Emblems* (Leiden: Brill, 1969).

76 Jacob, *Strangers Nowhere in the World*, 43.

77 Pamela H. Smith, *The Business of Alchemy: Science and Culture in the Holy Roman Empire* (Princeton: Princeton University Press, 1994).

78 Florian Ebeling, *The Secret History of Hermes Trismegistus* (Ithaca: Cornell University Press, 2007).

79 On Sendivogius see Roman Bugaj, *Michał Sędziwój (1566–1636): Życie i Pisma*. (Wrocław: Ossolineum, 1968); Rafał T. Prinke, 'Nolite de me inquirere (Nechtĕtje se po mnĕ ptáti): Michael Sendivogius', in *Alchymie a Rudolf II. Hledání tajemství přírody ve středni Evropĕ 16. a 17. století*, Ivo Purš and Vladimír Karpenko, eds. (Prague: Artefactum, 2011), 317–334; Rafał T. Prinke and Mike A. Zuber, 'Alchemical Patronage and the Making of an Adept: Letters of Michael Sendivogius to Emperor Rudolf II and his Chamberlain Hans Popp', *Ambix* 65 (2018): 324–355.

80 Michael Sendivogius, *Novvm lvmen chymicvm tractatus duodecim* (N.P. [Prague?], 1604), 107–109. I have used the translation by Arthur Edward Waite in *The Hermetic Museum* (London: J. Elliot & Co., 1893) vol. 2, 111. The sense was fractured in Sendivogius, *A New Light of Alchymie*, John French trans. (London, 1650), 49 where *cosmopolita sum* is rendered as 'I am one that can live anywhere.'

81 Rafał Prinke, 'New Light on the Alchemical Writings of Michael Sendivogius (1566–1636)', *Ambix* 63 (2016), 217–243 at 228 suggests that Sendivogius's statement was informed by his identification as a 'citizen of the world' in Bartosz Paprocki, *Ogrod krolwesky w Ktorem o początku Cesarzow Rzymskich, Arcyxiążąt Rakuskich Krolow, Polskich, Czeskych, Xiążąt Slanskich, Ruskich, Litewskich, Pruskich rozrodzienia ich krotko opisane naidziesz* (Prague: Sedlčanský, 1599), vol. 3, sig. CXLIv, where he is compared to Socrates and Diogenes because of his 'virtue and learning' which 'give settlement to everyone everywhere'.

82 Jacob, *Strangers Nowhere in the World*, 95–121.

83 For the later example of Johann Friedrich Böttger (1682–1719) see Janet Gleeson, *The Arcanum: The Extraordinary True Story of the Invention of European Porcelain* (London: Bantam Press, 1998).

84 See further Prinke, 'New Light', 226–228. William R. Newman, *Gehennical Fire: The Lives of George Starkey, an American Alchemist in the Scientific Revolution* (Chicago: University of Chicago Press, 2003), 1–8. In Leigh T.I. Penman, 'The Hidden History of the Cosmopolitan Concept: Heavenly Citizenship and the Aporia of World Community', *Journal of the Philosophy of History* 9 (2015): 284–305 at 297–298 I mistakenly ventured that Sendivogius himself created the story of the cosmopolitan adept as a means to protect his identity.

85 [Sendivogius], *Cosmopolite, dat is: burgher der werelt. Ofte Het nieuwe licht van de wetenschap van natuurlijcke dinghen* (Amsterdam, 1627); [Sendivogius], *Cosmopolite ou nouvelle lumiere de la physique naturelle* (The Hague, 1639).

86 On Starkey see Newman, *Gehennical Fire*; Harold Jantz, 'America's First Cosmopolitan', *Proceedings of the Massachusetts Historical Society*, 3rd Series, 84 (1972): 3–25.

87 Newman, *Gehennical Fire*, 59.

88 George Ripley, *The Morrow of Alchemy* (London, 1654), 60.

89 Walter Pagel, 'The Paracelsian Elias Artista and the Alchemical Tradition', in *Kreatur und Kosmos. Internationale Beiträge zur Paracelsusforschung*, Rosemarie Dilg-Frank, ed. (New York and Stuttgart: Gustav Fischer Verlag, 1981), 6–19; Antoine Faivre, 'Elie Artiste, ou le messie des philosophes de la nature', *Aries* 2 (2002): 119–152 and 3 (2003): 25–54.

90 On Bruno see Vincenzo Spampanato, *Vita di Giordano Bruno, con documenti editi e inediti*, 2 vols. (Messina: G. Principato, 1921); Hilary Gatti, *Giordano Bruno and Renaissance Science: Broken Lives and Organizational Power* (Ithaca, NY: Cornell University Press, 1999); Ingrid D. Rowland, *Giordano Bruno: Philosopher/Heretic* (Chicago: University of Chicago Press, 2009).

91 Alberto A. Martinez, 'Giordano Bruno and the Heresy of Many Worlds', *Annals of Science* 73 (2016): 345–374; Jole Shackelford, 'Giordano Bruno as the First Scientific Martyr', in *Galileo Goes to Jail, and Other Myths about Science and Religion*, Ronald L. Numbers ed. (Cambridge, MA: Harvard University Press, 2009), 59–67. Conversely, Philipp Melanchthon, *Initia doctrinae physicae*, 2nd ed. (Wittenberg, 1550), 43r used the vocabulary in an argument against cosmic pluralism.

92 Giordano Bruno, *La cena de le ceneri* ([London], 1584) cited in Giordano Bruno, *The Expulsion of the Triumphant Beast*, Arthur D. Imerti, trans. and ed. (New Brunswick, NJ: Rutgers University Press, 1964), 19.

93 Bruno, *Expulsion of the Triumphant Beast*, 72.

94 On Haberweschel see J.B. Miltner, 'Haberveslové z Habernfeldu', *Památky archeologické* 8 (1868): 46–56; Nicolette Mout, 'Ondřej Habervešl of Habernfeld and the Thirty Years' War: His Writings, the War and International Politics', in *Mezi Baltem a Uhrami. Komenský, Jednota bratrská a svět středoevropského protestantismu*, Vladimír Urbánek, Lenka Řezníková, eds. (Prague: Filosofia, 2006), 149–165; Vladimír Urbánek, *Eschatologie, vědění a politika: Příspěvek k dějinám myšlení pobělohorského exilu* (České Budějovice: Jihočeská univerzita v Českých Budějovicích, 2008), 145–229.

95 Mercurius Cosmopolita [i.e. Andreas Haberweschel], *Pentalogos in Libri cujusdam Gallico idiomate evulgati quatuor discursuum: De la methode, Dioptrique, Meteorique, & Geometrique* (The Hague, 1640). See further Erik-Jan Bos, 'Mercurius Cosmopolita *alias* Andreas von Habernfeld. The Hermetic Response to Descartes', forthcoming.

96 Bos, 'Mercurius Cosmopolita', unpag.

97 Robert Boyle, *Occasional Reflections upon Several Subjects* (London, 1665), 186; reprinted in Michael Hunter and Edward B. Davis eds., *The Works of Robert Boyle* (London: Pickering & Chatto, 1999), vol. 5, 166.

Chapter 6

1. Louis Dupré, *Enlightenment and the Intellectual Foundations of Modern Culture* (New Haven: Yale University Press, 2005).
2. Peter Gay, *The Enlightenment: An Interpretation* (New York: Knopf, 1966), 13–14.
3. Appiah, *Cosmopolitanism*, xiv.
4. Jeremy Adler et al., 'Theresa May's Rejection of Enlightenment Values', in *The Guardian* (London), 10 October 2016, archived online at https://www.theguardian.com/politics/2016/oct/09/theresa-may-rejection-of-enlightenment-values (accessed 21 March 2020).
5. Paul Hazard, *Die Herrschaft der Vernunft. Das europäische Denken im 18. Jahrhundert* (Hamburg: Hoffmann und Campe, 1949), 350–352.
6. Jacob, *Strangers Nowhere in the World*, 10–11; Hayden, *Cosmopolitan Global Politics*.
7. David Sorkin, *The Religious Enlightenment* (Princeton: Princeton University Press, 2008); David Sorkin, *Moses Mendelssohn and the Religious Enlightenment* (London: Peter Halban, 2012).
8. Anton M. Matytsin and Dan Edelstein, eds., *Let There Be Enlightenment: The Religious and Mystical Sources of Rationality* (Baltimore: Johns Hopkins University Press, 2018); Jeffrey D. Burson and Anton M. Matytsin, *The Skeptical Enlightenment: Doubt and Certainty in the Age of Reason* (Liverpool: Liverpool University Press, 2019). For a work in a similar spirit see Dale K. van Klay, *The Religious Origins of the French Revolution: From Calvin to the Civil Constitution, 1560–1791* (New Haven: Yale University Press, 1996).
9. Albrecht, *Kosmopolitismus*; Heuvel, 'Cosmopoli(ti)sme'; Scuccimarra, *I confini del mondo*; Sigrid Thielking, *Weltbürgertum: Kosmopolitische Ideen in Literatur und politischer Publizistik seit dem achtzehnten Jahrhundert* (Munich: Fink, 2000); Pauline Kleingeld, 'Six Varieties of Cosmopolitanism in Late Eighteenth-Century Germany', *Journal of the History of Ideas* 60/3 (1999): 505–524; Kleingeld, *Immanuel Kant*.
10. Joseph-Honoré Remí, *Le Cosmopolisme, publié a Londres a l'occasion du mariage de Louis Auguste, Dauphin de France* (Amsterdam, 1770).
11. Jean-Marie-Bernard Clément, *Petit Dictionnaire de la cour et de la ville* (Paris 1788), 69.
12. Hazard, 'Cosmopolite', 356–358.
13. Johann Fiebiger, *Dissertatio inauguralis de quaestione an et quatenus vidua superstes defuncto marito repetere* (Erfurt: Hering, 1730), 10–11 invoked 'Titius

civis Cosmopolitanus' as an archetypal 'man on the Clapham omnibus' in his legal discourse. Pauline Kleingeld, 'Six Varieties of Cosmopolitanism', 505–506 notes that the Hamburg *Patriotische Gesselschaft* of the 1720s also employed cosmopolitan terminology.

14 Humphrey Prideaux, *A Letter to a Deist* (London, 1696), 72–73; David Irish, *Levamen infirmi: or, cordial counsel to the sick and diseased Containing* [...] *A miscellany of pious discourses, concerning the attributes of God; with ejaculations and prayers, according to scripture rule* (London, 1700), 94.

15 Joseph Addison et al., *The Spectator with Sketches of the Lives of the Authors and Explanatory Notes*, 8 vols. (London, 1797), vol. 1, 260 (9 May 1711).

16 Jacob, *Strangers Nowhere in the World*, passim.

17 On early modern literacy see David Cressy, 'Literacy in Context: Meaning and Measurement in Early Modern England', in *Consumption and the World of Goods*, John Brewer and Roy Porter eds. (London: Routledge, 1993), 305–319.

18 D.T. Starnes, 'English Dictionaries of the Seventeenth Century', *Studies in English* 17 (1937): 33. See further Gabriele Stein, *The English Dictionary before Cawdrey* (Berlin: De Gruyter, 1985).

19 Blount, *Glossographia*, sig. L4r.

20 [Walter William Skeat], 'Report upon "Ghost-Words", or Words which have no real Existence', *Transactions of the Philological Society*, S.N. (1886): 350–374.

21 For example, Coles, *An English Dictionary*, sig. I1r; Nathan Bailey, *An Universal Etymological English Dictionary* (London, 1724), sig. Dd2r; Steven Poole, *A Word for Every Day of the Year* (London: Quercus, 2019), 123. The word was used in Robert Norton, *The Gunner: Shewing the Whole Practise of Artillery* (London, 1628), 30, but as a synonym for a theodolite. See Leo Wiener, 'English Lexicography', *Modern Language Notes* 11/6 (1896): 176–183 at 182.

22 *Dictionnaire universel françois et latin ... nouvelle édition* (Paris, 1721), vol. 2, 270. On this work, see John Considine, *Academy Dictionaries, 1600–1800* (Cambridge: Cambridge University Press, 2014), 30–31.

23 Ephraim Chambers, *Cyclopædia, or, An universal dictionary of arts and sciences* (London, 1728), 335.

24 Johann Leonhard Frisch, ed. *Neues Frantzösisch-Teutsches und Teutch-Frantzösisches Wörter-Buch*, 2nd ed. (Leipzig, 1737), 548.

25 Marie Leca-Tsiomis, *Écrire l'Encyclopédie: Diderot: De l'usage des dictionnaires à la grammaire philosophique* (Oxford: Voltaire Foundation, 1999), 75–84, 139–142.

26 Robert Darnton, *The Business of Enlightenment: A Publishing History of the Encyclopédie, 1775–1800* (Cambridge, MA: Harvard University Press, 1979), 4; Daniel Rosenberg, 'An Eighteenth-Century Time Machine: The *Encyclopedia* of Denis Diderot', *Réflexions historiques* 25/2 (1999): 227–250 at 227.

27 Denis Diderot, 'Cosmopolitain ou Cosmopolite', *Encyclopédie ou Dictionnaire raisonné des sciences, des arts et des métiers*, vol. 4, (Paris, 1751), 47.
28 Jason Ā. Josephson-Storm, *The Myth of Disenchantment: Magic, Modernity and the Birth of the Human Sciences* (Chicago: University of Chicago Press, 2017), 57.
29 Eric M. Steel, *Diderot's Imagery. A Study of a Literary Personality* (New York: Haskell House, 1966), 103–105 documents Diderot's use of alchemical metaphor in his works. See however Jean Ehrard, 'Matérialisme et naturalisme: Les sources occultistes de la pensée de Diderot', *Cahiers de l'Association internationale des études françaises* 13 (1961): 189–201, which documents a more ambivalent attitude. The generally favourable articles in the *Encyclopédie* on 'Alchemy' and 'The Alchemist' were likely written by Paul-Jacques Malouin (1701–1778). I thank Didier Kahn for his thoughts on this problem. In contrast to Diderot's omission of Sendivogius from the story of cosmopolitanism, Gilles Ménage's *Dictionnaire étymologique de la langue françoise. Nouvelle Édition* (Paris 1750), vol. 2, 51–56 contained a lavish entry for 'Cosmopolite', which concentrated solely on the life and works of Sendivogius.
30 Andrew Ramsay Campbell, *Essay philosophique sur le gouvernement civil*, 2nd ed. (London, 1721), 21; Lucian, *Oeuvres*, N. Perrot D'Ablancourt, ed. and trans. (Cologne: 1670), 199. On Campbell see Andrew Mansfield, *Ideas of Monarchical Reform: Fénelon, Jacobitism and the Political Works of the Chevalier Ramsay* (Manchester: Manchester University Press, 2015); Burnet, *Histoire de ce qui s'est passé de plus mémorable en Angleterre* (The Hague, 1735), vol. 2, 287.
31 Jean-Pierre de Crousaz, *Examen du Pyrrhonisme ancien & moderne* (The Hague, 1733), 24.
32 La Mothe Le Vayer, *Quatre dialogues*, 200–201; La Mothe Le Vayer, *The Great Prerogative*, 100–101.
33 Montesquieu, *Pensées et fragments inédits de Montesquieu*, Baron Gaston de Montesquieu, ed. (Bordeaux, 1899) vol. 1, 15; see further Schlereth, *The Cosmopolitan Ideal*, 191.
34 Mark Hulliung, *The Autocritique of Enlightenment: Rousseau and the Philosophes*, 2nd ed. (London: Routledge, 2014); Reginald James White, *The Anti-Philosophers: A Study of the Philosophes in Eighteenth-Century France* (London: MacMillan, St. Martin's Press, 1970). Conal Condren, Stephen Gaukroger and Ian Hunter, eds. *The Philosopher in Early Modern Europe: The Nature of a Contested Identity* (Cambridge: Cambridge University Press, 2006).
35 A.N. Whitehead, *Science and the Modern World* (New York: Macmillan, 1928), 86. Cf. Schlereth, *The Cosmopolitan Ideal*, 158–159.
36 On intellectual links see Ira O. Wade, *The Clandestine Organization and Diffusion of Philosophic Ideas in France from 1700 to 1750* (New York: Octagon, 1967); Miguel

Benítez, *La Face cachée des Lumières: Recherches sur les manuscrits philosophiques clandestins de l'âge classique* (Paris and Oxford: Voltaire Foundation, 1996).
37 Goodman, *Republic of Letters*.
38 The best edition is César Chesneau du Marsais, *Les Philosophe: Texts and Interpretation*, Herbert Dieckmann, ed. and trans. (St. Louis: Washington University Press, 1948). See further Gianluca Mori, 'Du Marsais philosophe clandestin: textes et attributions', in *La Philosophie clandestine à l'Age classique*, Antony McKenna and Alain Mothu, eds. (Paris and Oxford: Voltaire Foundation, 1997), 169–192. Allen Wood, 'Philosophy: Enlightenment Apology, Enlightenment Critique', in *What is Philosophy?* C.P. Ragland and Sarah Heidt, eds. (New Haven: Yale University Press, 2001), 96–120 at 104, suggests that Diderot himself revised Du Marsais's essay for publication.
39 César Chesneau du Marsais, 'Philosopher', *The Encyclopedia of Diderot & d'Alembert Collaborative Translation Project*, Dena Goodman, trans., Dena Goodman. Ann Arbor: Michigan Publishing, University of Michigan Library, 2002. http://hdl.handle.net/2027/spo.did2222.0000.001 (accessed 2 September 2017). Originally published as 'Philosophe', *Encyclopédie ou Dictionnaire raisonné des sciences, des arts et des métiers* (Paris, 1765), vol. 12, 509–511.
40 See Chapters 4 and 5.
41 du Marsais, 'Philosopher'.
42 du Marsais, 'Philosopher'.
43 Charles Palissot de Montenoy, *Les Philosophes, comédie en trois actes, en vers, représentée pour la première fois par les comédiens français ordinaires du Roi, le 2 mai 1760* (Paris, 1760), 72: 'Le véritable Sage est un Cosmopolite'. See Hazard, 'Cosmopolite', 359–360 for further contemporary examples.
44 Frederick Grimm, *Correspondence littéraire, philosophique et critique* (Paris 1877), vol. 4, 69–70.
45 David Hume, *Letters of David Hume*, J.Y.T. Greig, ed. (Oxford: Oxford University Press 1932), vol. 1, 470 (Hume to Gilbert Elliot, 2 September 1764).
46 Denis Diderot, *Correspondance*, Georges Roth, ed. (Paris, 1955), vol. 8, 116.
47 Remí, *Le Cosmopolisme*, 19; Denis Diderot, *Diderot on Art: The Salon of 1765 and Notes on Painting*, John Goodman, trans. (New Haven: Yale University Press, 1995), 156–157.
48 Remí, *Le Cosmopolisme*, 19–20.
49 Schlereth, *The Cosmopolitan Ideal*; M.R. de Labriolle, 'Le "Journal étranger" dans l'histoire du cosmopolitisme littéraire', *Studies on Voltaire and the Eighteenth Century* 56 (1967): 783–797.
50 See Iring Fetscher, *Rousseaus politische Philosophie. Zur Geschichte des demokratischen Freiheitsbegriffs* (Berlin: Suhrkamp, 1975); Brooke, *Philosophic Pride*, passim.

51 Anthony Pagden, *The Enlightenment: And Why it Still Matters* (Oxford: Oxford University Press, 2013), 274.
52 Jean-Jacques Rousseau, *Discours sur l'origine de l'inégalité parmi les hommes* (Paris, 1755), 325–326.
53 Louis-Charles Fougeret de Monbron, *Le Cosmopolite ou Le Citoyen du monde* (Paris, 1750). Georg Cavallar, 'Educating Émile: Jean-Jacques Rousseau on Cosmopolitanism', *The European Legacy* 17 (2012): 485–499 also links de Monbron to Rousseau's critiques, albeit in a later period. De Monbron's attitude recalls that of the protagonist of Pierre de l'Eussa, *Comedie du cosmopolite* (1604).
54 A readable account of Rousseau's life is provided by Leo Damrosch, *Jean-Jacques Rousseau: Restless Genius* (New York: Mariner, 2007).
55 Jean-Jacques Rousseau, 'Émile', in *Oeuvres complètes*, Bernard Gagnebin and Marcel Raymond, eds. (Paris: Gallimard, 1959–1995), vol. 4, 249.
56 Helena Rosenblatt, 'Rousseau the anti-Cosmopolitan', *Daedalus* 137/3 (2008): 59–67. Compare, however, the conclusions of Fetscher, *Rousseaus politische Philosophie*, 77–79.
57 Rousseau, *Oeuvres complètes*, vol. 4, 249; Jimmy Casas Klausen, *Fugitive Rousseau: Slavery, Primitivism, and Political Freedom* (Oxford: Oxford University Press, 2017), 174.
58 [Ernst August Anton von Göchhausen], *Enthüllung des Systems der Weltbürger-Republik. In Briefen aus der Verlassenschaft eines Freymaurers* (Rome [i.e. Leipzig], 1786). On Göchhausen see Albrecht, *Kosmopolitismus*, 97–99.
59 Andreas Önnerfors, 'Cosmopolitanism and What Is "Secret": Two Sides of Enlightened Ideas Concerning World Citizenship', in *The Idea of Kosmopolis*, 65–86; J.M. Roberts, *The Mythology of the Secret Societies* (London: Secker & Warburg, 1972).
60 [Göchhausen], *Enthüllung des Systems der Weltbürger-Republik*, 190.
61 Surveyed in Roberts, *The Mythology of the Secret Societies*.
62 Clément, *Petit Dictionnaire*, 69. Clément's source was likely Rousseau's famous 1763 statement in a letter to Paul Usteri: 'The patriotic spirit is an exclusive spirit, which makes us look on everyone but our fellow citizens as strangers, and almost as enemies.'
63 David A. Bell, *The Cult of the Nation in France. Inventing Nationalism, 1680–1800* (Cambridge, MA: Harvard University Press, 2003).
64 Cited in Hazard, 'Cosmopolite', 360.
65 Hazard, 'Cosmopolite', 361–362.
66 Heuvel, 'Cosmopolite, Cosmopoli(ti)sme', 9.
67 Roberts, *The Mythology of the Secret Societies*, passim.

68 Maximilien Robespierre, *Correspondance de Maximilien et Augustin Robespierre*, Georges Michon, ed. (Paris: Librairie Nizet et Bastard, 1941), vol. 2, 75–76 (Philippe-François-Joseph le Bas and Louis Antoine Léon de Saint-Just to Robespierre, 24 frimaire An. 2 [e.g. 14 November 1793]).
69 Derrida, *On Cosmopolitanism*. See further Theodore W. Jennings, *Reading Derrida/Thinking Paul: On Justice* (Stanford: Stanford University Press, 2006), 120–122; Gideon Baker, 'Cosmopolitanism as Hospitality: Revisiting Identity and Difference in Cosmopolitanism', *Alternatives* 34 (2009): 107–128.
70 Nussbaum, 'Patriotism and Cosmopolitanism', 3–6.
71 Tihanov, 'Cosmopolitanism in the Discursive Landscape of Modernity', 136.
72 This is the subject of Kleingeld, *Kant and Cosmopolitanism*.
73 See for example Charles-Irénée Castel de Saint-Pierre, *Abrégé du projet de paix perpétuelle inventé par le roi Henri le Grand... approprié à l'état présent des affaires générales de l'Europe* (Paris, 1729). On these discourses see further Tihanov, 'Cosmopolitanism in the Discursive Landscape of Modernity'.
74 Immanuel Kant, *Eternal Peace and Other International Essays*, Mary Campbell, trans. and ed. (New York: World Peace Foundation, 1914), 62.
75 Kant, *Eternal Peace*, 89.
76 Francis Cheneval, *Philosophie in weltbürgerlicher Bedeutung. Über die Entstehung und die philosophischen Grundlagen des supranationalen und kosmopolitischen Denkens der Moderne* (Basel: Schwabe, 2002).
77 Nussbaum, 'Kant and Stoic Cosmopolitanism'. 1–25.
78 Georg Cavallar, 'Cosmopolitanisms in Kant's Philosophy', *Ethics & Global Politics* 5 (2012): 95–96. Kleingeld, *Kant and Cosmopolitanism*; Frederick C. Beiser, 'Moral Faith and the Highest Good', in *The Cambridge Companion to Kant and Modern Philosophy*, Paul Guyer, ed. (Cambridge: Cambridge University Press, 2006): 588–629.
79 Immanuel Kant, *Gesammelte Schriften. Erste Abtheilung.* (Berlin: Walter de Gruyter, 1968), vol. 6, 131, 134.
80 Cavallar, *Kant's Embedded Cosmopolitanism: History, Philosophy, and Education for the World* (Berlin: De Gruyter, 2010), 39.
81 Kant, *Practical Philosophy*, 240.
82 See for example Christopher J. Insole, 'Kant on Christianity, Religion and Politics: Three Hopes, Three Limits', *Studies in Christian Ethics* 29/1 (2016): 14–33; Allen W. Wood, *Kant's Moral Religion* (Ithaca, NY: Cornell University Press, 2009); Cheneval, *Philosophie in weltbürgerlicher Bedeutung*, passim.
83 Kant *Gesammette, Schriften*, vol. 6, 34.

84 James DiCenso, *Kant, Religion, and Politics* (Cambridge: Cambridge University Press, 2011).
85 See further Mark Larrimore, 'Sublime Waste: Kant on the Destiny of the "Races"', in *Civilization and Oppression*, Catherine Wilson, ed. (Alberta: University of Calgary Press, 1999), 99–125; Raphaël Lagier, *Les races humaines selon Kant* (Paris: Presses Universitaires de France, 2004); Thomas E. Hill, Jr. and Bernard Boxill, 'Kant and Race', in *Race and Racism*, Bernard Boxill, ed. (Oxford: Oxford University Press, 2000), 448–471; Lucy Allais, 'Kant's Racism', *Philosophical Papers* 45 (2016): 1–36.
86 Kleingeld, *Kant and Cosmopolitanism*, 107.
87 Carl L. Becker, *The Heavenly City of the Eighteenth-Century Philosophers* (New Haven: Yale University Press, 1936), 31.

Epilogue

1 Poulsen, 'Anarchasis Cloots and the Birth of Modern Cosmopolitanism', 88.
2 Schlereth, *The Cosmopolitan Ideal*, 158–161.
3 Sheldon Pollock, Homi K. Bhabha, H.K., Carol A. Breckenridge and Dipesh Chakrabarty, 'Cosmopolitanisms', *Public Culture* 12 (2000): 577–589 at 577.
4 Richard W. Miller, 'The Cosmopolitanism Controversy Needs a Mid-Life Crisis', in *Cosmopolitanism versus Non-Cosmopolitanism: Critiques, Defenses, Reconceptualizations*, Gillian Brock, ed. (Oxford: Oxford University Press, 2013), 272–293 at 272.
5 Appiah, *Cosmopolitanism*; Martha C. Nussbaum, *The Cosmopolitan Tradition: A Noble but Flawed Ideal* (Cambridge, MA: The Belknap Press of Harvard University, 2019).
6 Max Bearak, 'Theresa May criticized the term "citizen of the world" but half the world identifies that way', *Washington Post*, 5 October 2016. https://www.washingtonpost.com/news/worldviews/wp/2016/10/05/theresa-may-criticized-the-term-citizen-of-the-world-but-half-the-world-identifies-that-way/?utm_term=.09b7d2c1638c? (accessed 31 March 2020).
7 Amulya Shankar, '"Cosmopolitan" is a dog whistle word once used in Nazi Germany and Communist Russia', *PRI*, 3 August 2017, https://www.pri.org/stories/2017-08-03/cosmopolitan-dog-whistle-word-once-used-nazi-germany-and-communist-russia (accessed 31 March 2020).

Bibliography

Manuscripts

London, British Library, Ms. Add. 59861.
London, British Library, Ms. Harley 249.
London, British Library, Ms. Cotton Vitellius C.VII.
Lübeck, Bibliothek der Hansestadt Lübeck, Ms. hist. 4° 25.
Oxford, Bodleian Library, Ms. Ashmole 1789.
Paris, Bibliothèque nationale de France, Ms. lat. 3401.
Paris, Bibliothèque nationale de France, Ms. fr. 2116.
Prague, National Museum, Ms. VI D 17.
Sheffield, University Library, Ms. 61 (Hartlib Papers).

Primary sources

Adams, Thomas, *The Diuells Banquet Described in sixe Sermons*. London, 1614.
Adams, Thomas, *Englands Sicknes, comparatively conferred with Israels, Diuided into two sermons*. London, 1615.
Adams, Thomas, *Plaine-Dealing, or, a Precedent of Honestie*. London, 1616.
Adams, Thomas, *Eirenopolis: the citie of peace Surueyed and commended to all Christians*. London, 1622.
Adams, Thomas, *A Commentary or Exposition upon the Divine Second Epistle General, Written by the Blessed Apostle St. Peter*. London, 1633.
Addison, Joseph et al., *The Spectator with Sketches of the Lives of the Authors and Explanatory Notes*. 8 vols. London, 1797.
Ambrose, *Letters*. Mary Melchior Beyenka, trans. New York: Fathers of the Church, 1954.
Ambrose, *Opera omnia*. Milan, 1876.
Andreae, Johann Valentin, *Christianopolis*. Edward P. Thompson, trans. and ed. Dordrecht: Kluwer, 1999.
Andreae, Johann Valentin, *Gesammelte Schriften*. Wilhelm Schmidt-Biggemann, ed. 19 vols. Stuttgart: frommann-holzboog, 1994ff.

Andreae, Johann Valentin, *Menippus, sive dialogorvm satyricorum centuria*. Cosmopoli [Straßburg?], 1618.

Andreae, Johann Valentin, *A Modell of a Christian Society*. John Hall, trans. Cambridge, 1647.

Andreae, Johann Valentin, *Mythologiæ Christianiæ libri tres*. Straßburg, 1619.

Andreae, Johann Valentin, *De reipublicæ Christianopolitanæ descriptio*. Straßburg, 1619.

Andreae, Johann Valentin, *Theca gladii spiritus*. Straßburg, 1616.

Aneau, Barthélemy, *Alector, Histoire Fabuleuse*. Lyon, 1560.

Aneau, Barthélemy, *Alector ou le coq. Histoire fabuleuse.* Marie Madeleine Fontaine, ed. 2 vols. Geneva: Droz, 1996.

Aneau, Barthélemy, *ΑΛΕΚΤΟΡ: The Cock. Containing the First Part of the Most Excellent and Mytheologicall Historie of the Valorous Squire Alector; Sonne to the Renowned Prince Macrobius Franc-Gal and the Peerelesse Princesse Priscaraxe, Queene of High Tartary*. London, 1590.

Aneau, Barthélemy, *Juris prudentia. A primo et divino sui ortu, ad nobilem Biturigum academiam deducta*. Lyon: ad Signo Sagittarii, 1554.

Anthony, Francis [Michael Maier], *The Apologie, or defence of a verity heretofor published concerning a medicine called aurum potabile*. London, 1616.

Augustine, *The City of God*. Marcus Dodd, trans. New York: Modern Library, 1950.

Bacon, Francis, *The Essayes or Counsels, Civill and Morall*. Michael Kiernan, ed. Oxford: Clarendon Press, 1985.

Bacon, Francis, *The History of the Reign of King Henry VII*. Brian Vickers, ed. Cambridge: Cambridge University Press, 1998.

Bacon, Francis, *The Major Works*. Brian Vickers, ed. Oxford: Oxford University Press, 2008.

Bailey, Nathan, *An Universal Etymological English Dictionary.* London, 1724.

Barlow, William, *Magneticall aduertisements*. London, 1616.

Barlow, William, *The nauigators supply Conteining many things of principall importance belonging to nauigation, with the description and vse of diuerse instruments framed chiefly for that purpose; but seruing also for sundry other of cosmography in generall.* London, 1597.

du Bartas, Guillaume, *Du Bartas his Diuine Weekes and Workes*. Joshua Sylvester, trans. London, 1641.

Barton, Thomas, *ΛΟΓΟΣ ΑΓΩΝΙΟΣ or, a Sermon of the Christian Race, preached before his Majesty at Christ-Church in Oxford, May 9 1643.* [London], 1643.

Bates, William, *A short description of the blessed place and state of the saints above in a discourse upon the words of Our Blessed Saviour, John XIV, 2*. London, 1687.

Bellarmino, Roberto, *De æterna felicitate sanctorvm libri qvinqve*. Cologne, 1626.

Bennefield, Samuel, *A Commentary or Exposition vpon the third Chapter of the Prophecie of AMOS. Deliuered In VXII. Sermons*. London, 1628.

Bergerac, Cyrano de, *Satyrical characters and handsome descriptions in letters written to severall persons of quality*. London, 1658.

Besold, Christoph, *Axiomatum de Consilio Politico Appendicula: quæ ad pietatem inprimis ducit*. Tübingen: Eberhard Wild, 1622.

Besold, Christoph, 'Anhang der Spanischem Monarchi Campanellæ. Ob zu wünschen/ daß alle Christliche Herrschafften/ einem einigen Ober-Haupt vnderworffen weren?' in Campanella, *Von der Spannischen Monarchy* . . . No Place, 1623.

Birken, Sigmund von, *HochFürstlicher Brandenburgischer Ulysses / oder Verlauf der LänderReise / welche . . . Christian Ernst / Marggraf zu Brandenburg . . . Durch Teutschland / Frankreich / Italien und die Niederlande . . . hochlöblichst verrichtet*. Bayreuth, 1669.

Blount, Thomas, *The Academie of Eloquence. Containing a Compleat English Rhetorique*. London, 1654.

Blount, Thomas, *Glossographia, or A dictionary, interpreting all such hard vvords, whether Hebrew, Greek, Latin, Italian, Spanish, French, Teutonick, Belgick, British or Saxon; as are now used in our refined English tongue*. London, 1656.

Bodin, Jean, *The Colloquium of the Seven about Secrets of the Sublime*. Marion Leathers Kuntz, ed., trans. and comm. University Park: Pennsylvania State University Press, 1975.

Bolton, Edmund, *Hypercritica or a Rule of Judgement for Writing* or reading our Historys. London, 1722.

Boulaese, Jehan, *Le Miracle de Laon en Lannoys*. Cambray: Lombard, 1566.

Boyle, Robert, *Occasional Reflections upon Several Subjects*. London, 1665.

de Britaine, William, *Human Prudence, or the Art by which a man may raise himself and fortune to grandeur*. London, 1680.

Bruno, Giordano, *La cena de le ceneri*. [London], 1584.

Bruno, Giordano, *The Expulsion of the Triumphant Beast*. Arthur D. Imerti, trans. and ed. New Brunswick, NJ: Rutgers University Press, 1964.

Bunyan, John, *The Pilgrim's Progress*. London 1679.

Bunyan, John, *Grace Abounding to the Chief of Sinners*. London, 1666.

Burnet, Thomas, *Histoire de ce qui s'est passé de plus mémorable en Angleterre*. The Hague, 1735.

C.R.E., *Theosophi eximii Epistola ad Anastasium Philaretum Cosmopolitam de sapientissima Fraternitate R.C*. Frankfurt: Johann Hofmann, 1619.

Campanella, Tomasso, *La Città del Sole: Dialogo Poetico. The City of the Sun: A Poetical Dialogue*. Daniel J. Donno, trans. Berkeley: University of California Press, 1981.

Campanella, Tomasso, *Von der Spannischen Monarchy* . . . No Place, 1623.

Campanella, Tomasso, *His advice to the King of Spain for attaining the universal monarchy of the world*. London, 1654.

Campbell, Andrew Ramsay, *Essay philosophique sur le gouvernement civil*. 2nd ed. London, 1721.

Castel de Saint-Pierre, Charles Irénée, *Abrégé du projet de paix perpétuelle inventé par le roi Henri le Grand . . . approprié à l'état présent des affaires générales de l'Europe*. (Paris, 1729).

Chambers, Ephraim, *Cyclopædia, or, An universal dictionary of arts and sciences*. London, 1728.

Charron, Pierre, *Of Wisdome three bookes*. Samson Leonard, trans. London, 1608.

Chesneau du Marsais, César, *Les Philosophe: Texts and Interpretation*. Herbert Dieckmann, ed. and trans. St. Louis: Washington University Press, 1948.

Chesneau du Marsais, César, 'Philosophe', in *Encyclopédie ou Dictionnaire raisonné des sciences, des arts et des métiers*. Paris, 1765, vol. 12, 509–511.

Clément, Jean-Marie-Bernard, *Petit Dictionnaire de la cour et de la ville*. Paris 1788.

Coles, Elisha, *An English Dictionary: Explaining The difficult Terms that are used in Divinity, Husbandry, Physick, Phylosophy, Law, Navigation, Mathematicks, and other Arts and Sciences* (London, 1677).

Comenius, Jan Amos, *The Labyrinth of the World and the Paradise of the Heart*. Howard Louthan and Andrea Sterk, trans. and eds. New York: Paulist Press, 1998.

Comenius, Jan Amos, *Lux e tenebris, novis radiis aucta. Hoc est: Solemnissimæ Divinæ Revelationes, in ususm seculi nostri factæ . . . qvomodo tandem Deus (deletâ Pseudo-Christianorum, Judæorum, Turcarum, Paganorum, & omnium sub Cœlo Gentium Babylonè) novam, verè Catholicam, donorum Dei luce plenè coruscantem Ecclesiam constituet; et qvis jam status ejus futurus sit ad finem usque seculi, explicatur*. No Place [Amsterdam]: No Printer, 1665.

Cosmopolite, Eusebe Philadelphe, *Le Reveille-matin des Francois, et de leurs voisins*. Edinburgh [Basel?], 1574.

Crook, Samuel, *TA ΔIAΦERONTA, or, Divine characters in two parts: acutely distinguishing the more secret and undiscerned differences between 1. the hypocrite in his best dresse of seeming virtues and formal duties, and the true Christian in his real graces and sincere obedience*. London, 1658.

de Crousaz, Jean-Pierre, *Examen du Pyrrhonisme ancien & moderne*. The Hague, 1733.

Dadraeus, Johannes, *Loci commvnes similivm et dissimilivm, ex omni propemodvm antiqvitate*. 3rd ed. Venice, 1583.

Dee, John, *General and Rare Memorials Pertayning to the Perfect Arte of Navigation*. London, 1577.

Dee, John, *A Letter, Containing a moste briefe Discourse Apologeticall, with a plaine Demonstration, and feruent Protestation, for the lawfull, sincere, very faithfull and Christian course, of the Philosophicall studies and exercises, of a certaine studious Gentleman: An ancient Seruaunt to her most excellent Maiesty Royall.* London, 1599.

Dee, John, *The Limits of the British Empire.* Ken MacMillan with Jennifer Abeles, eds. Westport & London: Praeger, 2004.

Diderot, Denis, 'Cosmopolitain ou Cosmopolite', *Encyclopédie ou Dictionnaire raisonné des sciences, des arts et des métiers.* Paris, 1751, vol. 4, 47.

Diderot, Denis, *Correspondance.* Georges Roth, ed. Paris, 1955.

Diderot, Denis, *Diderot on Art: The Salon of 1765 and Notes on Painting.* John Goodman, trans. New Haven: Yale University Press, 1995.

Drant, Thomas, *The divine lanthorne, or, A sermon preached in S. Pauls Church.* London, 1637.

Ellis, Clement, *The Gentle Sinner, or England's Brave Gentlemen.* London, 1660.

Erasmus, *Collected Works of Erasmus. Volume 9. The Correspondence, 1522 to 1523.* R.A.B. Mynors, trans. James M. Estes, annotations. Toronto: University of Toronto Press, 1989.

Erasmus, *Apophthegmatum opus cum primis frugiferum.* Leiden, 1533.

Estienne, Henri, *Deux dialogues du nouveau langage françois italianizé.* Paris, 1578.

Everaerts, Anthonius, *Cosmopolitae historia naturalis: comprehendens humani corporis atomiam & anatomicam delineationem, ab ipsis primis foetus rudimentis in utero, usque ad perfectum & adultum statum, lumine praeclaro generationem hominis & efformationem exhibens.* Leiden, 1686.

Faret, Nicolas, *L'honneste Homme, Das ist: Der Ehrliebende Welt-Mann/ Oder Die von vielen Leuten gesuchte schöne Kunst/ wie einer an grosser Herren Höfen ... sich beliebet und belobet machen könne.* Leipzig, 1648.

Fiebiger, Johann, *Dissertatio inauguralis de quaestione an et quatenus vidua superstes defuncto marito repetere.* Erfurt, 1730.

Ford, Simon, *The Fall and Funeral of Northampton, in an elegy, Late Published in Latin [...] Since, made English.* London, 1677.

Fougeret de Monbron, Louis-Charles, *Le Cosmopolite ou Le Citoyen du monde.* Paris, 1750.

Frisch, Johann Leonhard, ed. *Neues Frantzösisch-Teutsches und Teutch-Frantzösisches Wörter-Buch.* 2nd ed. Leipzig, 1737.

Gearing, William, *God's Soveraignty displayed.* London, 1667.

Gibbon, Charles, *The order of equalitie Contriued and diuulged as a generall directorie for common sessements.* London, 1604.

Göchhausen, Ernst August Anton von, *Enthüllung des Systems der Weltbürger-Republik. In Briefen aus der Verlassenschaft eines Freymaurers.* [Leipzig], 1786.

Goodwin, George, *Melissa religionis Pontificae ejusdemque apostrophe*. London, 1620.

Goodwin, George, *Babels balm: or The honey-combe of Romes religion With a neate draining and straining-out of the rammish honey thereof*. John Vicars, trans. London, 1624.

Grapaldi, Francisco Maria, *De partibus aedium*. Parma, 1516.

Grimaldus, Laurentius, *De optimo senatore libri duo*. Venice, 1568.

Grimaldus, Laurentius, *The Counsellor. Exactly pourtraited in two Bookes. Wherin the Offices of Magistrats, The happie life of Subiectes, and the felicitie of Common-weales is pleasantly and pithilie discoursed*. London, 1593.

Grießmann, Valentin, *Πρόδρομος εὐμενής, καὶ ἀποτρεπτικός Exhibens enneadem quaestionum generalium De Haeresibus ex orco redivivis: Das ist: Getrewer Eckhart*. Gera: Andreas Mamitzsch, 1623.

Grimm, Frederick, *Correspondence littéraire, philosophique et critique*. Paris, 1877.

Guazzo, Stefano, *Lettere del Stefano Gvazzo, Gentilhuomo di Casale di Monserrato*. Venice, 1590.

[Gühler, Michael], *Clavis Apocalyptica*. London, 1651.

[Haberweschel, Andreas] Mercurius Cosmopolita, *Pentalogos in Libri cujusdam Gallico idiomate evulgati quatuor discursuum: De la methode, Dioptrique, Meteorique, & Geometrique*. The Hague, 1640.

Hakluyt, Richard, *Principal Navigations, Voyages, and Traffiques, and Discoveries of the English Nation*. London, 1598.

Heydon, John, *Eugenius Theodidactus. The prophetical trumpeter sounding an allarum to England illustrating the fate of Great Britain, past, present, and to come*. London, 1655.

Hondius, Jodocus, *Typus totius orbis terrarum. In quo & Christiani militis certamen super terram (in pietatis studiosi gratiam) graphicè designatur*. [Antwerp?]: No Printer, [c. 1596].

Hooker, Richard, *Of the Lawes of Ecclesiastical Politie*. R.W. Church, ed. Oxford: Oxford University Press, 1868.

Howell, James, *A German diet, or, The ballance of Europe*. London, 1653.

Hume, David, *Letters of David Hume*. J.Y.T. Greig, ed. Oxford: Oxford University Press 1932.

Irish, David, *Levamen infirmi: or, cordial counsel to the sick and diseased Containing [...] A miscellany of pious discourses, concerning the attributes of God; with ejaculations and prayers, according to scripture rule*. London, 1700.

Kant, Immanuel, *Kant: Political Writings*. H.S. Reiss, H.B. Nisbet, eds. Cambridge: Cambridge University Press, 1991.

Kant, Immanuel, *Eternal Peace and Other International Essays*. Mary Campbell, trans. and ed. New York: World Peace Foundation, 1914.

Kant, Immanuel, *Gesammelte Schriften. Erste Abtheilung.* 9 vols. Berlin: Walter de Gruyter, 1902–1923.

Kuhlmann, Quirinus, *A. Z! Quirin Kuhlman a Christian Jesuelit his Quinary of Slingstones, against the Goliath of all Kindreds, Peoples and Languages.* Paris, 1680.

Kuhlmann, Quirinus, A.Z. *Salomon a Kaiserstein Cosmopolita de monarchia jesuelitica ultimo ævo reservata ad politicos aulicosque orbis terrarium.* London, 1682.

La Mothe Le Vayer, François de, *Quatre dialogues faits a l'imitation des anciens par Orasius Tubero.* Frankfurt, 1604, i.e. 1630.

La Mothe Le Vayer, François de, *The Great Prerogative of a Private Life.* London, 1678.

l'Eussa, Pierre de, *Comédie du cosmopolite représentée en la ville de Mouldon, le dimanche 14 jour d'octobre 1604, à l'entrée de son nouveau Baillif, magnifique et très honnoré seigneur Hans Rudolph d'Erlach, gentilhomme de la cité de Berne.* [Berne], 1605.

Lipsius, Justus, *A direction for trauailers.* John Stradling, trans. and ed. London, 1592.

Lipsius, Justus, *Epistolarum selectarum III. Centuriae.* Antwerp, 1601.

Lipsius, Justus, *Physiologia Stoicorum libri tres.* Antwerp: Plantin, 1604.

Lotichius, Johann-Peter, *Paradoxon sive de febribus in genere dissertatio theorico-practica.* Frankfurt, 1627.

Lyly, John, *Euphues: The Anatomy of Wit.* London, 1578.

Maier, Michael, *Atalanta fugiens hoc est emblemata nova de secretis naturae chymica.* Oppenheim, 1617.

Melanchthon, Philipp, *Initia doctrinae physicae. Dictata in academia Vuitebergensi. Iterum edita.* Wittenberg, 1550.

Ménage, Gilles, *Dictionnaire étymologique de la langue françoise. Nouvelle Édition.* Paris, 1750.

Montaigne, Michel de, *Essays.* John Florio, trans. London, 1603.

Montesquieu, *Pensées et fragments inédits de Montesquieu.* Baron Gaston de Montesquieu, ed. Bordeaux, 1899.

More, Henry, *Conjectura cabbalistica or, a conjectural essay of interpreting the minde of Moses.* London, 1653.

More, Thomas, *La Republique d'Utopie . . . Traduite nouuellement de Latin.* Lyon, 1559.

[Morsius, Joachim], *Anastasii Philareti Cosmopolitæ epistola sapientissime F.R.C. remissa.* Philadelphia, [1618].

[Morsius, Joachim], *Magische Propheceyung . . . Paracelsi von Entdeckung seiner 3. Schätzen . . .* Philadelphia, 1625.

[Morsius, Joachim], *Nuncius Olympicus: Von etzlichen geheimen Bücheren und Schrifften . . .* Philadelphia, 1626.

[Morsius, Joachim], *Eine wunderbarliche Vision eines Catholischen Einsiedlers.* Philadelphia, 1626.

[Morsius, Joachim], *Ein güldener Discurs. Von der Freyheit des Gewissens vnd Glaubens*... No Place: No Printer, 1636.

Naudé, Gabriel, *Advis pour dresser une bibliothèque*. Paris, 1627.

Naudé, Gabriel, *Instructions concerning erecting of a library presented to my lord, the President De Mesme*. John Evelyn, trans. London, 1661.

Nebrija, Antonio de, *Dictionarium latino-hispanicum*. Antwerp, 1553.

Nicolay, Nicolas de, *Les quatre premiers livres des navigations et peregrinations Orientales*. Lyon, 1568.

Nicolay, Nicolas de, *The nauigations, peregrinations and voyages, made into Turkie*. London, 1585.

Norton, Robert, *The Gunner: Shewing the Whole Practise of Artillery*. London, 1628.

Ortelius, Abraham, 'VTOPIÆ TYPVS, EX Narratione Raphaelis Hythlodæi, Descriptione D. Thomas Mori, Delineatione Abrahami Ortelij', [Antwerp: 1595].

Ortelius, Abraham, *Epistolae*. J.H. Hessels, ed. Cambridge, 1887.

Palissot de Montenoy, Charles, *Les Philosophes, comédie en trois actes, en vers, représentée pour la première fois par les comédiens français ordinaires du Roi, le 2 mai 1760*. Paris, 1760.

Paprocki, Bartosz, *Ogrod krolwesky w Ktorem o początku Cesarzow Rzymskich, Arcyxiążąt Rakuskich Krolow, Polskich, Czeskych, Xiążąt Slanskich, Ruskich, Litewskich, Pruskich rozrodzienia ich krotko opisane naidziesz*. Prague: Daniel Sedlčanský, 1599.

Philo of Alexandria, *Scriptoris eloquentissimi ac philosophi summi*. Sigismund Gelen, trans. Louvain, 1555.

Plato, *The Republic*. P. Shorey, trans. Cambridge, MA: Loeb Classical Library, 1935.

Postel, Guillaume, *Guillaume Postel et Jean Boulaese. De summopere (1566) et Le Miracle de Laon (1566)*. Irena Backus, trans. and ed. Geneva: Droz, 1995.

Postel, Guillaume, *Description et charte de la terre Saincte, quie est la propriété de Iesus Christ*. No Place, [1561].

Postel, Guillaume, *De la République des Turcs: et là où l'occasion s'offrera, des meurs et loy de tous Muhamedistes*. Poitiers, 1560.

Postel, Guillaume, *Le livre de la concorde entre le Coran et les Évangiles*. No Place, 1553.

Postel, Guillaume, *Quatuor librorum de orbis terrae concordia Primus*. Paris, 1543.

Postel, Guillaume, *Πανδενωσια: compositio omnium dissidorum*. Basel, 1547.

Postel, Guillaume, *Les premiers éléments d'Euclide chrestien, pour la raison de la divine et ethernelle verité demonstrer*. Paris, 1579.

Postel, Guillaume, *La tierce partie des orientales histoires, ou est exposée la condition, puissance et revenu de l'Empire Turquesque*. Poitiers, 1560.

Postel, Guillaume, *L'histoire memorable des expeditions depuys la deluge faictes par les Gauloys ou Francoys*. Paris, 1552.

Postel, Guillaume, *Candelabri typici in Mosis tabernaculo . . . interpretatio*. Venice, 1548.
Postel, Guillaume, *De nativitate mediatoris ultima, nunc futura et toti orbi terrarum in singulis ratione praeditis manifestanda, opus*. Paris, 1547.
Prideaux, Humphrey *A Letter to a Deist*. London, 1696.
Pufendorf, Samuel von (praes.) Andreas von Ulcken (resp.) *De obligatione adversus patriam*. Heidelberg: Wyngaerden, 1663.
Purchas, Samuel, *Hakluytus posthumus or Purchas his Pilgrimes*. 5 vols. London, 1625.
Purchas, Samuel, *Purchas his pilgrim Microcosmus, or the historie of man. Relating the wonders of his generation, vanities in his degeneration, necessity of his regeneration*. London, 1619.
Purchas, Samuel, *Purchas his Pilgrimage. Or Relations of the World and the Religions observed in all Ages and Places discovered, from the Creation vnto this Present. In foure Parts*. London, 1614.
Reeve, Thomas, *God's Plea for Nineveh, or, London's precedent for mercy delivered in certain sermons within the city of London*. London, 1657.
Remí, Joseph-Honoré, *Le Cosmopolisme, publié a Londres a l'occasion du mariage de Louis Auguste, Dauphin de France*. Amsterdam, 1770.
Renaudot, Theophraste ed., *Recueil général des questions traitées és conférences du Bureau d'adresse*. Paris, 1634.
Renaudot, Theophraste ed., *A general collection of discourses of the virtuosi of France, upon questions of all sorts of philosophy, and other natural knowledg made in the assembly of the Beaux Esprits at Paris, by the most ingenious persons of that nation*. G. Havers, trans. London, 1664.
Ripley, George, *The Marrow of Alchemy*. London, 1654.
de la Rivière, Polycarp, *L'Adieu du Monde, ou Le mépris de ses vaines grandeurs & plaisirs périssables*. Lyon, 1619.
Robespierre, Maximilien, *Correspondance de Maximilien et Augustin Robespierre*. Georges Michon, ed. 3 vols. Paris: Librairie Nizet et Bastard, 1941.
Rousseau, Jean-Jacques, *Discours sur l'origine de l'inégalité parmi les hommes*. Paris, 1755.
Rousseau, Jean-Jacques, *Oeuvres complètes*. Bernard Gagnebin and Marcel Raymond, eds. Paris: Gallimard, 1959–1995.
Rumsey, Walter, *Organon Salutis. An Instrument to cleanse the Stomach, As also divers new Experiments of the virtue of Tobacco and Coffee: How much they conduce to preserve humane health*. London, 1657.
Sendivogius, Michael, *Novvm lvmen chymicvm tractatus duodecim*. [Prague?], 1604.
Sendivogius, Michael, *Cosmopolite, dat is: burgher der werelt. Ofte Het nieuwe licht van de wetenschap van natuurlijcke dinghen*. Amsterdam, 1627.

Sendivogius, Michael, *Cosmopolite ou nouvelle lumiere de la physique naturelle*. The Hague, 1639.
Sendivogius, Michael *A New Light of Alchymie*. John French, trans. London, 1650.
Thomas, Thomas, *Dictionarium, summa fide ac diligentissime*. London, 1600.
Verdier, Antoin de, *Les bibliothèques françoises de la Croix du Maine et Du Verdier. Nouvelle Édition*. Paris, 1773.
Vicars, John, *A prospectiue glasse to looke into heauen, or The coelestiall Canaan described Together with the soules sacred soliloquie*. London, 1618.

Secondary sources

Adler, Jeremy, et al., 'Theresa May's Rejection of Enlightenment Values', *The Guardian* (London), 10 October 2016.
Albrecht, Andrea, *Kosmopolitismus. Weltbürgerdiskurse in Literatur, Philosophie und Publizistik um 1800*. Berlin: De Gruyter, 2005.
Allais, Lucy, 'Kant's Racism', *Philosophical Papers* 45 (2016): 1–36.
Andersson, Bo, Lucinda Martin, Leigh T.I. Penman, and Andrew Weeks, eds. *The World of Jacob Böhme*. Leiden: Brill, 2018.
Appiah, Kwame Anthony, *Cosmopolitanism: Ethics in a World of Strangers*. New York: Norton, 2006.
Armitage, David, *The Ideological Origins of the British Empire*. Cambridge: Cambridge University Press, 2000.
Armitage, David, 'The Elizabethan Idea of Empire', *Transactions of the Royal Historical Society* 14 (2004): 269–277.
Arnold, Jafe, 'Esoteric Imperialism: The Solomonic-Theurgic Mystique of John Dee's British Empire', *Endeavour* 43 (2019): 17–24.
Augustijn, Cornelis, *Erasmus: His Life, Work and Influence*. J.C. Grayson, trans. Toronto: University of Toronto Press, 1991.
Backus, Irena, *Le miracle de Laon. Le déraisonable, le raisonnable, l'apocalyptique et le politique dans les recits du miracle de Laon (1566–1578)*. Geneva: Droz, 1994.
Baker, Gideon, 'Cosmopolitanism as Hospitality: Revisiting Identity and Difference in Cosmopolitanism', *Alternatives* 34 (2009): 107–128.
Balcar, Lubomír, 'Theologické srovnání Komenského "Labyrintu světa's Bunyanovou knihou *Pilgrim's Progress*"', *Archiv pro Badání o Životě a Spisech J.A. Komenského* 14 (1938): 113–125.
Baldry, H.C., *The Unity of Mankind in Greek Thought*. Cambridge: Cambridge University Press, 1965.

Ball, Philip, *Curiosity: How Science Became Interested in Everything*. Chicago: University of Chicago Press, 2013.

Barber, Peter, 'The Christian Knight, the Most Christian King and the Rulers of Darkness', *The Map Collector* 52 (1990): 8–13.

Barbour, Reid, *English Epicures and Stoics: Ancient Legacies in Early Stuart Culture*. Amherst, MA: University of Massachusetts Press, 1998.

Bearak, Max, 'Theresa May Criticized the Term "Citizen Of The World" but Half The World Identifies that Way', *Washington Post*, 5 October 2016.

Becker, Carl L., *The Heavenly City of the Eighteenth-Century Philosophers*. New Haven: Yale University Press, 1936.

Beiser, Frederick C., 'Moral Faith and the Highest Good', in *The Cambridge Companion to Kant and Modern Philosophy*. Paul Guyer, ed. Cambridge: Cambridge University Press, 2006, 588–629.

Bell, David A., *The Cult of the Nation in France: Inventing Nationalism, 1680–1800*. Cambridge, MA: Harvard University Press, 2003.

Benedict, Philip, *Graphic History: The Wars, Massacres, and Troubles of Tortorel and Perrissin*. Geneva: Droz, 2007.

Benítez, Miguel, *La Face cachée des Lumières: Recherches sur les manuscrits philosophiques clandestins de l'âge classique*. Paris and Oxford: Voltaire Foundation, 1996.

Bernát, Libor, *Mikuláš Drábik: Vizionár, mystik a kazateľ Jednoty bratskej*. Trenčin: Trenčianske múzeum v Trenčíne, 2017.

Besse, Jean-Marc, *Les grandeurs de la terre. Aspects du savoir géographique à la Renaissance*. Lyon: ENS Editions, 2003.

Beugnot, Bernard, 'La fonction du dialogue chez La Mothe Le Vayer', *Cahiers de l'AIEF* 24 (1972): 31–41.

Beyer, Jürgen and Leigh T.I. Penman, 'Printed Autobibliographies from the Sixteenth and Seventeenth Centuries', in *Documenting the Early Modern Book World: Inventories and Catalogues in Manuscript and Print*. Malcolm Walsby and Natasha Constantinidou, eds. Leiden: Brill, 2013, 161–184.

Beyer, Jürgen, *Lay Prophets in Lutheran Europe, 1500–1750*. Leiden: Brill, 2017.

Billig, Michael, *Banal Nationalism*. London: Sage, 1995.

Biot, Brigitte, 'Barthélemy Aneau, lecteur de l'*Utopie*', *Moreana* 121 (1995): 11–28.

Biot, Brigitte, *Barthélemy Aneau, régent de la Renaissance lyonnaise*. Paris: Champion, 1995.

Blankert, A., 'Heraclitus en Democritus. In het bijzonder in de nederlandse kunst van de 17de eeuw', *Nederlands Kunsthistorisch Jaarboek* 18 (1967): 31–124.

Blekastad, Milada, *Comenius: Versuch eines Umrisses von Leben, Werk und Schicksal des Jan Amos Komenský*. Oslo and Prague: Universitets Forlaget and Academia Praha, 1969.

Blumenberg, Hans, *The Legitimacy of the Modern Age*. Robert M. Wallace, trans. Cambridge: MIT Press, 1983.

Bohman, James and Matthias Lutz-Bachmann, eds. *Perpetual Peace: Essays on Kant's Cosmopolitan Ideal*. Cambridge, MA: MIT Press, 1997.

Bouman, José and Cis van Heertum, *Divine Wisdom, Divine Nature: The Message of the Rosicrucian Manifestoes in the Visual Language of the Seventeenth Century*. Amsterdam: In de Pelikaan, 2016.

Boutcher, Warren, *The School of Montaigne in Early Modern Europe*. Toronto: University of Toronto Press, 2014.

Bouwsma, William J., *Concordia Mundi: The Career and Thought of Guillaume Postel, 1510-1581*. Cambridge, MA: Harvard University Press, 1957.

Bouwsma, William J., 'Postel and the Significance of Renaissance Cabalism', *Journal of the History of Ideas* 15 (1954): 218-232.

Brecht, Martin, *Johann Valentin Andreae, 1586-1654*. Göttingen: Vandenhoeck & Ruprecht, 2008.

Brecht, Martin, 'Die Aufnahme von Arndts "Vier Bücher vom wahren Christenthum"', in *Frömmigkeit oder Theologie: Johann Arndt und die 'Vier Bücher vom wahren Christenthum'*. Hans Otte and Hans Schneider, eds. Göttingen: Vandenhoeck & Ruprecht, 2007, 231-262.

Brecht, Martin, 'Chiliasmus in Württemberg im 17. Jahrhundert', *Pietismus und Neuzeit* 14 (1988): 25-49.

Breuer, Dieter, ed. *Frömmigkeit in der frühen Neuzeit: Studien zur religiösen Literatur des 17. Jahrhunderts in Deutschland*. Amsterdam: Rodopi, 1984.

Brooke, Christopher, *Philosophic Pride: Stoicism and Political Thought from Lipsius to Rousseau*. Princeton: Princeton University Press, 2012.

Brown, E., 'The Emergence of Natural Law and the Cosmopolis', in *The Cambridge Companion to Ancient Greek Political Thought*. S. Salkever, ed. Cambridge: Cambridge University Press, 2009, 331-363.

Brown, Garrett Wallace, *Grounding Cosmopolitanism: From Kant to the Idea of a Cosmopolitan Constitution*. Edinburgh: Edinburgh University Press, 2009.

Brown, John, *The Sermons of Thomas Adams, the Shakespeare of Puritan Theologians*. London, 1909.

Brunstetter, Daniel R., 'La Mothe le Vayer and Political Skepticism', in *Skepticism and Political Thought in the Seventeenth and Eighteenth Centuries*. John Christian Laursen and Gianni Paganini, eds. Toronto: University of Toronto Press, 2000, 36-54.

Bugaj, Roman, *Michał Sędziwój (1566-1636): Życie i Pisma*. Wrocław: Ossolineum, 1968.

Burson, Jeffrey D. and Anton M. Matytsin, *The Skeptical Enlightenment: Doubt and Certainty in the Age of Reason*. Liverpool: Liverpool University Press, 2019.

Bury, Emmanuel, *Littérature et politesse: l'invention de l'honnête homme (1580-1750)*. Paris: Presses Universitaires de France, 1996.

Busch, H.J. and Axel Horstman, 'Kosmopolit/Kosmopolitismus', *Historisches Wörterbuch der Philosophie*. Joachim Ritter and Karlfried Gründer, eds. 8 vols. Basel: Schwabe & Co., 1976, vol. 4, 1155–1158.

Camino, Mercedes Maroto, *Producing the Pacific: Maps and Narratives of Spanish Exploration (1567-1606)*. Amsterdam: Rodopi, 2005.

Carey, Francis, ed. *Apocalypse and the Shape of Things to Come*. London: British Museum Press, 1999.

Cargill Thompson, W.D.J., 'The Philosopher of the "Politic Society": Richard Hooker as a Political Thinker', in *Studies in the Reformation: Luther to Hooker*. C.W. Dugmore, ed. London: Athlone Press, 1980, 131–191.

Casanova, Pascale, *The World Republic of Letters*. Cambridge, MA: Harvard University Press, 2004.

Cavallar, Georg, *Kant's Embedded Cosmopolitanism: History, Philosophy, and Education for the World*. Berlin: De Gruyter, 2010.

Cavallar, Georg, 'Educating Émile: Jean-Jacques Rousseau on Cosmopolitanism', *The European Legacy* 17 (2012): 485–499.

Cavallar, Georg, 'Cosmopolitanisms in Kant's Philosophy', *Ethics & Global Politics* 5 (2012): 95–118.

Cave, Terence, *Thomas More's Utopia in Early Modern Europe: Paratexts and Contexts*. Manchester: Manchester University Press, 2012.

Chapple, Anne S., 'Robert Burton's Geography of Melancholy', *Studies in English Literature* 33 (1993): 99–130.

Charles-Daubert, Françoise, *Les Libertins érudits en France au XVIIe siècle*. Paris: Presses Universitaires de France, 1998.

Cheneval, Francis, *Philosophie in weltbürgerlicher Bedeutung. Über die Entstehung und die philosophischen Grundlagen des supranationalen und kosmopolitischen Denkens der Moderne*. Basel: Schwabe, 2002.

Chin, Tamara T., 'What is Imperial Cosmopolitanism? Revisiting *Kosmopolitēs* and Mundanus', in *Cosmopolitanism and Empire*. Myles Lavan, Richard E. Payne and John Weisweiler, eds. New York: Oxford University Press, 2016, 129–152.

Chyutin, Michael, 'The New Jerusalem: Ideal City', *Dead Sea Discoveries* 1 (1994): 71–97.

Čiževsky, Dmitri, 'Comenius' *Labyrinth of the World*: Its Themes and their Sources', *Harvard Slavic Studies* 1 (1970): 85–135.

Collinson, Patrick, *The Religion of Protestants: The Church in English Society, 1559-1625*. Oxford: Oxford University Press, 1979.

Condren, Conal, Stephen Gaukroger and Ian Hunter, eds. *The Philosopher in Early Modern Europe: The Nature of a Contested Identity*. Cambridge: Cambridge University Press, 2006.

Considine, John, *Academy Dictionaries, 1600–1800*. Cambridge: Cambridge University Press, 2014.

Cosgrove, Denis E., *Apollo's Eye: A Cartographic Genealogy of the Earth in the Western Imagination*. Baltimore: Johns Hopkins University Press, 2001.

Cotter, Cory S., 'Anglo-Dutch Dissent: British Dissenters in the Netherlands, 1662–88'. Unpublished PhD dissertation, University of Virginia, 2011.

Coulmas, Peter, *Weltbürger: Geschichte einer Menschheitssehnsucht*. Reinbeck: Rowohlt, 1990.

de Courcelles, Dominique, *Des femmes et des livres: France en Espagnes XIVe–XVIIe siècle*. Paris: L'ecole des Chartes, 1999.

Cressy, David, 'Literacy in Context: Meaning and Measurement in Early Modern England', in *Consumption and the World of Goods*. John Brewer and Roy Porter eds. London: Routledge, 1993, 305–319.

Dalton, Susan, *Engendering the Republic of Letters: Reconnecting Public and Private Spheres*. Montreal: McGill-Queen's University Press, 2003.

Damrosch, Leo, *Jean-Jacques Rousseau: Restless Genius*. New York: Mariner, 2007.

Darnton, Robert, *The Business of Enlightenment: A Publishing History of the Encyclopédie, 1775–1800*. Cambridge, MA: Harvard University Press, 1979.

Davis, J.C., *Utopia and the Ideal Society: A Study of English Utopian Writing, 1516–1700*. Cambridge: Cambridge University Press, 1981.

Derrida, Jacques, *Adieu to Emmanuel Levinas*, trans. P.A. Brault and M. Naas. Stanford: Stanford University Press, 1999.

Derrida, Jacques, *On Cosmopolitanism and Forgiveness*. London: Routledge, 2001.

Desan, Philippe, *Montaigne: A Life*. Steven Rendell and Lisa Neal, trans. Princeton: Princeton University Press, 2017.

Destombes, Marcel, 'Guillaume Postel cartographe', in *Guillaume Postel 1581–1981. Actes du Colloque International d'Avranches 5–9 septembre 1981*. Paris: Guy Trédaniel, 1985, 361–371.

DiCenso, James, *Kant, Religion, and Politics*. Cambridge: Cambridge University Press, 2011.

Dickson, Donald R., *The Tessera of Antilia: Utopian Brotherhoods and Secret Societies in Early Modern Germany*. Leiden: Brill, 1999.

Dietze, Walter, *Quirinus Kuhlmann. Ketzer und Poet. Versuch einer monographischen Darstellung von Leben und Werk*. Berlin: Rütten & Loening, 1963.

Dimmock, Matthew, 'Faith, Form and Faction: Samuel Purchas's *Purchas His Pilgrimage* (1613)', *Renaissance Studies* 28 (2014): 262–278.

Dreitzel, Horst, 'Zehn Jahre Patria in der politischen Theorie in Deutschland: Prasch, Pufendorf, Leibniz, Becher, 1662 bis 1672', in *Patria und Patrioten vor dem Patriotismus. Pflichten, Rechte, Glauben und die Rekonfigurierung europäischer Gemeinwesen im 17. Jahrhundert*. Wiesbaden: Harrassowitz, 2005, 367–534.

Dülmen, Richard von, *Die Utopie einer christlichen Gesellschaft: Johann Valentin Andreae (1586-1654)*. Stuttgart-Bad Cannstatt, 1978.

Dunning, Benjamin, *Aliens and Sojourners: Self as Other in Early Christianity*. Philadelphia: University of Pennsylvania Press, 2009.

Dupré, Louis, *Enlightenment and the Intellectual Foundations of Modern Culture*. New Haven: Yale University Press, 2005.

Ebeling, Florian, *The Secret History of Hermes Trismegistus*. Ithaca: Cornell University Press, 2007.

Edighoffer, Roland, '"Errores in Patria" zur Ambivalenz der Schöpfung bei Johann Valentin Andreae', in *Das Erbe des Christian Rosenkreuz. Johann Valentin Andreae 1586-1986 und die Manifeste der Rosenkreuzbruderschaft 1614-1616*. F.A. Jansen, ed. Amsterdam: In de Pelikaan, 1988, 48–62.

Edighoffer, Roland, *Rose-Croix et société idéale selon Johann Valentin Andreae*. 2 vols. Paris: Arma Artis, 1981–1987.

Edwards, Robert R., '"The Metropole and the Mayster-Toun": Cosmopolitanism and Late Medieval Literature', in *Cosmopolitan Geographies: New Locations in Literature and Culture*. Vinay Dharwadker, ed. New York and London: Routledge, 2001, 33–62.

Ehrard, Jean, 'Matérialisme et naturalisme: Les sources occultistes de la pensée de Diderot', *Cahiers de l'Association internationale des études francaises* 13 (1961): 189–201.

Elias, Norbert, *The Civilising Process: Sociogenetic and Psychogenetic Investigations*. Edmund Jephcott, trans. Oxford: Blackwell, 2000.

Enenkel, Karl. A.E. ed., *Transformations of the Classics via Early Modern Commentaries*. Leiden: Brill, 2013.

Engamarre, Max, 'La Bible de Jérôme Bolsec. Un témoin de l'émergence de la chronologie historique modern', in *Esculape et Dionysos: mélanges en l'honneur de Jean Céard*. Jean Dupèbe et al., eds. Geneva: Droz, 2008, 847–866.

Engberg-Pedersen, Troels, *Paul and the Stoics*, Louisville, KY: Knox, 2000.

Engberg-Pedersen, Troels, *Cosmology and Self in the Apostle Paul: The Material Spirit*. Oxford: Oxford University Press, 2010.

Engel, Gisla, et al., eds., *Geschlechterstreit am Beginn der europäischen Moderne: die Querelle des femmes*. Frankfurt am Main: Helmer, 2004.

Erdeljan, Jelena, *Chosen Places: Constructing New Jerusalems in Slavia Orthodoxa*. Leiden: Brill, 2017.

Eusterschulte, Anna and Günter Frank, eds. *Cicero in der Frühen Neuzeit*. Stuttgart-Bad Cannstatt: frommann-holzboog, 2017.

Faivre, Antoine, 'Elie Artiste, ou le messie des philosophes de la nature', *Aries* 2 (2002): 119–152 and 3 (2003): 25–54.

Feingold, Mordechai, 'And Knowledge Shall Be Increased: Millenarianism and the Advancement of Learning Revisited', *The Seventeenth Century* 28 (2013): 363–393.

Feldmeier, Reinhard, *Die Christen als Fremde: Die Metapher der Fremde in der antiken Welt, im Urchristentum und im 1. Petrusbrief*. Tübingen: Mohr-Siebeck, 1992.

Fetscher, Iring, *Rousseaus politische Philosophie. Zur Geschichte des demokratischen Freiheitsbegriffs*. Berlin: Suhrkamp, 1975.

Fiorillo, Vanda, 'La Patria, come Stato dei padri. La *obligatia ergo patriam* nella teoria politica di Samuel Pufendorf', in *Patria e nazione. Problemi di identità di appartenenza: Problemi di identità e di appartenenza*. Vanda Fiorillo and Gianluca Dioni, eds. Milan: Franco Angeli, 2013, 111–144.

Fontaine, Marie Madeleine, 'Barthélemy Aneau et la *Jurisprudentia*', in *Esculape et Dionysos: mélanges en l'honneur de Jean Céard*. Geneva: Droz, 2008, 1001–1112.

Forshaw, Peter J., 'The Early Alchemical Reception of John Dee's *Monas Hieroglyphica*', *Ambix* 52 (2005): 247–269.

Forster, Leonard, 'Quirinus Kuhlmann in Moscow 1689: An Unnoticed Account', *Germano-Slavica* 5 (1978): 317–323.

Freeman, Kathleen and Hermann Diel, *Ancilla to the Pre-Socratic Philosophers: A Complete Translation of the Fragments*. Cambridge, MA: Harvard University Press, 1948.

Friedeburg, Robert V., 'In Defense of Patria: Resisting Magistrates and the Duties of Patriots in the Empire from the 1530s to the 1640s', *Sixteenth Century Journal* 32 (2001): 357–382.

Friedeburg, Robert von, 'The Juridification of Natural Law: Christoph Besold's Claim for a Natural Right to Believe What One Wants', *The Historical Journal* 53/1 (2010): 1–19.

Friedeburg, Robert von, *Luther's Legacy: The Thirty Years War and the Modern Notion of 'State' in the Empire, 1530s to 1790s*. Oxford: Oxford University Press, 2016.

Fukuyama, Francis, *The End of History and the Last Man*. New York: Free Press, 1992.

Funk, Francis Xavier, *Disascalia et constitutiones apostolorum*. Paderborn, 1906.

Gatti, Hilary, *Giordano Bruno and Renaissance Science: Broken Lives and Organizational Power*. Ithaca, NY: Cornell University Press, 1999.

Gay, Peter, *The Enlightenment: An Interpretation*. New York: Knopf, 1966.

Genrich, Tom, *Authentic Fictions: Cosmopolitan Writing of the Troisème République*. Bern: Peter Lang, 2004.

Geyer, Hermann, *Verborgene Weisheit. Johann Arndts 'Vier Bücher vom Wahren Christentum' als Programm einer spiritualistisch-hermetischen Theologie*. 2 vols. Berlin: De Gruyter, 2001.

Gilly, Carlos, 'Das Sprichwort "Die Gelehrten die Verkehrten" oder der Verrat der Intellektuellen im Zeitalter der Glaubensspaltung', in *Forme e destinazione del messagio religioso*. A. Rotondò, ed. Florence: Olschki, 1991: 229–375.

Gilly, Carlos, *Adam Haslmayr: Der erste Verkünder der Manifeste der Rosenkreuzer*. Amsterdam: In de Pelikaan, 1994.

Gilly, Carlos, *Cimelia Rhodostaurotica: Die Rozenkreuzer im Spiegel der zwischen 1610 und 1660 entstandenen Handschriften und Drucke*. 2nd ed. Amsterdam: In de Pelikaan, 1994.

Gilly, Carlos, 'Don Quijote und Rosenkreuz: Die *Chymische Hochzeit* als alchemokritischer Ritterroman', *Recherches Germaniques* 13 (2018): 47–62.

Gilly, Carlos and Pleun van der Kooij, *Fama Fraternitatis. Das Urmanifest der Rosenkreuzer Bruderschafft*. Haarlem: Rozekruis Pers, 1999.

Gleeson, Janet, *The Arcanum: The Extraordinary True Story of the Invention of European Porcelain*. London: Bantam Press, 1998.

Goodman, Dena, *The Republic of Letters: A Cultural History of the French Enlightenment*. Cornell: Cornell University Press, 1984.

Goodman, Nan, *The Puritan Cosmopolis: The Law of Nations and the Early American Imagination*. Oxford: Oxford University Press, 2018.

Gordon, Andrew and Bernhard Klein, eds. *Literature, Mapping, and the Politics of Space in Early Modern Britain*. Cambridge: Cambridge University Press, 2002.

Gouhier, Henri, *Les Premières Pensées de Descartes: Contribution à l'histoire de l'Anti-Renaissance*. Paris, 1958.

Grafton, Anthony, *Defenders of the Text: The Traditions of Scholarship in an Age of Science, 1450–1800*. Cambridge, MA: Harvard University Press, 1994.

Grafton, Anthony and Lisa Jardine, *From Humanism to the Humanities: Education and the Liberal Arts in Fifteenth- and Sixteenth-Century Europe*. Cambridge: Cambridge University Press, 1986.

Greaves, Richard L., *Glimpses of Glory: John Bunyan and English Dissent*. Stanford: Stanford University Press, 2002.

Green, Jonathan, *Printing and Prophecy: Prognostication and Media Change, 1450–1550*. Ann Arbor: University of Michigan Press, 2011.

Greenblatt, Stephen. *The Swerve: How the World Became Modern*. New York: W.W. Norton, 2011.

Greengrass, Mark, 'Montaigne and the Wars of Religion', in *The Oxford Handbook of Montaigne*. Philippe Desan, ed. Oxford: Oxford University Press, 2016, 138–157.

Grenfell, Joanne Woolway, 'Do Real Knights Need Maps? Charting Moral, Geographical and Representational Uncertainty in Edmund Spenser's *The Faerie Queene*', in *Literature, Mapping, and the Politics of Space in Early Modern Britain*.

Andrew Gordon and Bernhard Klein, eds. Cambridge: Cambridge University Press, 2001, 224–238.

Hahn, Juergen, *The Origins of the Baroque Concept of Peregrinatio*. Chapel Hill: University of North Carolina Press, 1973.

Haran, Alexandre Y., *Le lys et le globe. Messianisme dynastique et rêve impérial en France aux xvie et xviie siècles*. Paris: Champ Vallon, 2000.

Harris, Ian, *The Mind of John Locke: A Study of Political Theory in its Intellectual Setting*. Revised ed. Cambridge: Cambridge University Press, 1998.

Harrison, Peter, 'Curiosity, Forbidden Knowledge, and the Reformation of Natural Philosophy in Early Modern England', *Isis* 92 (2001): 265–290.

Harwood, Jeremy, *To the End of the Earth: 100 Maps that Changed the World*. Cape Town: Stuik Publishing, 2006.

Hayden, Patrick, *Cosmopolitan Global Politics*. Farnham: Ashgate, 2005.

Hayden-Roy, Patrick Marshall, *The Inner Word and the Outer Word: A Biography of Sebastian Franck*. Zürich: Peter Lang, 1994.

Hazard, Paul, 'Cosmopolite', in *Mélanges d'histoire littéraire générale et comparée offerts à Ferdinand Baldensperger*. 2 vols. Paris: Champion, 1930, vol. 1, 354–364.

Hazard, Paul, *Die Herrschaft der Vernunft. Das europäische Denken im 18. Jahrhundert*. Hamburg: Hoffmann und Campe, 1949.

Headley, John, *Tomasso Campanella and the Transformation of the World*. Princeton, NJ: Princeton University Press, 1997.

Heater, Derek, *World Citizenship and Government: Cosmopolitan Ideas in the History of Western Political Thought*. London: Palgrave, 1996.

Held, David, *Cosmopolitanism: Ideals, Realities, and Deficits*. Cambridge: Polity Press 2010.

Helgerson, Richard, 'The Folly of Maps and Modernity', in *Literature, Mapping, and the Politics of Space in Early Modern Britain*. Andrew Gordon and Bernhard Klein, eds. Cambridge: Cambridge University Press, 2001, 241–262.

Hentsch, Thierry, *Imagining the Middle East*. Fred A. Read, trans. Montréal: Black Rose Books, 1992.

Heuvel, Gerd van den, 'Cosmopolite, Cosmopoli(ti)sme', *Handbuch politisch-sozialer Grundbegriffe in Frankreich 1680–1820. Heft 6*, Rolf Reichardt et al. eds. Munich: Oldenbourg, 1986, 41–55.

Hill, Jr., Thomas E. and Bernard Boxill, 'Kant and Race', in *Race and Racism*. Bernard Boxill, ed. Oxford: Oxford University Press, 2000, 448–471.

Hobsbawm, Eric, *Nations and Nationalism since 1780*. Cambridge: Cambridge University Press, 1990.

Hochstrasser T.J. and Peter Schröder, *Early Modern Natural Law Theories: Contexts and Strategies in the Early Enlightenment*. Dordrecht: Kluwer, 2002.

Hoffmann, George, *Reforming French Culture: Satire, Spiritual Alienation, and Connection to Strangers*. Oxford: Oxford University Press, 2017.

Honess, Claire E., *From Florence to the Heavenly City. The Poetry of Citizenship in Dante*. Abingdon & New York: Legenda, 2006.

Hooft, Stan van and Wim Vandekerckhove, eds. *Questioning Cosmopolitanism*. New York: Springer, 2010.

Horowitz, Maryanne Cline, 'The Stoic Synthesis of the Idea of Natural Law in Man: Four Themes', *Journal of the History of Ideas* 35 (1974): 3–16.

Horsman, Matthew and Andrew Marshall, *After the Nation-State: Citizens, Tribalism and the New World Disorder*. London: Harper Collins, 1994.

Houston, Chloë, *The Renaissance Utopia: Dialogue, Travel, and the Ideal Society*. London: Routledge, 2014.

Hulliung, Mark, *The Autocritique of Enlightenment: Rousseau and the Philosophes*. 2nd ed. London: Routledge, 2014.

Hunter, G.K., *John Lyly: The Humanist as Courtier*. Cambridge, MA: Harvard University Press, 1962.

Hunter, Ian, *The Secularisation of the Confessional State: The Political Thought of Christian Thomasius*. Cambridge: Cambridge University Press, 2007.

Huntington, Samuel P., 'The Clash of Civilisations?', *Foreign Affairs* 72/3 (1993): 22–49.

Insole, Christopher J., 'Kant on Christianity, Religion and Politics: Three Hopes, Three Limits', *Studies in Christian Ethics* 29/1 (2016): 14–33.

Jacob, Margaret C., *Strangers Nowhere in the World: The Rise of Cosmopolitanism in Early Modern Europe*. Philadelphia: University of Pennsylvania Press, 2006.

Jacob, Margaret C., 'The Cosmopolitan as a Lived Category', *Daedelus* 137 (2008): 18–25.

Jacob, Margaret C., 'Assessing the Cosmopolitan', *Eighteenth-Century Studies* 47/3 (2014).

Jantz, Harold, 'America's First Cosmopolitan', *Proceedings of the Massachusetts Historical Society*, 3rd Series, 84 (1972): 3–25.

Jennings, Theodore W., *Reading Derrida/Thinking Paul: On Justice* (Stanford: Stanford University Press, 2006).

John Dee's Books in the Royal College of Physicians' Library. A Handlist (London: Library of the Royal College of Physicians, [2016]).

de Jong, H.M.E., *Michael Maier's Atalanta Fugiens: Sources of an Alchemical Book of Emblems*. Leiden: Brill, 1969.

Josephson-Storm, Jason Ā., *The Myth of Disenchantment: Magic, Modernity and the Birth of the Human Sciences*. Chicago: University of Chicago Press, 2017.

Josten, C.H. 'A Translation of John Dee's *Monas hieroglyphica* (Antwerp, 1564), with an Introduction and Annotations', *Ambix* 12 (1964), 84–221.

Junzt, Friedrich Wilhelm von, *Von unaussprechlichen Kulten*. Düsseldorf: [No Printer], 1839.

Kahn, Didier, 'Between Alchemy and Antitrinitarianism: Nicholas Barnaud (ca. 1539-1604?)', in *Socinianism and Arminianism: Antitrinitarians, Calvinists and Cultural Exchange in Seventeenth Century Europe*. Martin Mulsow, Jan Rohls, eds. Leiden: Brill, 2005.

Keller, Vera, *Knowledge and the Public Interest, 1575–1725*. Cambridge: Cambridge University Press, 2016.

Keller, Vera and Leigh T.I. Penman, 'From the Archives of Scientific Diplomacy: Science and Shared Interests of Samuel Hartlib's London and Frederick Clodius's Gottorf', *ISIS* 106 (2015): 17–42.

Kennedy, Simon P., 'Richard Hooker as Political Naturalist', *Historical Journal* 62 (2018): 1–18.

Klay, Dale K. van, *The Religious Origins of the French Revolution: From Calvin to the Civil Constitution, 1560–1791*. New Haven: Yale University Press, 1996.

Kleingeld, Pauline, 'Six Varieties of Cosmopolitanism in Late Eighteenth-Century Germany', *Journal of the History of Ideas* 60/3 (1999): 505–524.

Kleingeld, Pauline, *Kant and Cosmopolitanism: The Philosophical Ideal of World Citizenship*. Cambridge: Cambridge University Press, 2012.

Koselleck, Reinhart, 'Einleitung', in *Geschichtliche Grundbegriffe: Historisches Lexikon zur politisch-sozialen Sprache in Deutschland*. Otto Brunner, Werner Conze and Reinhart Koselleck, eds. Stuttgart: Ernst Klett Verlag, 1972, vol. 1, xiii–xxvii.

Kötting, Bernhard, *Peregrinatio religiosa. Wallfahrten in der Antike und das Pilgerwesen in der alten Kirche*. Regensburg and Münster, 1950.

Kristeva, Julia, *Strangers to Ourselves*. Columbia: Columbia University Press, 1991.

Kruythooft, Cécile, 'Map of Utopia by Abraham Ortelius', *The Map Collector* 16 (1981): 10–14.

Kuntz, Marion Leathers, *Guillaume Postel, Prophet of the Restitution of all Things. His Life and Thought*. The Hague: M. Nijhoff, 1981.

Kvačala, Ján, ed. *Postelliana. Urkundliche Beiträge zur Geschichte der Mystik im Reformationszeitalter*. Juriev, 1915.

Kvačala, Ján, *Johann Valentin Andreä's Antheil an geheimen Gesellschaften*. Jurjew: Matthiessen, 1899.

de Labriolle, M.R., 'Le "Journal étranger" dans l'histoire du cosmopolitisme littéraire', *Studies on Voltaire and the Eighteenth Century* 56 (1967): 783–797.

Lagier, Raphaël, *Les races humaines selon Kant*. Paris: Presses Universitaires de France, 2004.

Larrimore, Mark, 'Sublime Waste: Kant on the Destiny of the "Races"', in *Civilization and Oppression*. Catherine Wilson, ed. Alberta: University of Calgary Press, 1999.

Leca-Tsiomis, Marie, *Écrire l'Encyclopédie: Diderot: De l'usage des dictionnaires à la grammaire philosophique*. Oxford: Voltaire Foundation, 1999.

Lee, Sang Meyng, *The Cosmic Drama of Salvation: A Study of Paul's Undisputed Writings from Anthropological and Cosmological Perspectives*. Tübingen: Mohr Siebeck, 2010.

Leibenguth, Erik, *Hermetische Poesie des Frühbarock, Die 'Cantilenae intellectuales' Michael Maiers, Edition mit Übersetzung, Kommentar und Bio-Bibliographie*. Tübingen: Max Niemeyer Verlag, 2002.

Lenke, Nils, Nicolas Roudet and Hereward Tilton, 'Michael Maier: Nine Newly Discovered Letters', *Ambix* 61 (2014): 1–47.

Leslie, Marina, *Renaissance Utopias and the Problem of History*. Ithaca: Cornell University Press, 1998.

Lestringant, Frank, *Écrire le monde à la Renaissance: quinze études sur Rabelais, Postel, Bodin et la littérature géographique*. Caen: Paradigme, 1993.

Lettevall, Rebecka and My Klockar Linder, eds. *The Idea of Kosmopolis: History, Philosophy, and Politics of World Citizenship*. Huddinge: Södertörns Höhskola, 2008.

Lievsay, John Leon, *Stefano Guazzo and the English Renaissance, 1575–1675*. Chapel Hill: University of North Carolina University Press, 1961.

Lilti, Antoine, *The World of the Salons: Sociability and Worldliness in Eighteenth-Century Paris*. Oxford: Oxford University Press, 2015.

Limbrick, Elaine, 'Montaigne and Socrates', *Renaissance and Reformation* 9/2 (1973): 46–57.

Lockey, Brian C., *Early Modern Catholics, Royalists, and Cosmopolitans: English Transnationalism and the Christian Commonwealth*. London: Ashgate, 2015.

Long, A.A., 'The Concept of the Cosmopolitan in Greek and Roman Thought', *Daedelus* 137 (2008): 50–58.

Louthan, Howard and Andrea Sterk, 'Introduction', in Comenius, *The Labyrinth of the World and the Paradise of the Heart*. Howard Louthan and Andrea Sterk, trans. and eds. New York: Paulist Press, 1998, 7–45.

Lutz, Cora E., 'Democritus and Heraclitus', *The Classical Journal* 49/7 (1954): 309–314.

Lutz, Cora E., 'Musonius Rufus: The Roman Socrates', *Yale Classical Studies* 10 (1947): 3–150.

MacMillan, Ken, 'Discourse on History, Geography, and Law: John Dee and the Limits of the British Empire, 1576–80', *Canadian Journal of History* 36:1 (2001): 1–25.

Maillard, Jean-François, 'Postel le Cosmopolite', in *Documents oubliés sur l'alchimie, la kabbale et Guillaume Postel*. S. Matton et al, eds. Geneva: Droz 2001, 199–222.

Malherbe, Abraham J., *Paul and the Popular Philosophers*. Minneapolis: Fortress Press, 1989.

Mansfield, Andrew, *Ideas of Monarchical Reform: Fénelon, Jacobitism and the Political Works of the Chevalier Ramsay*. Manchester: Manchester University Press, 2015.

Mansfield, Bruce, *Erasmus in the Twentieth Century*. Toronto: University of Toronto Press, 2003.

Markx, Francien, *E.T.A. Hoffmann, Cosmopolitanism, and the Struggle for German Opera*. Leiden: Brill, 2016.

Martinez, Alberto A., 'Giordano Bruno and the Heresy of Many Worlds', *Annals of Science* 73 (2016): 345–374.

Matytsin, Anton M. and Dan Edelstein, eds., *Let There Be Enlightenment: The Religious and Mystical Sources of Rationality*. Baltimore: Johns Hopkins University Press, 2018.

McCoy, Richard, *Alterations of State: Kingship in the English Reformation*. New York: Columbia University Press, 2002.

McGee, J.S., 'On Misidentifying Puritans: The Case of Thomas Adams', *Albion* 30 (1998): 402–418.

McKnight, Stephen A., *The Religious Foundations of Francis Bacon's Thought*. Columbia: University of Missouri Press, 2006.

Meyer, Jenny, 'Barthélemy Aneau's *Alector ou le coq* and the Paradox of Renaissance Cosmopolitanism', *Renaissance and Reformation* 38 (2015): 5–26.

Midelfort, H.C. Erik, *A History of Madness in Sixteenth-Century Germany*. Stanford: Stanford University Press, 1999.

Miller, Richard W., 'The Cosmopolitanism Controversy Needs a Mid-Life Crisis', in *Cosmopolitanism versus Non-Cosmopolitanism: Critiques, Defenses, Reconceptualizations*. Gillian Brock, ed. Oxford: Oxford University Press, 2013, 272–293.

Miltner, J.B., 'Haberveslové z Habernfeldu', *Památky archeologické* 8 (1868): 46–56.

Montgomery, John Warwick, *Cross and Crucible: Johann and Valentin Andreae, Phoenix of the Theologians*. 2 vols. Dordrecht: Kluwer, 1973.

More, Anna, 'Cosmopolitanism and Scientific Reason in New Spain: Carlos de Sigüenza y Góngora and the Dispute over the 1680 Comet', in *Science in the Spanish and Portuguese Empires, 1500–1800*. Daniela Bleichmar et al., eds. Stanford: Stanford University Press, 2009, 115–131.

Mori, Gianluca, 'Du Marsais philosophe clandestin: textes et attributions', in *La Philosophie clandestine à l'Age classique*. Antony McKenna and Alain Mothu, eds. Paris and Oxford: Voltaire Foundation, 1997, 169–192.

Moss, Ann, 'The *Politica* of Justus Lipsius and the Commonplace-Book', *Journal of the History of Ideas* 59 (1998): 421–436.

Moss, Ann, *Renaissance Truth and the Latin Language Turn*. Oxford: Oxford University Press, 2003.

Mout, Nicolette, 'Ondřej Habervešl of Habernfeld and the Thirty Years' War: His Writings, the War and International Politics', in *Mezi Baltem a Uhrami. Komenský, Jednota bratrská a svět středoevropského protestantismu*. Vladimír Urbánek, Lenka Řezníková, eds. Prague: Filosofia, 2006, 149–165.

Mulder, William, 'Style and the Man: Thomas Adams, Prose Shakespeare of Puritan Divines', *Harvard Theological Review* 48 (1955): 129–152.

Müller, Johannes, 'Transmigrant Literature: Translating, Publishing, and Printing in Seventeenth-Century Frankfurt's Migrant Circles', *German Studies Review* 40/1 (2017): 1–21.

Nava, Mica, *Visceral Cosmopolitanism: Gender, Culture and the Normalisation of Difference*. Oxford and New York: Berg, 2007.

Neeb, Christoph, *Christlicher Hass wider die Welt. Philosophie und Staatstheorie des Johann Valentin Andreae (1586–1654)*. Frankfurt am Main: Peter Lang, 1999.

Needham, Catherine, 'The Idea of Cosmopolitanism in Eighteenth Century Letters', Unpublished M.A. diss., University of Illinois, 1919.

Newman, William R., *Gehennical Fire: The Lives of George Starkey, an American Alchemist in the Scientific Revolution*. Chicago: University of Chicago Press, 2003.

Nussbaum, Martha C., 'Patriotism and Cosmopolitanism', *Boston Review*, October–November 1994, 3–6.

Nussbaum, Martha C., 'Kant and Stoic Cosmopolitanism', *The Journal of Political Philosophy* 5 (1997): 1–25.

Nussbaum, Martha C., *The Cosmopolitan Tradition: A Noble but Flawed Ideal*. Cambridge, MA: The Belknap Press of Harvard University, 2019.

Nussbaum, Martha C. and J. Cohen, eds., *For the Love of Country: Debating the Limits of Patriotism*. Boston: Beacon Press, 1996.

Nuti, Lucia, 'The World Map as an Emblem: Abraham Ortelius and the Stoic Contemplation', *Imago Mundi* 55 (2003): 38–55.

Obbink, D., 'The Stoic Sage in the Cosmic City', in *Topics in Stoic Philosophy*. K. Ierodiakonou, ed. Oxford: Oxford University Press, 1999, vol. 7, 178–195.

O'Brien, Karen, *Narratives of Enlightenment. Cosmopolitan History from Voltaire to Gibbon*. Cambridge: Cambridge University Press, 1997.

Ordine, Nuccio, *Giordano Bruno and the Philosophy of the Ass*. Henryk Baranski and Arielle Saiber, trans. New Haven: Yale University Press, 1996.

Pagden, Anthony, 'Stoicism, Cosmopolitanism, and the Legacy of European Imperialism', *Constellations* 7/1 (2000): 3–22.

Pagden, Anthony, *The Enlightenment: And Why it Still Matters*. Oxford: Oxford University Press, 2013.

Pagel, Walter, 'The Paracelsian Elias Artista and the Alchemical Tradition', in *Kreatur und Kosmos. Internationale Beiträge zur Paracelsusforschung*. Rosemarie Dilg-Frank, ed. New York and Stuttgart: Gustav Fischer Verlag, 1981, 6–19.

Painter, Douglas M., 'Humanist Insights and the Vernacular in Sixteenth-Century France', *History of European Ideas* 16 (1993): 67–73.

Papy, Jan, '"Italiam vestram amo supa omnes terras!" Lipsius's Attitude towards Italy and Italian Humanism of the late Sixteenth Century', *Humanistica Lovaniensia* 47 (1998): 245–277.

Papy, Jan, 'Erasmus, Europe, and Cosmopolitanism: The Humanist Image and Message in his Letters', in *Erasmo da Roterodam e la cultura europea. Atti dell'Incontro di Studi nel V centenario della laurea di Erasmo all'Università di Torino*. Pietro B. Rossi, ed. Florence: SISMEL-Edizioni del Galluzzo, 2008, 27–42.

Parry, Glyn, 'John Dee and the Elizabethan British Empire in its European Context', *The Historical Journal* 49 (2006): 643–675.

Parry, Glyn, *The Arch-Conjuror of England: John Dee*. New Haven and London: Yale University Press, 2011.

Pasche, Christophè, 'Comédie Jouée a Moudon en 1604', *Revue historique vaudoise* 8 (1900): 367–377.

Penman, Leigh T.I., '"Sophistical Fancies and Mear Chimaeras?" Traiano Boccalini's *Ragguagli di Parnaso* and the Rosicrucian Enigma', *Bruniana & Campanelliana* 15/1 (2009): 79–98.

Penman, Leigh T.I., 'The Hidden History of the Cosmopolitan Concept: Heavenly Citizenship and the Aporia of World Community', *Journal of the Philosophy of History* 9 (2015): 284–305.

Penman, Leigh T.I., '*Der Weg zu Christo*: Jacob Böhme and Pilgrimage', in *Grund und Ungrund. Der Kosmos des mystischen Philosophen Jacob Böhme*. Claudia Brink and Lucinda Martin, eds. Dresden: Sandstein Verlag, 2017, 68–81.

Penman, Leigh T.I., *Hope and Heresy: The Problem of Chiliasm in Lutheran Confessional Culture, 1570–1630*. Dordrecht: Springer, 2019.

Petry, Yvonne, *Gender, Kabbalah, and the Reformation: The Mystical Theology of Guillaume Postel*. Leiden: Brill, 2004.

Pierik, Roland and Wouter Werner, eds. *Cosmopolitanism in Context: Perspectives from International Law and Political Theory*. Cambridge: University of Cambridge Press, 2010.

Pinson, Yona, *The Fools' Journey: A Myth of Obsession in Northern Renaissance Art*. Turnhout: Brepols, 2008.

Pollock, Sheldon, Homi K. Bhabha, Carol A. Breckenridge and Dipesh Chakrabarty, 'Cosmopolitanisms', *Public Culture* 12 (2000): 577–589.

Poole, Steven, *A Word for Every Day of the Year*. London: Quercus, 2019.

Popkin, Richard H., *The History of Scepticism from Savonarola to Bayle*. 3rd ed. Oxford: Oxford University Press, 2003.

Postel, Claude, *Les écrits de Guillaume Postel publiés en France et leurs éditeurs (1538–1579)*. Geneva: Droz, 1992.

Postel, Claude, *L'homme prophétique. Science et magie à la Renaissance*. Paris: Les Belles Lettres, 1999.

Poulsen, Frank Ejby, 'Anarchasis Cloots and the Birth of Modern Cosmopolitanism', in *Critique of Cosmopolitan Reason: Timing and Spacing the Concept of World Citizenship*. Rebecka Lettevall and Kristian Petrov, eds. Bern: Peter Lang, 2014, 87–117.

Prinke, Rafał T., 'Beyond Patronage: Michael Sendivogius and the Meanings of Success in Alchemy', in *Chymia: Science and Nature in Medieval and Early Modern Europe*. M. López Pérez, D. Kahn and M.R. Bueno, eds. Newcastle upon Tyne: Cambridge Scholars Press, 2010, 175–231.

Prinke, Rafał T., 'Nolite de me inquirere (Nechtětje se po mně ptáti): Michael Sendivogius', in *Alchymie a Rudolf II. hledání tajemství přírody ve středni Evropě 16. a 17. století*, Ivo Purš and Vladimír Karpenko, eds. Prague: Artefactum, 2011, 317–334.

Prinke, Rafał T., 'New Light on the Alchemical Writings of Michael Sendivogius (1566–1636)', *Ambix* 63 (2016): 217–243.

Prinke, Rafał T. and Mike A. Zuber, 'Alchemical Patronage and the Making of an Adept: Letters of Michael Sendivogius to Emperor Rudolf II and his Chamberlain Hans Popp', *Ambix* 65 (2018): 324–355.

Ramachandran, Ayesha, 'How to Theorize the "World": An Early Modern Manifesto', *New Literary History* 48 (2017): 655–684.

Richter, Daniel S. *Cosmopolis: Imagining Community in Late Classical Athens and the Early Roman Empire*. Oxford: Oxford University Press, 2011.

Robbins, Bruce, 'Actually Existing Cosmopolitanism', in *Cosmopolitics: Thinking and Feeling beyond the Nation*. Bruce Robbins and Pheng Cheoh, eds. Minneapolis: University of Minnesota Press, 1998, 1–19.

Roberts, J.M., *The Mythology of the Secret Societies*. London: Secker & Warburg, 1972.

Roberts, Julian and Andrew D. Watson, eds. *John Dee's Library Catalogue*. London: The Bibliographical Society, 1990.

Roldanus, Johannes, 'Références patristiques au "chrétien-êtranger" dans les trois premiers siècles', *Cahiers de Biblia Patristica* 1 (1987): 27–52.

Rosenberg, Daniel, 'An Eighteenth-Century Time Machine: The *Encyclopedia* of Denis Diderot', *Réflexions historiques* 25/2 (1999): 227–250.

Rosenblatt, Helena, 'Rousseau the anti-Cosmopolitan', *Daedalus* 137/3 (2008): 59–67.

Rosenfeld, Nancy, *John Bunyan's Imaginary Writings in Context*. New York and London: Routledge, 2018.

Rowland, Ingrid D., *Giordano Bruno: Philosopher/Heretic*. Chicago: University of Chicago Press, 2009.

Rummel, Erika, *The Confessionalization of Humanism in Reformation Germany*. Oxford: Oxford University Press, 2000.

Runia, David T., 'The Idea and the Reality of the City in the Thought of Philo of Alexandria', *Journal of the History of Ideas* 61 (2000): 361–379.

Salazar, Philippe-Joseph, *'La Divine Sceptique.' Ethique et rhétorique au 17eme siècle; autour de La Mothe Le Vayer*. Tübingen: Gunter Narr Verlag, 2000.

Salvadori, Stefania, 'From Spiritual Regeneration to Collective Reformation in the Writings of Christoph Besold and Johann Valentin Andreae', *Aries* 14 (2014): 1–19.

Sanahuja, Lorena Cebolla, *Toward Kantian Cosmopolitanism*. London: Palgrave Macmillan, 2017.

Sasaki, Chikara, *Descartes's Mathematical Thought*. New York & Dordrecht: Springer, 2003.

Scaltsas, Theodore and Andrew S. Mason, eds. *The Philosophy of Epictetus*. Oxford: Oxford University Press, 2010.

Scattola, Merio, 'Before and After Natural Law: Models of Natural Law in Ancient and Modern Times', in *Early Modern Natural Law Theories: Contexts and Strategies in the Early Enlightenment*. T.J. Hochstrasser and M. Schröder, eds. Dordrecht: Springer, 2003, 1–30.

Scattola, Merio, *Dalla virtù alla scienza: la fondazione e la trasformazione della disciplina politica nell'età moderna*. Milan: Angeli, 2003.

Schelkshorn, Hans, 'The Change of Geographical Worldviews and Francisco De Vitoria's Foundation of a Modern Cosmopolitanism', in *Between Creativity and Norm-Making: Tensions in the Early Modern Era*. Leiden: Brill, 2012, 165–188.

Schlereth, Thomas J., *The Cosmopolitan Ideal in Enlightenment Thought: Its Form and Function in the Ideas of Franklin, Hume, and Voltaire, 1694–1790*. Notre Dame and London: The University of Notre Dame Press, 1977.

Schlesinger, Roger, *In the Wake of Columbus: The Impact of the New World on Europe, 1492–1650*, 2nd ed. New York: Harlan Davidson, 2006.

Schmidt, Peer, *Spanische Universalmonarchie oder 'teutsche Libertet.' Das spanische Imperium in der Propaganda des Dreißigjährigen Krieges*. Stuttgart: Franz Steiner Verlag, 2001.

Schmidt-Biggemann, Wilhelm, 'Salvation through Philology: The Poetical Messianism of Quirinus Kuhlmann (1651–1689)', in *Toward the Millennium: Messianic Expectations from the Bible to Waco*. P. Schäfer and M. R. Cohen, eds. Leiden: Brill, 1998, 259–298.

Schnabel, Werner Wilhelm, 'Exulantenlieder. Über Konstituierung und Verfestigung von Selbst- und Fremdbildern mit literarischen Mitteln', in *Frühneuzeitliche Stereotype. Zur Produktivität und Restriktivität sozialer Vorstellungsmuster.* Mirosława Czarnecka and Thomas Borgstedt et al., eds. Berne: Peter Lang, 2010, 317–353.

Schneider, Heinrich, *Joachim Morsius und sein Kreis. Zur Geistesgeschichte des 17. Jahrhunderts.* Lübeck: Quitzlow, 1929.

Schofield, M., *The Stoic Idea of the City*. Cambridge: Cambridge University Press, 1991.

Schunka, Alexander, 'Constantia im Martyrium. Zur Exilliteratur des 17. Jahrhunderts zwischen Humanismus und Barock', in *Frühneuzeitliche Konfessionskulturen.* Thomas Kaufmann, Anselm Schubert and Kaspar von Greyerz, eds. Gütersloh: Gütersloher Verlagshaus, 2008, 175–200.

Sellevold, Kirsti, 'The French Versions of Utopia', in *Thomas More's* Utopia *in Early Modern Europe: Paratexts and Contexts.* Terence Cave, ed. Manchester and New York: Manchester University Press, 2008, 67–86.

Shackelford, Jole, 'Giordano Bruno as the First Scientific Martyr', in *Galileo Goes to Jail, and Other Myths about Science and Religion.* Ronald L. Numbers, ed. Cambridge, MA: Harvard University Press, 2009, 59–67.

Shankar, Amulya, '"Cosmopolitan" Is a Dog Whistle Word Once Used in Nazi Germany and Communist Russia', *PRI*, 3 August 2017.

Shantz, Douglas, 'Homeless Minds: The Migration of Radical Pietists, their Writings, and Ideas in Early Modern Europe', in *Pietism in Germany and North America 1680-1820.* Jonathan Strom et al., eds. Farnham: Ashgate, 2009, 85–100.

Scuccimarra, Luca, *I Confini del Mondo. Storia del cosmopolitismo dall'Antichità al Settecento*. Bologna: Il Mulino, 2006.

Secret, François, *Postelliana*. Nieuwkoop: B. de Graaf, 1981.

Serjeantson, Richard, 'Natural Knowledge in the *New Atlantis*', in *Francis Bacon's New Atlantis*. Bronwen Price, ed. Manchester: Manchester University Press, 2002, 82–105.

Sherlock, Peter, *Monuments and Memories in Early Modern England*. Aldershot: Ashgate, 2008.

Sherman, William, *John Dee: The Politics of Reading and Writing in the English Renaissance*. Amherst: University of Massachusetts Press, 1995.

Shirley, Rodney, 'Who Was Epichtonius Cosmopolites?' *The Map Collector* 18 (1982): 40–41.

Shirley, Rodney, *The Mapping of the World: Early Printed World Maps, 1472-1750*. London: Holland Press, 1983.

[Skeat, Walter William], 'Report upon "Ghost-Words", or Words which Have No Real Existence', *Transactions of the Philological Society*, S.N. (1886): 350–374.

Skinner, Quentin, 'Rhetoric and Conceptual Change', *Finnish Yearbook of Political Thought* 3 (1999): 60–73.

Skinner, Quentin, 'Language and Social Change', in *Quentin Skinner and his Critics*. James Tully, ed. Princeton: Princeton University Press, 1988, 119–133.

Skinner, Quentin, 'Meaning and Understanding in the History of Ideas', in Quentin Skinner, *Visions of Politics: Regarding Method*. Cambridge: Cambridge University Press, 2002, vol. 1, 57–89.

Smith, Anthony D., *Chosen Peoples: Sacred Sources of National Identity*. Oxford: Oxford University Press, 2004.

Smith, Pamela H., *The Business of Alchemy: Science and Culture in the Holy Roman Empire*. Princeton: Princeton University Press, 1994.

Solomon, Howard M., *Public Welfare, Science, and Propaganda in Seventeenth-Century France: The Innovations of Théophraste Renaudot*. Princeton: Princeton University Press, 1972.

Sorkin, David, *The Religious Enlightenment*. Princeton: Princeton University Press, 2008.

Sorkin, David, *Moses Mendelssohn and the Religious Enlightenment*. London: Peter Halban, 2012.

Spampanato, Vincenzo, *Vita di Giordano Bruno, con documenti editi e inediti*. 2 vols. Messina: G. Principato, 1921.

Steel, Eric M., *Diderot's Imagery. A Study of a Literary Personality*. New York: Haskell House, 1966.

Stein, Gabriele, *The English Dictionary before Cawdrey*. Berlin: De Gruyter, 1985.

Stępkowski, Aleksander, ed. *O senatorze doskonałym studia: Prace upamiętniające postać i twórczość Wawrzyńca Goślickiego*. Warsaw: Kancelaria Senatu, 2009.

Teyssandier, Bernard, 'L'ethos érudit dans l'*Avis pour dresser une bibliothèque* de Gabriel Naudé', *Littératures Classiques* 66/2 (2008), 115–131.

Thielking, Sigrid, *Weltbürgertum: Kosmopolitische Ideen in Literatur und politischer Publizistik seit dem achtzehnten Jahrhundert*. Munich: Fink, 2000.

Thompson, C.R., 'Erasmus as Internationalist and Cosmopolitan', *Archiv für Reformationsgeschichte* 46 (1955): 167–195.

Tihanov, Galin, 'Cosmopolitanism in the Discursive Landscape of Modernity: Two Enlightenment Articulations', in *Enlightenment Cosmopolitanism*. David Armstrong and Galin Tihanov, eds. London: Legenda and Routledge, 2011.

Tihanov, Galin, 'Whose Cosmopolitanism? Genealogies of Cosmopolitanism', in *Whose Cosmopolitanism? Critical Perspectives, Relationalities and Discontents*. Nina Glick Schiller, Andrew Irving, eds. Oslo: Berghan Books, 2014.

Tilton, Hereward, *The Quest for the Phoenix: Spiritual Alchemy and Rosicrucianism in the Work of Count Michael Maier (1569–1622)*. Berlin: Walter de Gruyter, 2003.

Tracy, James, *The Politics of Erasmus: A Pacifist Intellectual and His Political Milieu.* Toronto: University of Toronto Press, 1978.

Turnbull, David, 'Cook and Tupaia, a Tale of Cartographic Méconnaissance?' in *Science and Exploration in the Pacific: European Voyages to the Southern Oceans in the Eighteenth Century.* Margarette Lincoln, ed. Woodbridge: Boydell, 1998, 117–132.

Turnbull, G.H., 'John Hall's Letters to Samuel Hartlib', *The Review of English Studies* Vol. 4, 15 (1953): 221–233.

Turnbull, G.H., 'Johann Valentin Andreae's Societas Christiana', *Zeitschrift für Deutsche Philologie* 73 (1954): 407–432 and 74 (1955): 151–185.

Turner, James, *Philology: The Forgotten Origins of the Humanities.* Princeton: Princeton University Press, 2014.

Turner, John D., 'Allogenes the Stranger', in *The Nag Hammadi Scriptures.* Marvin Meyer, ed. (New York: Harper & Collins, 2008), 679–700.

Urbánek, Vladimír, *Eschatologie, vědění a politika: Příspěvek k dějinám myšlení pobělohorského exilu.* České Budějovice: Jihočeská univerzita v Českých Budějovicích, 2008.

Vertovec, Steven and Robin Cohen, eds. *Conceiving Cosmopolitanism: Theory, Context, and Practice.* Oxford: Oxford University Press, 2002.

Wade, Ira O., *The Clandestine Organization and Diffusion of Philosophic Ideas in France from 1700 to 1750.* New York: Octagon Books, 1967.

Wang, Andreas, *Der 'Miles Christianus' im 16. und 17. Jahrhundert und seine mittelalterliche Tradition. Ein Beitrag zum Verhältnis von sprachlicher und graphischer Bildlichkeit.* Frankfurt: Peter Lang, 1975.

Weeks, Andrew, *Valentin Weigel: German Religious Dissenter, Speculative Theorist and Advocate of Tolerance.* Albany: SUNY Press, 2000.

Weiss, Judith, 'Structure amid the Chaos: The Quadruple Structure in Guillaume Postel's Thought', *The Journal of Religion* 99/3 (2019): 361–382.

Welman, Kathleen Anne, *Making Science Social: The Conferences of Théophraste Renaudot, 1633–1642.* Norman, OK: University of Oklahoma Press, 2003.

Werner, Elke Anna, 'Triumphierende Europa – Klagende Europa. Zur visuellen Konstruktion europäischer Selbstbilder in der Frühen Neuzeit', in *Europa- Stier und Sternenkranz. Von der Union mit Zeus zum Staatenverbund.* Roland Alexander Ißler and Almut-Barbara Renger, eds. Göttingen: Vandenhoeck & Ruprecht, 2009, 241–260.

White, Howard B., *Peace Among the Willows: The Political Philosophy of Francis Bacon.* The Hague: Martinus Nijhoff, 1968.

White, Reginald James, *The Anti-Philosophers: A Study of the Philosophes in Eighteenth-Century France.* London: MacMillan, St. Martin's Press, 1970.

Whitehead, A.N., *Science and the Modern World*. New York: Macmillan, 1928.

Whitfield, Peter, *The Image of the World: 20 Centuries of World Maps*. London: The British Library, 1994.

Wilding, Michael, 'A Biography of Edward Kelly', in *Mystical Metal of Gold: Essays on Alchemy and Renaissance Culture*. Stanton J. Linden, ed. New York: AMS Press, 2007, 35–114.

Wilkinson, Robert John, *The Kabbalistic Scholars of the Antwerp Polyglot Bible*. Leiden: Brill, 2007.

Williams, George Huntston, *The Radical Reformation*. 3rd ed. Kirksville, MO: Truman State University Press, 1995.

Wintle, Michael, 'Renaissance Maps and the Construction of the Idea of Europe', *Journal of Historical Geography* 25 (1999): 137–165.

Wolfe, Jessica L., 'The Cosmopolitanism of *The Adages*: The Classical and Christian Legacies of Erasmus' Hermeneutics of Accommodation', in *Cosmopolitanism and the Middle Ages*. John M. Ganim and Shayne Aaron Legassie, eds. New York: Springer, 2013, 207–230.

Wood, Allen W., 'Philosophy: Enlightenment Apology, Enlightenment Critique', in *What Is Philosophy?* C.P. Ragland and Sarah Heidt, eds. New Haven: Yale University Press, 2001, 96–120.

Wood, Allen W., *Kant's Moral Religion*. Ithaca, NY: Cornell University Press, 2009.

Yewbrey, Graham, 'John Dee and the "Sidney Group": Cosmopolitics and Protestant "Activism" in the 1570s'. Unpublished PhD dissertation, University of Hull, 1981.

Index

Abraham (biblical) 5, 23, 24, 33
Adam (biblical) 5, 6, 20, 68, 76, 94, 95
Adams, Thomas 78
Addison, Joseph 107
Agrippa, Heinrich Cornelius 70, 88
alchemy 28, 34, 98–102, 103, 111
Allogenes the Stranger 6
Ambrose of Milan 6, 7
America 27, 41, 43, 51, 91, 124
Andreae, Johann Valentin
    Christianopolis 59, 65–66
    Cosmoxenus 68–69
    Mythologiae Christianiae 69–70
    Rosicrucianism 71–73, 75
    Turris Babel 72
Aneau, Barthélemy 59–60, 94, 116, 120
Anglicanism 67, 76
Anthony, Francis 98–99
antisemitism 129
anticlericalism 57, 70, 73, 75
apocalypticism 23–24, 30–33, 37, 42, 46, 74–75, 97
Apostolic Constitutions 6
Aristotle 70, 76, 102, 103, 112
Arius Didymus 94
Arndt, Johann 70–71, 75
atheism 79, 120
Augustine 7, 56, 61, 124

Babylon 57, 74–75
Bacon, Francis 60–62, 66, 85
Barlow, William 42
Barnaud, Nicholas 74
Barton, Thomas 81
Bates, William 83
Bayle, Pierre 112
Becher, Johann Joachim 99
Bennefield, Sebastian 79
Bergerac, Cyrano 88
Besold, Christoph 30, 36, 80
Birken, Sigismund von 83

Blount, Thomas 85, 93, 108
Bodin, Jean 41, 43
Böhme, Jacob 73
Bolsec, Jérôme 87
Bolton, Edmund 80
Botero, Giovanni 36
Boulaese, Jehan 21–22
Boyle, Robert 101, 103–104
Braun, Georg 51–52
Bruno, Giordano 101–102, 103
Bunyan, John 57–52
Burton, Robert 46

Campanella, Tomasso 30, 35, 59–60
cartography 43, 45–51, 53–62
Chambers, Ephraim 109–110, 111
Charles V 51, 52
Charron, Pierre 87
Christian Soldiers 53–56, 57, 68–69, 74
Chrysippus of Soli 94
Cicero 5, 7, 29, 59, 67, 94, 113
citizenship
    heavenly 29, 30, 54–56, 66, 80, 83, 104, 106, 124, 130
    terrestrial 1–2, 121, 130
city
    of heaven 2, 82, 130
    of the universe 92, 111–112
    of the world 5, 8, 9, 29, 56, 99, 101
Cleanthes of Assos 94
Clément Jean-Marie-Bernard de 118, 119
Cloots, Anarchasis 112, 119, 120
Comenius, Jan Amos 36, 56–57
commerce 99, 129
communism 10, 120
conspiracy 76, 118
Coornhert, Dirck Volckertszoon 49, 50
Cornutus, Lucius Annaeus 46
cosmopolitan vocabulary 3, 5–10, 30, 67–68, 104, 119–120, 127–128

cosmopolitan identity
    as elite 88, 117, 129
    as everyman 86–89, 98, 118–119, 120
    women and 88–89
cosmopolitanism
    in early modernity 8–9, 125, 127–128
    in Enlightenment 105–106
    French Revolution 119
    ideal 127–128
    meta-discourse 104, 106–107, 114, 116, 125, 128
    modern scholarship 10–12, 105–106, 128–130
    sacred conceptions of 3–4, 5–6, 9, 15–16, 106–108, 113
    secular conceptions of 2, 4, 5, 106, 113
cosmopolitics 28, 29, 30, 32, 39, 42
Cosmoxenus 66, 68–69, 80
Crooke, Samuel 66, 81
Crousaz, Jean-Pierre de 111
Cyclopædia (1728), 109
cynics, cynicism 5, 9, 22, 86, 100

Dee, John
    cosmopolitan 12, 16, 24–25, 28–29, 32
    imperialism 25, 29, 31–33
    Postel and 24, 26
    prophecy 27–28, 31
    reception 41, 123
deism 107, 112, 115, 116
Democritus of Abdera 8, 47, 49–51
Descartes, René 75–76, 103
devotional literature 56–58, 70–71
dictionaries 85–86, 107–112, 119
Dictionnaire universel 109, 110
Diderot, Denis 8, 110–112, 114–115, 118, 129–130
Diogenes of Sinope 5, 22, 77, 83, 95, 100, 107, 109, 127
Diogenes Laërtius 7
Doneau, Hughes 74
Drabík, Mikuláš 36
duty 81–82

Ecclesia spiritualis 4, 7
Edgar the Peaceful 32, 51
Elias (prophecy) 19, 23, 101

Elizabeth I 28, 31, 33–35, 76
Encyclopédie (1751) 110–115, 117, 128
enlightenment 105–106, 114, 121, 128
Epictetus 7, 67, 90
Erasmus of Rotterdam 1–3, 8, 47, 55
Estienne, Henri 87
Euclid 24
European Union 5, 129
Everaert, Anthonius 98
exploration, voyages of 42–43

Faret, Nicolas 88
Ferdinand I Holy Roman Emperor 19, 21
Ficino, Marsilio 89
Fontenelle, Bernard de 113
fools 46–49
    see also jesters
'Fool's Cap' maps 45–49, 50–51
Franck, Sebastian 73
Freemasons 118
French Revolution 106, 118–120, 121
Frisch, Johann Leonard 110, 111

Gearing, William 79–80
geography 12, 20, 39, 40, 42, 46, 53, 54
Gibbon, Charles 95
Göchhausen, Ernst August von 118, 119
Gomer 18, 21, 33
Goodwin, George 74–75
Gourmount, Jean de 48, 50, 51–53
Grapaldi, Francisco Erasmus 7
Grießmann, Valentin 76, 83
Grimaldus, Laurentius 30–31, 34, 40, 86–87, 95, 113
Grimm, Friedrich Melchior von 114
Guazzo, Stefano 86

Haberweschel von Habernfeld, Andreas 103–104
Habsburgs 18, 27–28, 36
Hakluyt, Richard 41, 43
Hartlib, Samuel 62–63
heaven 6, 50, 53–58, 72, 79, 94, 103
Hebrews 5–7, 19, 23, 30, 60, 94–95, 97, 127
Heemskerck, Marten van 49
Henri III of Anjou 74
Henri IV of France 53
Heraclitus 47, 49–51
Hercules 40, 68, 70

Hermes Trismegistus 100, 103–104
Hess, Tobias 71
Holy Roman Empire 18, 51, 82
Homo viator 7, 54–56, 59–62, 65–68, 102, 103, 113
Hondius, Jodocus 53–55
honnête homme 88
Hooker, Richard 95, 113
hospitality 3, 59, 120, 121
Howell, James 93
Huguenots 74
human rights 121–122
humanism 7, 15–16, 86, 89–92, 112
Hume, David 112, 114–115

Illuminati 118
imperialism 15–37, 51, 59–60, 94–95, 100
individualism 117

Jacobins 119
James I of England 43
Jerusalem 6, 7, 19, 22, 29, 32, 42, 54–56, 61, 66, 101, 102, 103
jesters 45–46, 48, 50
Jesuits 18, 118
Jesus 7, 26, 55, 60, 80, 90, 97
Jews 118, 129
Journal étranger 116
Juvenal 46

Kabbalah 19, 97
Kant, Immanuel
    cosmopolitanism 9, 11, 105, 121–122
    Perpetual Peace 121, 123
    philosophical chiliasm 123
    racism 123–124
    and Reformation 122–124
    religion 122–123
Kelly (Kelley), Edward 34, 35
knowledge 89, 100, 103
Koran 18, 20
Kuhlmann, Quirinus 30, 36–37

La Mothe Le Vayer, François de 92, 106, 111, 112, 113
law
    divine 5, 32, 59, 72, 94, 97, 117
    moral 94, 96

    natural 72, 94, 96, 97, 113, 116, 121
    universal 94, 96, 97, 121–122
Leibniz, Gottfried Wilhelm 105
L'Eussa, Pierre de 91
Lipsius, Justus 8, 90, 93
Locke, John 81
Lotich, Johann Peter 98
Louis XIV 92
Loyola, Ignatius 17, 18
Lyly, John 87

Maier, Michael 98–99
maps 43–55
Marcus Aurelius 80
Marsais, César Chesneau du 112
Maximilian II Holy Roman Emperor 26, 33, 35
May, Theresa 129, 130
medicine 98–100, 107
Mehmed IV 37
Mercator, Gerardus 53
Miller, Steve 129–130
Mirandola, Pico di 70
missionaries 16, 17, 20
modernity 97, 105, 120, 122, 123
Monbron, Louis-Charles Fougeret de 117
Montaigne, Michel de 91, 92, 93, 94, 106
Montenoy, Charles Palissot de 114
Montesquieu 111–112, 117
More, Henry 97
More, Thomas 58–59
Morsius, Joachim 75, 83
Moses 5, 94, 100
Mother Zuana 19, 22, 23, 24
Münster, Johann 52

nationalism 10, 119
Naudé, Gabriel 41, 92
neoplatonism 100, 102
neostoics, neostoicism 78, 83, 90–92, 99, 112–113
Newton, Isaac 105
Nicolay, Nicolas de 40
Noah 18, 40
Noyers, Pierre de 101

Ortelius, Abraham 39, 47, 58
Ottoman Empire 15, 16, 36

Paracelsus 70, 73
Passions 90, 93, 114
Patria 95, 96, 97, 118, 119, 130
patriotism 10, 88, 91, 93, 95, 118, 129
Paul of Tarsus 2, 35, 66, 80, 95
peace
    perpetual 120–121
    Thirty Years' War and 96, 120
    universal 15–16, 18, 22, 23–24
Peregrinatio 40, 53–55, 90–91
Persius, Aulus Flaccus 46
Philo of Alexandria 5–6, 7, 23, 40, 68, 77, 94
Philosophes 4, 92, 104–117, 118–120, 124, 128, 130
pilgrims 2, 56, 76
    see also homo viator
Plantin, Christophe 49
Plato 5–6, 9, 87, 100, 112
Pliny 46
Plutarch 94, 95
Pomponazzi, Pietro 89
Pontanus, Henri 51
Postel, Guillaume
    cosmopolite 12, 15–17, 19, 22–25
    messianism 19–20, 24, 47, 102
    missionary 17–18, 19
    prophecy 18, 19–21
    reception 41, 109, 123
Pufendorf, Samuel von 96, 121
Purchas, Samuel 42–43, 45, 77–78, 80
Puritans 57, 67, 76–79, 81
Putsch, Johann 52
Pyrrhonism 12, 13, 111
Pythagoras 40, 92

querelle des femmes 88–89

reason 20, 30, 77, 112
reason of state (*ratio status*) 81–82, 93
rebirth (spiritual) 68–69, 71–73
Reeves, Thomas 79
reformation
    magisterial 101–102
    universal 22, 62, 71, 73, 76, 98, 101
Remí, Joseph-Honoré 115
Renaudot, Théophraste 88
republic of letters 1, 89–93, 99, 112, 115

Les Réveille-matin des François 74, 75, 83
Richelieu, Armand Jean du Plessis (Cardinal) 88
Ripley, George 101
Robespierre, Maximilien 119
Rosicrucians 71–73, 75–76, 98, 118
Rouelle, Guillaume François 111
Rousseau, Jean-Jacques
    and cosmopolites 116–117, 118
    Discourse on Inequality 117
    Émile 117
    and *philosophes* 116, 118
Rudolf II 34, 100
Rufus, Gaius Musonius 8
Rumsey, Walter 99

Salic law 18, 31
scepticism 87, 92
science and natural philosophy 83, 97–98, 103
scientific revolution 97, 105
secrecy 94, 100, 101
secularization 86, 97–98, 105
Sendivogius, Michael 100, 109, 111
Seneca 77, 83
Shakespeare, William 47, 78, 93
sin 53–55, 57, 59, 68
Socrates 7, 8, 59, 67, 77, 87, 91, 95, 107
Solomon (biblical) 37, 61
sovereignty 95
Starkey, George 101
statesmanship 25–27, 40–41, 56, 86, 95, 97
stoics, stoicism 2, 5, 7, 8, 9, 11, 22, 29, 31, 49, 67, 86, 94, 96, 98, 114
Stradling, John 90
strangers 2, 5–6, 35, 40, 56–58, 73
supercessionism 6, 9

Tatars 37, 91
Thirty Years' War 67, 92, 96, 122
Trump, Donald 129

Ulcken, Andreas von 96
universalism 16, 18, 122
utopia 57–58, 65–67

vanity 46, 56–58, 63, 103
Vicars, John 79, 83
vices 78, 79, 88, 90
virtues 78, 87, 88, 91–93, 115
Vos, Marten de 54

Wierix, Jeronimus 54, 57
world empire (Christian) 20, 123
world republic (Kant) 123

worldliness 4, 50, 66–69, 76–79, 88, 104

Xavier, Francis 17
xenophobia 91, 119

Zeno of Citium 94
Zion 55, 57
Zohar 19

www.ingramcontent.com/pod-product-compliance
Lightning Source LLC
Chambersburg PA
CBHW072236290426
44111CB00012B/2119